Indiana CORE Elementary Education

SECRETS

Study Guide
Your Key to Exam Success

Indiana CORE Test Review for
The Indiana CORE Assessments
for Educator Licensure

Dear Future Exam Success Story:

First of all, **THANK YOU** for purchasing Mometrix study materials!

Second, congratulations! You are one of the few determined test-takers who are committed to doing whatever it takes to excel on your exam. **You have come to the right place.** We developed these study materials with one goal in mind: to deliver you the information you need in a format that's concise and easy to use.

In addition to optimizing your guide for the content of the test, we've outlined our recommended steps for breaking down the preparation process into small, attainable goals so you can make sure you stay on track.

We've also analyzed the entire test-taking process, identifying the most common pitfalls and showing how you can overcome them and be ready for any curveball the test throws you.

Standardized testing is one of the biggest obstacles on your road to success, which only increases the importance of doing well in the high-pressure, high-stakes environment of test day. Your results on this test could have a significant impact on your future, and this guide provides the information and practical advice to help you achieve your full potential on test day.

Your success is our success

We would love to hear from you! If you would like to share the story of your exam success or if you have any questions or comments in regard to our products, please contact us at **800-673-8175** or **support@mometrix.com**.

Thanks again for your business and we wish you continued success!

Sincerely,
The Mometrix Test Preparation Team

Need more help? Check out our flashcards at: http://MometrixFlashcards.com/IndianaCORE

TABLE OF CONTENTS

INTRODUCTION 1

SECRET KEY #1 – PLAN BIG, STUDY SMALL 2
INFORMATION ORGANIZATION 2
TIME MANAGEMENT 2
STUDY ENVIRONMENT 2

SECRET KEY #2 – MAKE YOUR STUDYING COUNT 3
RETENTION 3
MODALITY 3

SECRET KEY #3 – PRACTICE THE RIGHT WAY 4
PRACTICE TEST STRATEGY 5

SECRET KEY #4 – PACE YOURSELF 6

SECRET KEY #5 – HAVE A PLAN FOR GUESSING 7
WHEN TO START THE GUESSING PROCESS 7
HOW TO NARROW DOWN THE CHOICES 8
WHICH ANSWER TO CHOOSE 9

TEST-TAKING STRATEGIES 10
QUESTION STRATEGIES 10
ANSWER CHOICE STRATEGIES 11
GENERAL STRATEGIES 12
FINAL NOTES 13

STUDENT DEVELOPMENT AND DIVERSITY 15

LEARNING PROCESSES AND ENVIRONMENTS 37

INSTRUCTION AND ASSESSMENT 67

PROFESSIONAL ENVIRONMENT 113

INDIANA CORE PRACTICE TEST 130

ANSWERS AND EXPLANATIONS 146

HOW TO OVERCOME TEST ANXIETY 165
CAUSES OF TEST ANXIETY 165
ELEMENTS OF TEST ANXIETY 166
EFFECTS OF TEST ANXIETY 166
PHYSICAL STEPS FOR BEATING TEST ANXIETY 167
MENTAL STEPS FOR BEATING TEST ANXIETY 168
STUDY STRATEGY 169
TEST TIPS 171
IMPORTANT QUALIFICATION 172

THANK YOU 173

ADDITIONAL BONUS MATERIAL 174

Introduction

Thank you for purchasing this resource! You have made the choice to prepare yourself for a test that could have a huge impact on your future, and this guide is designed to help you be fully ready for test day. Obviously, it's important to have a solid understanding of the test material, but you also need to be prepared for the unique environment and stressors of the test, so that you can perform to the best of your abilities.

For this purpose, the first section that appears in this guide is the **Secret Keys**. We've devoted countless hours to meticulously researching what works and what doesn't, and we've boiled down our findings to the five most impactful steps you can take to improve your performance on the test. We start at the beginning with study planning and move through the preparation process, all the way to the testing strategies that will help you get the most out of what you know when you're finally sitting in front of the test.

We recommend that you start preparing for your test as far in advance as possible. However, if you've bought this guide as a last-minute study resource and only have a few days before your test, we recommend that you skip over the first two Secret Keys since they address a long-term study plan.

If you struggle with **test anxiety**, we strongly encourage you to check out our recommendations for how you can overcome it. Test anxiety is a formidable foe, but it can be beaten, and we want to make sure you have the tools you need to defeat it.

Secret Key #1 – Plan Big, Study Small

There's a lot riding on your performance. If you want to ace this test, you're going to need to keep your skills sharp and the material fresh in your mind. You need a plan that lets you review everything you need to know while still fitting in your schedule. We'll break this strategy down into three categories.

Information Organization

Start with the information you already have: the official test outline. From this, you can make a complete list of all the concepts you need to cover before the test. Organize these concepts into groups that can be studied together, and create a list of any related vocabulary you need to learn so you can brush up on any difficult terms. You'll want to keep this vocabulary list handy once you actually start studying since you may need to add to it along the way.

Time Management

Once you have your set of study concepts, decide how to spread them out over the time you have left before the test. Break your study plan into small, clear goals so you have a manageable task for each day and know exactly what you're doing. Then just focus on one small step at a time. When you manage your time this way, you don't need to spend hours at a time studying. Studying a small block of content for a short period each day helps you retain information better and avoid stressing over how much you have left to do. You can relax knowing that you have a plan to cover everything in time. In order for this strategy to be effective though, you have to start studying early and stick to your schedule. Avoid the exhaustion and futility that comes from last-minute cramming!

Study Environment

The environment you study in has a big impact on your learning. Studying in a coffee shop, while probably more enjoyable, is not likely to be as fruitful as studying in a quiet room. It's important to keep distractions to a minimum. You're only planning to study for a short block of time, so make the most of it. Don't pause to check your phone or get up to find a snack. It's also important to **avoid multitasking**. Research has consistently shown that multitasking will make your studying dramatically less effective. Your study area should also be comfortable and well-lit so you don't have the distraction of straining your eyes or sitting on an uncomfortable chair.

The time of day you study is also important. You want to be rested and alert. Don't wait until just before bedtime. Study when you'll be most likely to comprehend and remember. Even better, if you know what time of day your test will be, set that time aside for study. That way your brain will be used to working on that subject at that specific time and you'll have a better chance of recalling information.

Finally, it can be helpful to team up with others who are studying for the same test. Your actual studying should be done in as isolated an environment as possible, but the work of organizing the information and setting up the study plan can be divided up. In between study sessions, you can discuss with your teammates the concepts that you're all studying and quiz each other on the details. Just be sure that your teammates are as serious about the test as you are. If you find that your study time is being replaced with social time, you might need to find a new team.

Secret Key #2 – Make Your Studying Count

You're devoting a lot of time and effort to preparing for this test, so you want to be absolutely certain it will pay off. This means doing more than just reading the content and hoping you can remember it on test day. It's important to make every minute of study count. There are two main areas you can focus on to make your studying count:

Retention

It doesn't matter how much time you study if you can't remember the material. You need to make sure you are retaining the concepts. To check your retention of the information you're learning, try recalling it at later times with minimal prompting. Try carrying around flashcards and glance at one or two from time to time or ask a friend who's also studying for the test to quiz you.

To enhance your retention, look for ways to put the information into practice so that you can apply it rather than simply recalling it. If you're using the information in practical ways, it will be much easier to remember. Similarly, it helps to solidify a concept in your mind if you're not only reading it to yourself but also explaining it to someone else. Ask a friend to let you teach them about a concept you're a little shaky on (or speak aloud to an imaginary audience if necessary). As you try to summarize, define, give examples, and answer your friend's questions, you'll understand the concepts better and they will stay with you longer. Finally, step back for a big picture view and ask yourself how each piece of information fits with the whole subject. When you link the different concepts together and see them working together as a whole, it's easier to remember the individual components.

Finally, practice showing your work on any multi-step problems, even if you're just studying. Writing out each step you take to solve a problem will help solidify the process in your mind, and you'll be more likely to remember it during the test.

Modality

Modality simply refers to the means or method by which you study. Choosing a study modality that fits your own individual learning style is crucial. No two people learn best in exactly the same way, so it's important to know your strengths and use them to your advantage.

For example, if you learn best by visualization, focus on visualizing a concept in your mind and draw an image or a diagram. Try color-coding your notes, illustrating them, or creating symbols that will trigger your mind to recall a learned concept. If you learn best by hearing or discussing information, find a study partner who learns the same way or read aloud to yourself. Think about how to put the information in your own words. Imagine that you are giving a lecture on the topic and record yourself so you can listen to it later.

For any learning style, flashcards can be helpful. Organize the information so you can take advantage of spare moments to review. Underline key words or phrases. Use different colors for different categories. Mnemonic devices (such as creating a short list in which every item starts with the same letter) can also help with retention. Find what works best for you and use it to store the information in your mind most effectively and easily.

Secret Key #3 – Practice the Right Way

Your success on test day depends not only on how many hours you put into preparing, but also on whether you prepared the right way. It's good to check along the way to see if your studying is paying off. One of the most effective ways to do this is by taking practice tests to evaluate your progress. Practice tests are useful because they show exactly where you need to improve. Every time you take a practice test, pay special attention to these three groups of questions:

- The questions you got wrong
- The questions you had to guess on, even if you guessed right
- The questions you found difficult or slow to work through

This will show you exactly what your weak areas are, and where you need to devote more study time. Ask yourself why each of these questions gave you trouble. Was it because you didn't understand the material? Was it because you didn't remember the vocabulary? Do you need more repetitions on this type of question to build speed and confidence? Dig into those questions and figure out how you can strengthen your weak areas as you go back to review the material.

Additionally, many practice tests have a section explaining the answer choices. It can be tempting to read the explanation and think that you now have a good understanding of the concept. However, an explanation likely only covers part of the question's broader context. Even if the explanation makes sense, **go back and investigate** every concept related to the question until you're positive you have a thorough understanding.

As you go along, keep in mind that the practice test is just that: practice. Memorizing these questions and answers will not be very helpful on the actual test because it is unlikely to have any of the same exact questions. If you only know the right answers to the sample questions, you won't be prepared for the real thing. **Study the concepts** until you understand them fully, and then you'll be able to answer any question that shows up on the test.

It's important to wait on the practice tests until you're ready. If you take a test on your first day of study, you may be overwhelmed by the amount of material covered and how much you need to learn. Work up to it gradually.

On test day, you'll need to be prepared for answering questions, managing your time, and using the test-taking strategies you've learned. It's a lot to balance, like a mental marathon that will have a big impact on your future. Like training for a marathon, you'll need to start slowly and work your way up. When test day arrives, you'll be ready.

Start with the strategies you've read in the first two Secret Keys—plan your course and study in the way that works best for you. If you have time, consider using multiple study resources to get different approaches to the same concepts. It can be helpful to see difficult concepts from more than one angle. Then find a good source for practice tests. Many times, the test website will suggest potential study resources or provide sample tests.

Practice Test Strategy

If you're able to find at least three practice tests, we recommend this strategy:

Untimed and Open-Book Practice

Take the first test with no time constraints and with your notes and study guide handy. Take your time and focus on applying the strategies you've learned.

Timed and Open-Book Practice

Take the second practice test open-book as well, but set a timer and practice pacing yourself to finish in time.

Timed and Closed-Book Practice

Take any other practice tests as if it were test day. Set a timer and put away your study materials. Sit at a table or desk in a quiet room, imagine yourself at the testing center, and answer questions as quickly and accurately as possible.

Keep repeating timed and closed-book tests on a regular basis until you run out of practice tests or it's time for the actual test. Your mind will be ready for the schedule and stress of test day, and you'll be able to focus on recalling the material you've learned.

Secret Key #4 – Pace Yourself

Once you're fully prepared for the material on the test, your biggest challenge on test day will be managing your time. Just knowing that the clock is ticking can make you panic even if you have plenty of time left. Work on pacing yourself so you can build confidence against the time constraints of the exam. Pacing is a difficult skill to master, especially in a high-pressure environment, so **practice is vital**.

Set time expectations for your pace based on how much time is available. For example, if a section has 60 questions and the time limit is 30 minutes, you know you have to average 30 seconds or less per question in order to answer them all. Although 30 seconds is the hard limit, set 25 seconds per question as your goal, so you reserve extra time to spend on harder questions. When you budget extra time for the harder questions, you no longer have any reason to stress when those questions take longer to answer.

Don't let this time expectation distract you from working through the test at a calm, steady pace, but keep it in mind so you don't spend too much time on any one question. Recognize that taking extra time on one question you don't understand may keep you from answering two that you do understand later in the test. If your time limit for a question is up and you're still not sure of the answer, mark it and move on, and come back to it later if the time and the test format allow. If the testing format doesn't allow you to return to earlier questions, just make an educated guess; then put it out of your mind and move on.

On the easier questions, be careful not to rush. It may seem wise to hurry through them so you have more time for the challenging ones, but it's not worth missing one if you know the concept and just didn't take the time to read the question fully. Work efficiently but make sure you understand the question and have looked at all of the answer choices, since more than one may seem right at first.

Even if you're paying attention to the time, you may find yourself a little behind at some point. You should speed up to get back on track, but do so wisely. Don't panic; just take a few seconds less on each question until you're caught up. Don't guess without thinking, but do look through the answer choices and eliminate any you know are wrong. If you can get down to two choices, it is often worthwhile to guess from those. Once you've chosen an answer, move on and don't dwell on any that you skipped or had to hurry through. If a question was taking too long, chances are it was one of the harder ones, so you weren't as likely to get it right anyway.

On the other hand, if you find yourself getting ahead of schedule, it may be beneficial to slow down a little. The more quickly you work, the more likely you are to make a careless mistake that will affect your score. You've budgeted time for each question, so don't be afraid to spend that time. Practice an efficient but careful pace to get the most out of the time you have.

Secret Key #5 – Have a Plan for Guessing

When you're taking the test, you may find yourself stuck on a question. Some of the answer choices seem better than others, but you don't see the one answer choice that is obviously correct. What do you do?

The scenario described above is very common, yet most test takers have not effectively prepared for it. Developing and practicing a plan for guessing may be one of the single most effective uses of your time as you get ready for the exam.

In developing your plan for guessing, there are three questions to address:

- When should you start the guessing process?
- How should you narrow down the choices?
- Which answer should you choose?

When to Start the Guessing Process

Unless your plan for guessing is to select C every time (which, despite its merits, is not what we recommend), you need to leave yourself enough time to apply your answer elimination strategies. Since you have a limited amount of time for each question, that means that if you're going to give yourself the best shot at guessing correctly, you have to decide quickly whether or not you will guess.

Of course, the best-case scenario is that you don't have to guess at all, so first, see if you can answer the question based on your knowledge of the subject and basic reasoning skills. Focus on the key words in the question and try to jog your memory of related topics. Give yourself a chance to bring the knowledge to mind, but once you realize that you don't have (or you can't access) the knowledge you need to answer the question, it's time to start the guessing process.

It's almost always better to start the guessing process too early than too late. It only takes a few seconds to remember something and answer the question from knowledge. Carefully eliminating wrong answer choices takes longer. Plus, going through the process of eliminating answer choices can actually help jog your memory.

Summary: Start the guessing process as soon as you decide that you can't answer the question based on your knowledge.

How to Narrow Down the Choices

The next chapter in this book (**Test-Taking Strategies**) includes a wide range of strategies for how to approach questions and how to look for answer choices to eliminate. You will definitely want to read those carefully, practice them, and figure out which ones work best for you. Here though, we're going to address a mindset rather than a particular strategy.

Your chances of guessing an answer correctly depend on how many options you are choosing from.

How many choices you have	How likely you are to guess correctly
5	20%
4	25%
3	33%
2	50%
1	100%

You can see from this chart just how valuable it is to be able to eliminate incorrect answers and make an educated guess, but there are two things that many test takers do that cause them to miss out on the benefits of guessing:

- Accidentally eliminating the correct answer
- Selecting an answer based on an impression

We'll look at the first one here, and the second one in the next section.

To avoid accidentally eliminating the correct answer, we recommend a thought exercise called **the $5 challenge**. In this challenge, you only eliminate an answer choice from contention if you are willing to bet $5 on it being wrong. Why $5? Five dollars is a small but not insignificant amount of money. It's an amount you could afford to lose but wouldn't want to throw away. And while losing $5 once might not hurt too much, doing it twenty times will set you back $100. In the same way, each small decision you make—eliminating a choice here, guessing on a question there—won't by itself impact your score very much, but when you put them all together, they can make a big difference. By holding each answer choice elimination decision to a higher standard, you can reduce the risk of accidentally eliminating the correct answer.

The $5 challenge can also be applied in a positive sense: If you are willing to bet $5 that an answer choice *is* correct, go ahead and mark it as correct.

Summary: Only eliminate an answer choice if you are willing to bet $5 that it is wrong.

Which Answer to Choose

You're taking the test. You've run into a hard question and decided you'll have to guess. You've eliminated all the answer choices you're willing to bet $5 on. Now you have to pick an answer. Why do we even need to talk about this? Why can't you just pick whichever one you feel like when the time comes?

The answer to these questions is that if you don't come into the test with a plan, you'll rely on your impression to select an answer choice, and if you do that, you risk falling into a trap. The test writers know that everyone who takes their test will be guessing on some of the questions, so they intentionally write wrong answer choices to seem plausible. You still have to pick an answer though, and if the wrong answer choices are designed to look right, how can you ever be sure that you're not falling for their trap? The best solution we've found to this dilemma is to take the decision out of your hands entirely. Here is the process we recommend:

Once you've eliminated any choices that you are confident (willing to bet $5) are wrong, select the first remaining choice as your answer.

Whether you choose to select the first remaining choice, the second, or the last, the important thing is that you use some preselected standard. Using this approach guarantees that you will not be enticed into selecting an answer choice that looks right, because you are not basing your decision on how the answer choices look.

This is not meant to make you question your knowledge. Instead, it is to help you recognize the difference between your knowledge and your impressions. There's a huge difference between thinking an answer is right because of what you know, and thinking an answer is right because it looks or sounds like it should be right.

Summary: To ensure that your selection is appropriately random, make a predetermined selection from among all answer choices you have not eliminated.

Test-Taking Strategies

This section contains a list of test-taking strategies that you may find helpful as you work through the test. By taking what you know and applying logical thought, you can maximize your chances of answering any question correctly!

It is very important to realize that every question is different and every person is different: no single strategy will work on every question, and no single strategy will work for every person. That's why we've included all of them here, so you can try them out and determine which ones work best for different types of questions and which ones work best for you.

Question Strategies

Read Carefully

Read the question and answer choices carefully. Don't miss the question because you misread the terms. You have plenty of time to read each question thoroughly and make sure you understand what is being asked. Yet a happy medium must be attained, so don't waste too much time. You must read carefully, but efficiently.

Contextual Clues

Look for contextual clues. If the question includes a word you are not familiar with, look at the immediate context for some indication of what the word might mean. Contextual clues can often give you all the information you need to decipher the meaning of an unfamiliar word. Even if you can't determine the meaning, you may be able to narrow down the possibilities enough to make a solid guess at the answer to the question.

Prefixes

If you're having trouble with a word in the question or answer choices, try dissecting it. Take advantage of every clue that the word might include. Prefixes and suffixes can be a huge help. Usually they allow you to determine a basic meaning. Pre- means before, post- means after, pro - is positive, de- is negative. From prefixes and suffixes, you can get an idea of the general meaning of the word and try to put it into context.

Hedge Words

Watch out for critical hedge words, such as *likely, may, can, sometimes, often, almost, mostly, usually, generally, rarely,* and *sometimes.* Question writers insert these hedge phrases to cover every possibility. Often an answer choice will be wrong simply because it leaves no room for exception. Be on guard for answer choices that have definitive words such as *exactly* and *always.*

Switchback Words

Stay alert for *switchbacks.* These are the words and phrases frequently used to alert you to shifts in thought. The most common switchback words are *but, although,* and *however.* Others include *nevertheless, on the other hand, even though, while, in spite of, despite, regardless of.* Switchback words are important to catch because they can change the direction of the question or an answer choice.

Face Value

When in doubt, use common sense. Accept the situation in the problem at face value. Don't read too much into it. These problems will not require you to make wild assumptions. If you have to go beyond creativity and warp time or space in order to have an answer choice fit the question, then you should move on and consider the other answer choices. These are normal problems rooted in reality. The applicable relationship or explanation may not be readily apparent, but it is there for you to figure out. Use your common sense to interpret anything that isn't clear.

Answer Choice Strategies

Answer Selection

The most thorough way to pick an answer choice is to identify and eliminate wrong answers until only one is left, then confirm it is the correct answer. Sometimes an answer choice may immediately seem right, but be careful. The test writers will usually put more than one reasonable answer choice on each question, so take a second to read all of them and make sure that the other choices are not equally obvious. As long as you have time left, it is better to read every answer choice than to pick the first one that looks right without checking the others.

Answer Choice Families

An answer choice family consists of two (in rare cases, three) answer choices that are very similar in construction and cannot all be true at the same time. If you see two answer choices that are direct opposites or parallels, one of them is usually the correct answer. For instance, if one answer choice says that quantity x increases and another either says that quantity x decreases (opposite) or says that quantity y increases (parallel), then those answer choices would fall into the same family. An answer choice that doesn't match the construction of the answer choice family is more likely to be incorrect. Most questions will not have answer choice families, but when they do appear, you should be prepared to recognize them.

Eliminate Answers

Eliminate answer choices as soon as you realize they are wrong, but make sure you consider all possibilities. If you are eliminating answer choices and realize that the last one you are left with is also wrong, don't panic. Start over and consider each choice again. There may be something you missed the first time that you will realize on the second pass.

Avoid Fact Traps

Don't be distracted by an answer choice that is factually true but doesn't answer the question. You are looking for the choice that answers the question. Stay focused on what the question is asking for so you don't accidentally pick an answer that is true but incorrect. Always go back to the question and make sure the answer choice you've selected actually answers the question and is not merely a true statement.

Extreme Statements

In general, you should avoid answers that put forth extreme actions as standard practice or proclaim controversial ideas as established fact. An answer choice that states the "process should be used in certain situations, if…" is much more likely to be correct than one that states the "process should be discontinued completely." The first is a calm rational statement and doesn't even make a definitive, uncompromising stance, using a hedge word *if* to provide wiggle room, whereas the second choice is a radical idea and far more extreme.

Benchmark

As you read through the answer choices and you come across one that seems to answer the question well, mentally select that answer choice. This is not your final answer, but it's the one that will help you evaluate the other answer choices. The one that you selected is your benchmark or standard for judging each of the other answer choices. Every other answer choice must be compared to your benchmark. That choice is correct until proven otherwise by another answer choice beating it. If you find a better answer, then that one becomes your new benchmark. Once you've decided that no other choice answers the question as well as your benchmark, you have your final answer.

Predict the Answer

Before you even start looking at the answer choices, it is often best to try to predict the answer. When you come up with the answer on your own, it is easier to avoid distractions and traps because you will know exactly what to look for. The right answer choice is unlikely to be word-for-word what you came up with, but it should be a close match. Even if you are confident that you have the right answer, you should still take the time to read each option before moving on.

General Strategies

Tough Questions

If you are stumped on a problem or it appears too hard or too difficult, don't waste time. Move on! Remember though, if you can quickly check for obviously incorrect answer choices, your chances of guessing correctly are greatly improved. Before you completely give up, at least try to knock out a couple of possible answers. Eliminate what you can and then guess at the remaining answer choices before moving on.

Check Your Work

Since you will probably not know every term listed and the answer to every question, it is important that you get credit for the ones that you do know. Don't miss any questions through careless mistakes. If at all possible, try to take a second to look back over your answer selection and make sure you've selected the correct answer choice and haven't made a costly careless mistake (such as marking an answer choice that you didn't mean to mark). This quick double check should more than pay for itself in caught mistakes for the time it costs.

Pace Yourself

It's easy to be overwhelmed when you're looking at a page full of questions; your mind is confused and full of random thoughts, and the clock is ticking down faster than you would like. Calm down and maintain the pace that you have set for yourself. Especially as you get down to the last few minutes of the test, don't let the small numbers on the clock make you panic. As long as you are on track by monitoring your pace, you are guaranteed to have time for each question.

Don't Rush

It is very easy to make errors when you are in a hurry. Maintaining a fast pace in answering questions is pointless if it makes you miss questions that you would have gotten right otherwise. Test writers like to include distracting information and wrong answers that seem right. Taking a little extra time to avoid careless mistakes can make all the difference in your test score. Find a pace that allows you to be confident in the answers that you select.

Keep Moving

Panicking will not help you pass the test, so do your best to stay calm and keep moving. Taking deep breaths and going through the answer elimination steps you practiced can help to break through a stress barrier and keep your pace.

Final Notes

The combination of a solid foundation of content knowledge and the confidence that comes from practicing your plan for applying that knowledge is the key to maximizing your performance on test day. As your foundation of content knowledge is built up and strengthened, you'll find that the strategies included in this chapter become more and more effective in helping you quickly sift through the distractions and traps of the test to isolate the correct answer.

Now it's time to move on to the test content chapters of this book, but be sure to keep your goal in mind. As you read, think about how you will be able to apply this information on the test. If you've already seen sample questions for the test and you have an idea of the question format and style, try to come up with questions of your own that you can answer based on what you're reading. This will give you valuable practice applying your knowledge in the same ways you can expect to on test day.

Good luck and good studying!

Student Development and Diversity

Sigmund Freud's Theory of Human Development

Freud proposed each psychosexual development stage revolves around the erogenous zone where pleasure focuses at the time. Freud divided the personality into three structures: the id, ego, and superego. During toddlerhood's (c. 1-3 years) anal stage, the ego emerges, providing a sense of self and reality, regulating id impulses unmediated during infancy's oral stage. Toilet-training is an important life event. If parents reward toilet use excessively, children may become possessive of bowel movements, deriving excessive pleasure from them. Overly strict toilet-training can cause anal fixation, manifested as either an anal-retentive (compulsively neat, overly structured, rigid, righteous, and stubborn) or anal-expulsive (sloppy, defiant of authority, and irresponsible) personality. Preschoolers (c. 3-5 years) are in Freud's phallic stage. The superego or conscience emerges, providing a moral compass, further governing the ego and id. Children discover their genitals, which become this stage's erogenous zone. In Freud's Oedipus complex during this stage, boys unconsciously desire their mothers, wishing to destroy their fathers as rivals. They fear paternal retribution, i.e., castration anxiety. They resolve the conflict through identification with the aggressor—emulating fathers. Freud saw elementary years as the latency period, wherein sexual impulses are suppressed in favor of developing social skills and relationships.

Erik Erikson's Theory of Human Development

Early Childhood Years

Erikson took major influences from Freud's theory in also viewing major life events, e.g., nursing during infancy; toilet-training during toddlerhood; exploration during preschool years; and school during school years as central to each developmental stage. But his orientation was psychosocial, not psychosexual: rather than Freud's focus on physical erogenous zones and parent-child relationships, Erikson focused on personal self-images and social interactions. In each of Erikson's stages, a nuclear conflict must be resolved. Toddlers (c. two to three years) confronting toilet-training experience autonomy vs. shame and doubt. In learning physical control, successful children develop independence; failing children develop self-doubt and shame. According to Erikson, preschoolers (c. three to five years) encounter the nuclear conflict of initiative vs. guilt. At these ages, they are exploring their environments and need to experiment with exercising personal control over their surroundings. Children who succeed in interacting with and manipulating their environments develop a sense of purpose. Children who fail in this endeavor by exerting excessive power, and/or by receiving disapproval from their parents for their efforts, develop guilt feelings. School-age (c. 6-11 years) children face industry vs. inferiority. Successful coping with new social and academic requirements develops feelings of competence; failure develops feelings of inadequacy.

Adolescence and Early Adulthood

Unlike his predecessor and strong influence, Sigmund Freud, Erikson believed people continue to develop throughout life. Hence he proposed stages for each life period until death. He identified the nuclear conflict characteristic of every stage as being identity vs. role confusion in adolescence (c. 12-18 years). Teenagers begin developing their individual personal identities. *Social relationships* are the focus of this stage. Teens that are successful in defining their personal roles and identities develop feelings of being *true to themselves*. Teens who fail in this endeavor develop *confusion about their roles* in life and *weak and/or poorly defined self-images*. Young adults (c. 19-40 years) are included in teenage years because Erikson's theory associates the final teen year as part of

- 15 -

young adulthood. This is Erikson's stage of intimacy vs. isolation. Once adolescents have defined their personal identities, they progress forming intimate, loving relationships with other young adults. *Relationships* are the focus of this stage. Successful individuals develop *strong relationships*; those failing develop *isolation and loneliness*.

Albert Bandura's Contributions to Education

Albert Bandura's social learning theory emphasized the importance of social interaction in learning. Bandura accepted principles of behaviorist learning theories like antecedent stimuli, behaviors, and consequent stimuli that punished or rewarded (reinforced) behaviors. However, internal cognitive processes, and social contexts of learning, became more central in Bandura's theory. Also, he believes learning does not necessarily change behavior. Bandura discovered children learned indirectly by watching others—i.e., vicarious or observational learning: seeing others receiving rewards for certain behaviors, they imitated those actions to obtain similar rewards. This discovery contradicted the empiricist claim that learning requires direct experience. Bandura also discovered children witnessing violent actions by living persons (cf. his Bobo doll experiments) or by people they saw in video recordings would then display more aggressive behaviors imitating what they observed. This influenced education and parenting: adults, realizing children's behavior was influenced not just directly by experiencing violence, but also indirectly by observing it, became more concerned about controlling what children observed. Bandura identified attention, retention, reproduction, and motivation as conditions necessary to modeling and observational learning. Bandura's concept of reciprocal determinism states individuals and environments mutually influence each other. His concept of self-efficacy identifies belief in one's individual competence to perform specific tasks and skills.

Jerome Bruner's Contributions to Education

Bruner, like Piaget and many others, embraces constructivist philosopher, i.e., by interacting with their environments, children actively construct their learning, knowledge, and realities. His emphasis on discovery learning is based on constructivism. He defined learning as not only remembering existing, culturally imparted or acquired ideas and actions, but moreover inventing or creating these on one's own. Bruner feels "culturally invented technologies" amplify human abilities, rather than providing all knowledge. He influenced education by advising that its goal should be producing autonomous learners. Bruner posited three modes of representation in child cognitive development. 1) Enactive representation: action-based information based on motor responses, retained in muscle memory, emerging in infancy. 2) Iconic representation: visual image-based information, emerging around 1-6 years of age. 3) Symbolic representation: coded or symbolic storage of information, emerging c. 7 years and older. For example, the category "dogs" symbolically represents all dog breeds, types, and individuals. We remember information symbolically in words, numbers, etc. Bruner's concept of the spiral curriculum enabled teaching complex ideas to all ages by initially structuring them simply and increasing difficulty gradually. Bruner (with Wood and Ross) originated the concept *scaffolding*—temporary, gradually withdrawn support matching student needs.

John Dewey's Contributions to Education

Psychologist, philosopher, educator, and social activist John Dewey was a prominent member of the Progressive social reform movement, a president of the American Psychological Association, a functional psychology pioneer, a Pragmatist and Instrumentalist philosopher, and the foremost theorist in modern American education. Like Rousseau and Froebel, he believed in experiential "learning by doing." He shifted schools from authoritarian and teacher-centered, rote-learning methods to democratic classrooms, relevant curricula, and participatory activities. He emphasized the social, interactive nature of the learning and educational processes. Dewey believed education not only conferred knowledge, but moreover taught children how to live. His humanist psychology and instrumental philosophy informed his opinions that education should enable children to realize their full potential, and to apply those abilities toward the greater good. He also viewed education as an important force for social reform and change. He believed education should not concentrate exclusively on being either child-centered or curriculum content-centered, but balance the two. Like Bruner, he believed education should prepare autonomous learners—who were also ethical and reflective. He also professionalized the role of teachers as social service providers producing higher character and community intelligence standards, not merely vocational trainers preparing students for work with limited job skills and information.

Jean Piaget's Theory of Cognitive Development

Piaget, like Bruner and others, believed in constructivism, i.e., children were not passive learners but actively constructed their own learning, knowledge, and worlds through interacting with their environments. He observed children as being "little scientists" from birth who experimented with and acted upon the environment to learn about it. Piaget formulated four stages of cognitive development. 1) Sensorimotor: infants respond to sensory input with motor responses. 2) Preoperational: wherein young children are *egocentric*, unable to see others' physical or mental perspectives. They think *intuitively*, not logically, unable to focus on more than one physical attribute of an object at a time (*centration*), categorize and classify, or follow structures and sequences of reasoning. They see things *animistically*, by attributing human qualities and behaviors to inanimate objects; and *magically*, by attributing events and others' actions to their own thoughts or words. 3) Concrete operations: school-age children can classify, perform other logical mental operations, and reverse them as long as they have concrete objects or events for reference. 4) Formal operations: preadolescents and adolescents develop the ability to perform abstract mental operations without concrete support, understanding and manipulating abstract concepts in math, philosophy, law, politics, etc. Piaget's theory influenced education, guiding educators not to present content to children who are not cognitively ready or able to understand; and introducing concepts and material appropriately to cognitive levels.

Lev Vygotsky's Contributions on Teaching Practices Today

Like theorists after him, e.g., Erikson, Bruner, Bandura, and others, Vygotsky, who lived during the Russian Revolution, stressed the importance of social interaction to learning. He differed from his contemporary Piaget's belief in invariant stages of cognitive development, believing instead that it varied among societies because culture heavily influenced it. Two of the most influential concepts in Vygotsky's theories were the more knowledgeable other (MKO), i.e., a person (or a computer, software program, etc. can be included) with a higher level of skill or understanding—whether peer, older child, or adult—than a given student; and the zone of proximal development (ZPD), which interact with one another. The ZPD is the distance between two levels of cognitive development: (1) the level of actual development, where a student can accomplish something independently; and (2) the level of potential development, where a student can accomplish something with guidance or assistance from an MKO. Vygotsky emphasized ability and potential above knowledge: what one could learn was more important than what one already knew. He also was first to prove that self-talk or inner speech (whose existence others agreed to, but not its cognitive value) was important to activity self-regulation, social competence, and learning.

Lawrence Kohlberg's Theory of Moral Development

Kohlberg based his theory on Piaget's two stages of moral development, heteronomous (other-directed) morality and autonomous (self-directed) morality; but Kohlberg extended these to three distinct levels and six stages, with each level encompassing two stages. Similarly to Erikson's belief regarding psychosocial development, Kohlberg believed moral development continued throughout life. Kohlberg's level one is preconventional morality. In stage one, obedience and punishment, young children (and some adults) view rules as absolute and fixed; obedience averts punishment. In stage two, individualism and exchange, children judge actions by whether they meet one's own interests or needs. They can understand and appreciate *reciprocity,* but only if it also is in one's best interests. At level two, conventional morality, stage three involves interpersonal relationships, nicknamed *"good boy-good girl."* Conforming to meet social roles and expectations, concern for how choices affect relationships, and being "nice" predominate. Stage four, maintaining social order, focuses on respecting authority, doing one's duty, following rules, maintaining law and order, and considering overall society. Level three is postconventional morality. In stage five, social contract and individual rights, people still find laws and rules important, but only with individual members' agreement. By stage six, universal ethical principles, individuals apply internalized justice principles, regardless whether they conflict with rules and laws.

Bloom's Taxonomy

Bloom organized learning into a hierarchy of six cognitive levels, from simplest to most challenging. Remembering involves retaining, recalling, retrieving, recognizing, reproducing, or repeating names, facts, lists, and other pieces of information. Understanding requires also being able to find, identify, select, describe, explain, discuss, review, restate, and/or translate information, rather than only remembering it. Applying requires learners to interpret information they understand; to use it appropriately, e.g., for solving problems; to illustrate, demonstrate, or dramatize it; write about it, etc. Analyzing means that learners must be able not only to remember, understand, and apply information, but moreover to break it down into component parts; assign information to different categories; make comparisons and contrasts between and among pieces or sets of information; use information to make calculations; differentiate and discriminate among different information; examine information; question its truth, accuracy, or credibility; experiment with it; test its veracity; and criticize information. Evaluating demands the learner assess and appraise information, make estimates and/or predictions based on it, rate it, judge it, and defend it. Creating, the highest level, involves proposing, developing, planning, designing, formulating, preparing, collecting, composing, organizing, and managing information, including both original ideas and/or original uses of existing information.

Physical and Cognitive Characteristics of Typically Developing Children

Early Childhood

Physically, children gain c. 2.5 inches and 5-7 pounds, decreasing yearly. Preschoolers become taller and slimmer, losing baby fat. Preschooler heads are less oversized for bodies than top-heavier toddlers', but still somewhat large. *Cognitively*, continuing brain maturation plus wider life experiences enable significant progress in attention, planning, and language. Reasoning develops from 4-7 years, but is not logical. By 5 years, gross motor skills gain automaticity, and fine motor skills improve significantly.

Middle and Late Childhood

Physically, growth is slow and consistent—2-3 inches and 5-7 pounds annually. Heads and waists become smaller proportionately to height. Bones and muscle tissue strengthen. Motor skills gain

- 18 -

coordination and smoothness. By 10-12 years, fine motor coordination and manipulative skills approximate adults'. *Cognitively*, brain circuitry continues developing, especially in the prefrontal cortex, improving cognitive control, attention, and reasoning. In Piaget's concrete operations stage, children can reason logically and reverse mental operations, but need physical objects, events, or examples for reference.

Adolescence

Physically, uberty combines physical and sexual maturation with hormonal changes. *Cognitively*, structural changes improve information-processing, reasoning, decision-making, and self-control. However, though the emotion-related amygdala matures earlier, the prefrontal cortex controlling emotions only matures by 18-25 years. Adolescents reach Piaget's formal operations, understanding abstract concepts and performing and manipulating entirely mental operations.

Linguistic, Affective, and Moral Characteristics of Children with Typical Development

Early Childhood

linguistic : greater sensitivity to spoken phonological features; linguistic rule systems understanding; learning and applying syntactic rules to speech; dramatic vocabulary development; changing speech "registers" and styles based on situation, improving conversational skills.

Affective: by 4-5 years, self-awareness; self-conscious emotions like guilt and pride; understanding of and ability to discuss both personal and others' emotions, causes and results, increase.

Moral: most are at Kohlberg's level one of preconventional reasoning with external punishments and rewards until c. 9 years.

Middle and Late Childhood

Linguistic: understanding the alphabetic principle; categorizing; whereas younger children respond sentence-sequentially, e.g., prompted "dog" and saying "barks"; or "eat" and "lunch"; older children respond with like parts of speech, saying "cat" or "horse" to "dog," and "drink" to "eat." From age 6-11, vocabulary grows from c. 14,000-40,000 words. Complex grammar comprehension develops, and metalinguistic awareness, knowing, and thinking about language.

Affective: more varied coping strategies. Self-regulation and self-efficacy influence achievement.

Moral: many are at Kohlberg's level two conventional reasoning, stage 3, "good boy-good girl", adopting parental morality.

Adolescence

Linguistic: skills advance, including complex spoken and written sentences; writing stories following story grammar rules; consistently accurate inferences from text; understanding figurative language, idioms, and metaphors.

Moral: Kohlberg's postconventional reasoning is possible—recognizing alternatives, social contracts, and developing universal moral standards transcending laws.

Considerations for Judging Typical vs. Atypical Child Development

Although the majority of children develop skills in each domain at similar ages and in similar patterns, individual differences dictate normal variance in each. Each child's personal history, characteristics, family history, and environment influence the rates and patterns of their development. This is why experts commonly indicate not exact ages, but ranges for normal

- 19 -

developmental signs. Also, slowly emerging skills more often indicate delays; skills differing in form, function, and quality more often indicate disorders. While most children with typical motor development sit up unassisted at around 6 months, some take longer; if a child cannot maintain a sitting position by 10 months, this could indicate a movement or motor delay disorder. An infant whose legs stiffen whenever s/he attempts to roll over could also have a motor disorder. Older children who cannot dress or undress, eat with utensils, draw with crayons, or cut with scissors may have atypical motor development. Two-year-olds having vocabularies of below 50 words and using no or few two- or three-word combinations are considered "late talkers," who may have speech or language delays. Also, some children excel in receptive understanding of spoken language, yet have expressive verbal difficulties.

Detecting Atypical and Typical Cognitive, Social, Emotional, and Moral Development in Children

With intellectual development, the common standard for suspecting atypical or delayed development is an IQ score two standard deviations or more below the average for a standardized test. With adaptive development, age range-appropriate criteria are used; for example, a normal 3-year-old is expected to toilet independently, but not to tie shoes until about 5-6 years. Parents do not expect 6-year-olds to cook or sew. Typical adaptive development is often gauged through comparison to age peers. However, not all children lagging behind peers have developmental disorders or delays: considerable individual variance is normal. Parents can assess children's social skills development by downloading informal checklists, many available online, indicating social skills according to age levels. Innate temperament is one factor in emotional development: some children jump fearfully at unexpected noises, others laugh; some get angry, others cry at the same stimulus. Cognitive and emotional development interact, as evidenced in toddlers: most 3-year-olds begin developing self-control of their emotions via growing cognitive development. This progresses from initially separate cognitive and emotional processes—e.g., a child is immersed in stacking blocks until another child takes a block; emotion overwhelms the first child. Eventually, toddlers learn and remember other ways to respond than screaming or hitting.

Developmental Milestones in Physical, Cognitive, and Linguistic Domains

2- to 6-Month-Olds

Physically, 2-month-olds can hold up their heads, start pushing up from stomach-lying, and their limb movements become smoother. Cognitively, they track moving objects visually, recognize people from distances, attend to faces, and fuss or cry showing boredom when activities do not change. Linguistically, they coo, gurgle, and turn heads toward sounds. Four-month-olds can hold heads steadily unsupported; may roll over stomach-to-back; bring hands to mouths; swing at hanging toys, or hold and shake toys; push down with legs when feet touch hard surfaces; and push up from stomach on elbows. They express happiness and sadness, respond to affection, reach for things they see, reach one-handed, track moving objects laterally, recognize familiar people and objects from distances, and closely observe faces. They start babbling, with expression; imitate heard sounds; and differentiate crying to express hunger, fatigue, or pain. Six-month-olds roll over front-to-back and back-to-front, begin sitting unsupported, support standing weight on legs, bounce, rock, and crawl backward and forward. They look at nearby objects, bring objects to mouth, display curiosity and try to obtain out-of-reach objects, and start passing objects hand-to-hand. They respond to sounds with vocalization, enjoy taking turns with parents making sounds, babble vowel strings, start including consonants, respond to their names, and vocalize pleasure and displeasure.

3 , 4 , and 5-Year-Olds

Socially and affectively, 3-year-olds typically show affection for others spontaneously; imitate adults and peers; show concern for crying friends; take turns during games and activities; display wide ranges of emotions; and understand the meanings of *mine*, *yours*, *his*, and *hers*. They easily separate from parents, can dress and undress themselves, and may become upset over major changes in daily routines. Four-year-olds pretend-play at being parents, become progressively more creative when playing make-believe, like new activities, prefer playing with other children to playing alone, cooperate with peers, frequently cannot distinguish between fantasy and reality, and enjoy talking about their preferences and interests. Five-year-olds are more likely to follow rules than younger children. They want to be like their friends and want to please them. They typically enjoy acting, singing, and dancing. They demonstrate sympathy and concern for other people. They have developed awareness of gender. Unlike 4-year-olds, 5-year-olds typically can tell the difference between fantasy and reality. They demonstrate more independence, e.g., going on their own to visit a neighbor, though adults still need to supervise them. They are likely to alternate between being very cooperative and being very demanding.

Ways in Which Different Types of Student Development Can Respectively Interact

When a student's cognitive development is ahead of his/her physical development, the child is likely to become frustrated when s/he can conceive of many things mentally, but cannot execute them physically. This is especially of younger children still having more physical development to achieve. Conversely, when a student's physical development is ahead of his/her cognitive development, young children are apt inadvertently to damage property and/or harm peers, younger children, or pets. Linguistic development affects social development in that more advanced language levels often facilitate social communication—but not always: some children show advanced language skills development, yet lack commensurate social skills. In another way, some less linguistically advanced students are skilled at using nonverbal communication skills to support social interactions. Some young students also have superior emotional intelligence (EQ) without necessarily having equally high academic or linguistic skills. More advanced affective development in elementary-age children can influence their moral development: the more children are able to share, take others' perspectives, empathize, and engage in prosocial behaviors, the more able they are to understand and internalize less rigid, more mutual, and socially-oriented morality.

Linguistic development interacts with cognitive development: psychologists find very high positive correlations between vocabulary and intelligence test scores. Teachers can enhance adolescent linguistic mediation skills with exercises regarding literal vs. metaphorical word meanings, and enhance pragmatics (using language to meet needs) through question-asking skills instruction. Teens whose cognitive development precedes their physical development excel academically but not athletically may be stereotyped by peers as "nerds," and those with superior physical skills but lacking equal academic success as "jocks." Teens whose physical development far precedes their cognitive development may inadvertently harm others, particularly when rapidly gaining adult strength. Similarly, adolescent affective development influences cognitive development because the amygdala matures sooner, generating intense teen emotions; yet the prefrontal cortex, which will eventually control those emotions, does not mature until young adulthood. Affective maturity influences moral levels in that the more emotionally mature the student, the more able s/he is to relate to others' needs, use prosocial behaviors, and understand universal human rights. Teen social interactions are increasingly influenced by emotional intelligence (EQ) development. Both affective and social developments interact with moral development when teens must make difficult ethical decisions involving others in social contexts.

Supporting Cognitive Development During Early Childhood

Adults help children focus attention by preventing interruptions and distractions. Show interest in children's activities, and offer observations and reflections about what they believe children are trying to achieve. Presenting learning materials in new ways piques curiosity: spread green "grass" cloth over blocks, making a hill; arrange toy farm animals on it; arrange dolls "reading" books in classroom reading or library corners. Observe nearby objects and events, inviting children to go see what they are. Support mastery motivation with materials sufficiently challenging for interest without being impossible, express interest, encourage children, and share their joy when they show what they accomplished. Offering multisensory exploration modes, e.g., scent bottles, water, sand, cornstarch, etc., supports sensorimotor learning. Encourage object permanence by playing peek-a-boo, reading stories with flaps hiding pictures, and about people leaving and returning. Toys reacting differentially to actions, e.g., push lights, busy boxes, balls, etc., teach cause-and-effect. Stacking rings or cups, tunnels, toy houses, etc. promote spatial understanding. Play tools, phones, keys, paint, water, markers, etc. promote tool use comprehension. Scaffold play to the next level; supply materials, ideas, and language slightly increasing complexity and elaborating play. Discuss time concepts like now and later, before and after, today, yesterday, tomorrow, etc. Use language and toys introducing shape awareness, one-on-one correspondence, amounts, size comparisons, and numbers.

Home and Community Cultural Influences on Elementary School Student Achievement

Some research into high-ability or gifted talent development in bilingual Hispanic elementary school students has concluded that influential home factors include family values like respect, education, career, and family; maternal roles; extended family role models; emotional support; Spanish-language maintenance; trips to parental native countries; and Hispanic legacies. School factors include safe school environments, flexible grouping, and English-language support (when necessary). Research also finds teachers of high-ability or gifted Hispanic students frequently know little or nothing about home language spoken. They tend to assume if a student is not in ESL classes or programs, s/he is not bilingual; but in fact, many are both bilingual and biliterate. Teachers also demonstrate limited understanding of multicultural meanings and practices. Educational investigators advise, standards for assessing Hispanic students should reflect their cultural and ethnic backgrounds to be accurate and relevant. They state the need for establishing direct communication between Hispanic parents and schools, including information about gifted program identification procedures and home methods parents can use to help their children educationally. Another need is professional development to help faculty and staff understand differences in student cultural, language, and learning styles. Also, access for classroom teachers to information about Hispanic students' linguistic histories and present Spanish usage is advised.

Impacts of Community, Racial, and Cultural Differences

With American demographics rapidly changing, schools reflect societal racism. Racial and cultural differences cannot be overlooked anymore. It is not only necessary, but moreover healthy for minorities to express their racial and cultural identities. Teachers, administrators, school staff, parents—all school community members—must be involved in designing learning experiences founded on understanding and respect for racial and cultural diversity. While educational experts believe this requires the whole society to unite for success, they concede that as this has not occurred, the educational system must still strive for resolution of racial and cultural conflicts through collective efforts. While schools are desegregated, surrounding cities and suburbs are not. Neighborhoods, the foundations of American society, are subject to racial and economic limitations. Because children learn from each other, their education is strongly affected by community factors

Copyright © Mometrix Media. You have been licensed one copy of this document for personal use only. Any other reproduction or redistribution is strictly prohibited. All rights reserved.

of housing costs, incomes, lending policies, and racial and institutional discrimination. While some Latino parents believe bilingual education can overcome discrimination and black parents believe desegregation promotes equality, some Latino parents see desegregation as impeding their objectives by dissipating Latin influence and destroying bilingual programs. Experts call for compromise, noting that both must coexist by law.

Considerations Related to Children's School Readiness and Learning Readiness

The majority of children may enter school ready to learn, but not optimally; and have a range of cultural, environmental, and educational background experiences. Readiness works two ways: preparing children for school, and preparing schools for children. For educators to promote all children's learning, they must offer school environments recognizing background diversity, enabling comfortable transitions to successive learning levels, and supplying community supports as needed. School readiness is divided into readiness for school and readiness to learn. The former involves specific motor, cognitive, linguistic, and social skills enabling children to absorb school curriculum; the latter involves the developmental level where children are capable of learning specific materials. Educators differentiate traditional ideas of readiness placing responsibility on children vs. giving schools the responsibility to provide necessary services in the least restrictive environment to enable children to reach their full potentials. Also, readiness assessment criteria can have inappropriate expectations, not recognizing normal variations in individual development and learning natures and rates. Experts find three factors critical: recognizing and supporting individual cultural, linguistic, and other differences; addressing early life experience inequities to ensure that all children have access to opportunities promoting school success; and appropriate and reasonable expectations of children entering school.

Activities Teachers can Give Students in Grades K-6 to Help Them Develop

Grades K-2

Explain different examples of school success. Realize the relation between what you want to achieve and goal-setting. Describe a behavior you want to change. Give examples of academic and personal goals to set. Divide a goal into manageable steps.

Grades 1-3

Identify a situation you want to change. Explain how becoming what you want and school success are related. Identify progress you have made toward your goal. Explain how to improve your classroom behavior, e.g., paying attention, finishing assignments, raising your hand more, etc. Make a plan for improving your work in a certain school subject. Make a plan for a personal goal. Reward yourself for achievements using self-talk. Teachers can use puppet shows wherein puppets apply planning and goal-setting skills.

Grades 3-4

Explain how literary characters, people studied in social sciences, friends, and you have overcome goal obstacles. Identify people and conditions contributing to your goal achievement. Name steps for doing homework, studying for tests, organizing materials and spaces, etc. Name things interfering with goal achievement you could not change. Evaluate what you could have done differently to achieve a goal better.

Grades 4-6

Develop friendship and academic goals with action steps and dates, monitor progress, analyze step delays or changes, and evaluate your goal achievement level.

Instructional Methods That Reflect Individual Student Differences and Developmental Levels

Elementary grade students include wide ranges of individual differences. Teachers must pay attention to and address these differences to maximize the potential of each individual student. Many educational theorists and research studies show that when students receive instruction that responds to their developmental levels, as well as their learning profiles and personal interests, they find school more satisfying and achieve more success in said school. Teachers who differentiate instruction according to variable individual student learning needs are also recognized as more professional, competent, and creative educators. For example, elementary school teachers can vary instructional content by providing students with materials at different reading levels. They can record or procure some texts on tape for students with visual weaknesses and auditory strengths. They can make different vocabulary and/or spelling lists according to differing student readiness levels. They can present concepts in both visual and auditory modalities. They can assign reading buddies to students who are struggling readers—and/or to all students to enhance their reading skills. They can assign small groups for re-teaching skills or concepts to struggling learners, and for enriching the skills or thought processes of advanced students.

Classroom Instruction That Teachers Can Differentiate Among Students

Based on each student's learning profile, interests, readiness, and learning levels, teachers can differentiate classroom instruction. Four elements for differentiating instruction are: (1) content to learn; (2) the process students use to master content; (3) products students will produce, requiring practice, application, and extension and elaboration of what they learn in a unit; and (4) learning environment, i.e., how the classroom functions and how students experience it. Some examples of differentiating processes include: (1) set up interest centers where students can explore subcategories of class subjects they find most interesting. (2) Assign tiered activities with different levels of complexity, challenge, or support for acquiring the same skills and understanding. (3) Provide hands-on supports, like manipulatives, for students needing these. (4) Combine work commonly assigned to the entire class with individualized work for specific students into lists of tasks, making personal agendas to complete during designated and/or spare time. (5) Differentiate durations students take to finish tasks, allowing advanced students to examine topics in-depth and enable added support for struggling students.

Elements of Classroom Instruction That Teachers Can Differentiate Among Students

To address the needs of individual students in a class, teachers can differentiate things like (1) content; (2) processes and activities whereby students learn content; (3) products students create by applying and demonstrating what they learned; and (4) learning environment, i.e., how students perceive the classroom and how it functions. Some examples of differentiating products for elementary school students include: (1) design rubrics matching and extending various student skill levels. (2) Offer choices to students in how to demonstrate learning, like between writing a letter, creating a labeled art mural, or producing a puppet show. (3) Invite students to design their own product assignments, providing they include necessary components. (4) Give students options to work on projects in small groups or individually. Some examples of differentiating an elementary school learning environment include: (1) furnish materials reflecting diverse home and cultural backgrounds. (2) Establish clear guidelines matching individual student needs for independent work. (3) Ensure the classroom contains both areas for collaboration and areas for undistracted quiet work. (4) Help students realize some classmates need to sit quietly, while others must move about. (5) Develop routines enabling students to get help when teachers are temporarily busy with others.

Decision-Making and Goal-Setting Skills

Young people are able to develop some independence and recognize they have some control over their lives by learning to set goals. First, they must decide what they want to accomplish. This decision-making helps motivate children to achieve things, not for external rewards or to please other people, but for their own satisfaction. This helps them develop internal locus of control and intrinsic motivation. One step adults can help with is first defining what a goal is. They might use the analogy of a hockey or soccer goal. Explain that winning a goal is the end product of much hard work; setting a goal is describing what you want to get done or the place you want to get to, and that involves planning for something you want to understand or do better. Another step for adults to help children determine their priorities is by listening more than talking. Observing some strengths and needs is acceptable, but encourage children to talk about themselves. For example, observe a child has learned something, and ask what s/he next wants to do with this skill. Ask if a child is worried about anything in school that will be difficult.

Teach students how to talk about goals to understand and set them. For example, they must define what they want to accomplish, by when, and which related skills they already know. Children of any age may conceive unrealistic goals. For example, a child who has not learned how to ice skate may decide s/he wants to place ice hockey. Rather than squelching aspirations by telling the child this will be impossible or too difficult, help the child refine the goal into smaller associated goals as steps to the ultimate goal. For example, suggest setting the preliminary goal of learning ice skating. This generalizes to all goals: they are not accomplished all in one attempt, but rather involve series of many steps. Assist children with task analysis, breaking a goal down into its smaller component steps or skills. They can make each skill or step into a smaller or shorter-term goal toward the main goal. Help students make visual reminders, e.g., a worksheet with a drawing of a ladder, to list steps toward a goal on the rungs; a goal board with a drawing of a soccer goal, etc. Also help students track and mark their progress, and celebrate success.

Impacts of Student Substance Use and Abuse on Development and Learning

Not only are the physical and neurological development of younger children incomplete, even adolescents have yet to undergo full brain development. Therefore, using alcohol and other drugs can cause damage to their central nervous systems and other body systems and organs. Damage can be temporary or permanent, reversible or irreversible. In addition to interfering with attention in school, substance use can interfere with myelination, whereby brain and nerve cells develop coating sheaths, both protecting them and facilitating impulse and signal transmission. This process continues into young adulthood. The heart, lungs, liver, kidneys, other organs and systems are still developing and can be damaged, sometimes irreparably, at early ages. Substance use also undermines motivation to learn and achieve. Under the influence, students attend to the effects they experience, not acquiring new information or getting anything done. When use becomes abuse, addiction causes focus only on getting more of the needed substance to relieve withdrawal symptoms and reproduce the original high—which latter is impossible and leads to ingesting increasing amounts. Students neglect hygiene and schoolwork, attendance and grades fall, and dropouts become more common. Substance use and abuse triggers or exacerbates anxiety, depression, paranoia, schizophrenia, bipolar disorder, and other mental disorders.

Conditions Leading to Gang Involvement

The organizational structures and activities of gangs are extremely complex social phenomena. In low socioeconomic urban neighborhoods, gangs often develop in part to protect members against violence from adult criminals and other gangs. This positive motivation and protective benefit are still accompanied by undesirable effects. Gang involvement is more likely during adolescence, when students search to form personal identities. Many economically disadvantaged urban youth lack adult supervision, mentoring, and role models. Gang membership fills needs for group affiliation, belonging, identity, rules, and behavioral direction (even if behaviors are undesirable). Youth struggling to reconcile newly discovered abstractions and complexities find security in adversarial relationships among gangs, defining "us vs. them" mentalities that are less equivocal or contradictory. These enmities also provide concrete foes for youth feeling helpless to control or combat larger, seemingly unassailable foes of social ills like poverty, illiteracy, crime, discrimination, lack of opportunity, etc. Even in affluent communities, gangs may form to fulfill the same needs for social acceptance, allegiance, group identity, rules, etc.—sometimes particularly with inadequate parental or adult involvement, communication, and role modeling. Youth with unformed or unstable identities, vulnerable to peer pressure, are at higher risk for committing criminal acts as gang members. This can curtail their education, work, freedom, and life.

Types of Play Identified by Mildred Parten

(1) Unoccupied: not truly playing, simply observing anything of interest; a child may travel, stay still, move randomly, follow others, etc. (2) Solitary or independent play: playing alone, unaware or uninterested in others' activities. Two- and 3-year-olds do this more often than older children. (3) Onlooker behavior: observing others playing without participating, also more frequent among younger children. The child may talk about or otherwise interact socially, but not join the activity. (4) Parallel play (also called social coaction or adjacent play): playing near other children, but separately. The child might imitate other children's behaviors. This type is considered transitional from solitary and onlooker play to associative and cooperative play. (5) Associative play: showing interest in and interaction with others playing, but activities are not coordinated or organized. (6) Cooperative play: interested in both play activity and participants. Activities are organized; participants assume or assign roles. Group identification or identity may develop. Requiring greater organizational skills and social maturity, this is more common with children older than preschoolers and kindergarteners. Parten found these play types progressively more socially mature, as child communication skills and interaction opportunities increased. Others generally agree regarding types, but consider them not necessarily sequential and/or influenced by other factors, e.g., how well children know each other, etc.

Importance of Play to Early Childhood Development and Learning

The UN High Commission for Human Rights declares play every child's right. Pediatric research finds playing essential for healthy brain development. Playing develops physical strength, dexterity, cognitive and emotional strength, imagination, and early engagement and interaction with the environment. While exposure to letters and numbers promotes literacy, children learn about what people do, how they behave, and what they are thinking from playing, not from letters or numbers. By playing, children create and explore worlds they can master, enabling their overcoming fears and practicing adult roles. This helps them develop new skills, increasing their self-confidence and developing resiliency, which they will need for future challenges. Children learn sharing, group cooperation, conflict resolution, negotiation, self-advocacy, and leadership skills through unstructured play. Through child-driven play, they progress at their own paces, practice decision-making skills, and discover and pursue their own interests. Playing involves more healthful physical activity than passively watching TV, playing video games, etc. When young children's physical development precedes verbal development, they can express frustrations, experiences, and viewpoints through play better than language. Emotional-social development should be integrated with cognitive and academic learning. Research finds play enhances learning readiness, learning behaviors, problem-solving skills, and school adjustment.

Contemporary Model of the Whole Child Approach

The Association for Supervision and Curriculum Development (ASCD) and US Centers for Disease Control and Prevention (CDC) have collaborated to produce the Whole School, Whole Community, Whole Child (WSCC) model to coordinate public health, school health, and educational processes, policies, and practices to improve health and learning, which are interrelated. They say a whole child approach to learning, teaching, and community involvement means each child deserves to be safe, healthy, supported, engaged, and challenged. Related to this model, ASCD's Whole Child Initiative aims to help educators, policymakers, families, and community members realize a vision of educating the whole child through collaborative, sustainable action. ASCD's School Improvement Tool is a totally online needs assessment that educators in schools and districts worldwide can use to determine what practices to implement or improve to realize the whole-child education vision. The tool enables educators to survey, numerically score, and color-code schools regarding key criteria, e.g., all students enter school healthy, and learn about and practice healthy lifestyles; learn in physically and emotionally safe environments; are actively engaged in learning, connected to school and community, and supported by caring, qualified adults; have access to personalized learning; are challenged academically, prepared for college or employment success; and school whole-child approaches are sustainable.

Models of Developmentally Appropriate Instruction Related to Literacy Development

Direct or Explicit Instruction

Whole-class, small-group, and one-on-one learning. A teacher shows a class of 4-year-olds how to hold a book; points to the cover picture, inviting brainstorming about the book's subject; points to and reads aloud each title word; then reads them the book.

Centers

Individually-themed classroom areas for student selection, including computers, arts and crafts, gross and fine motor skills, etc. to enable meaningful, self-initiated, self-directed activity at students' own paces, stimulating language development and social interaction. Free play: students explore the physical environment, pretend, converse; pursue curiosity; and practice gross and fine motor skills and oral language skills. Students might construct buildings, make cookies, walk balance beams, paint, dress in costumes, etc. Letting students choose play areas facilitates self-exploration and using real-life manipulatives, informing all literacy instruction areas. Students develop learning styles and sense of the world.

Small-Group Instruction

Teacher modeling print reading; discussion of story events per page; problem-solving or predicting story endings and reasons; open-ended learning opportunities, meaningful to each group, focusing on each student's needs.

Guided Reading

Teacher and students read text fluently in unison with expression and connotation; then discuss the story, including teacher observations, reteaching; enrichment; self-monitoring; enabling analytical and critical reading patterns, enhancing phonemic awareness, phonics, comprehension, fluency, and reading confidence.

Student Diversity

Many people think of visible racial differences—African-American, Caucasian, Asian, Asian Indian, Hispanic, Native American, Pacific Islander, etc.—when they think of diversity. However, diversity also includes socioeconomic, from the highest wealthy tiers to the impoverished and everything in between; homelessness; living in transitional housing; all manners of disabilities, both obvious and "hidden"; intellectual and creative giftedness; urban, suburban, exurban, and rural living; different home cultures; learning English as a new language; illiterate families, parents with advanced degrees, and everything in between; younger and older ages than classmates; and many more. General principles include: treat students as individuals with unique, complex identities; ask open-ended questions, inviting reports of experiences and observations. Do not ask students to speak for their minority group. Pronounce every student's name correctly. Be aware of influences on student responses by making eye contact with everybody. Extend wait time to include more reflective and less assertive students. Ask questions challenging dominant students by drawing out quieter students in small groups; talk with and encourage students outside class. Vary teaching methods to address various learning styles and expand student strategy repertoires. Establish egalitarian norms and rules, promoting respect. Be cognizant of potential student performance anxiety in competitive settings, but not overprotective. Empathetically and tactfully give clear, straightforward standards, assessment criteria, and early feedback.

Native English speakers, including teachers, may take for granted the many idiomatic expressions we use, e.g., "between a rock and a hard place," "once in a blue moon," etc. But because they do not convey literal meanings, these sayings confuse students whose first language is not English, causing them to miss important concepts. Teachers should avoid using idioms. If they do, they should translate and/or explain them. All students benefit from linguistic redundancy, e.g., seeing print or writing while hearing speech; ELLs especially benefit. Teachers reinforce information by presenting it in multiple forms. They should also examine whether the examples they give assume or favor certain experiences or backgrounds, e.g., hobbies or activities preferred by one gender; examples based on regional, cultural, historical, or political knowledge unfamiliar to students from other countries, regions, or cultures. Teachers should provide diverse examples. They can learn some of these from their students. Teachers should not assume students who do not speak up do not know class material: Asian and other cultures find silence respectful and frown on attracting attention, while some students have learned responses to aversive consequences for participating. Teachers should also examine classroom humor to ensure jokes do not disparage any groups or differences, which occurs surprisingly often.

Cognitive Disabilities

(1) Intellectual disability (ID): students function intellectually two standard deviations or more lower than average age peers. Adaptive functioning may be equal, higher, or lower than intellectual functioning depending on strengths, background experience, and training. Students often learn the same ways as others, but at slower rates. Developmental milestones occur at later ages; learning accomplishments take longer periods to acquire. Emotional and social maturity often correspond to mental age, but also frequently advance beyond it with experience. Students have difficulty understanding abstract concepts, interpreting things literally and concretely. (2) Autism spectrum disorders (ASD): considered an emotional as well as cognitive disability, the spectrum ranges from profound to negligible impairment in activities of daily living and behavior. Intelligence ranges from profound ID to gifted. ASDs often impair social understanding and interaction, e.g., observing, interpreting, and producing nonverbal signals indicating emotions, attitudes, etc. Students have difficulty recognizing sarcasm, figurative language, humor; starting conversations; and conversational give-and-take. Behavioral characteristics include repetitive actions, restricted interests, rigid routines or schedules, focusing on one activity for long times, and difficulty transitioning among activities. (3) Specific learning disabilities: students are not intellectually

impaired, but have deficits processing linguistic and/or numeric information. Typically their school achievement is far behind their intellectual ability.

Auditory Disabilities

(1) One auditory disability not involving the hearing mechanism is central auditory processing disorder, a neurological deficit in interpreting the structure and meanings of speech sounds. Other auditory disabilities involve hearing loss. (2) Totally deaf students cannot hear any sound, often not even with hearing aids. (3) Hard of hearing students have hearing loss but some residual hearing. Hearing loss can be sensorineural, i.e., the cochlea, cochlear hair cells, and acoustic or auditory nerves do not function; or conductive, i.e., something in the outer or middle ear prevents conduction of sound waves, e.g., outer-ear wax buildup, middle-ear pus, fluid from otitis media infection, fused or immobilized middle-ear ossicles from otosclerosis, etc. Sensorineural hearing loss is irreversible, but cochlear implants enable hearing for some. Conductive hearing loss is most often treatable with surgery, medication, hearing aids, etc. Slight hearing loss, i.e., inability to hear whispering, is measured at 25-40 dB; mild hearing loss, i.e., understanding conversation with normal loudness up to 3-5 feet, 41-54 dB; moderate hearing loss, i.e., only understanding loud speech nearby, 55-69 dB; severe hearing loss, i.e., hearing only loud voices a foot away, 70-89 dB; profound hearing loss, i.e., feeling vibrations but not hearing tones, 90 dB or more. Noise-induced hearing loss is only at middle frequency (c. 4000 Hz).

Visual Impairments

The definition of 20/20 vision is reading at 20 feet from a Snellen eye chart what one normally should see. Comparably, 20/200 vision is reading at 20 feet what one should see at 200 feet. Legal blindness is defined as 20/200 after correction in the better eye. Low vision is described as anywhere from 20/200 to 20/70 after correction in the better eye and a visual field of 30 degrees or less. A visual field of 20 degrees or less is tunnel vision. Travel vision ranges from 5/200 to 10/200. Motion perception is 3/200 to 5/200, typically for moving objects. Seeing bright light from 3 feet away but not movement, i.e., below 3/200 vision, is light perception. Not seeing strong light directly in the eyes is total blindness. Students may be born blind or become blind adventitiously. Some children are born with congenital cataracts, causing opacity clouding the lenses and blindness unless surgically removed with a replacement lens implanted. Students with diabetes can develop diabetic retinopathy, i.e., vascular changes causing retinal hemorrhaging and blindness. Some students inherit glaucoma, wherein inner-eye fluid buildup creates pressure which causes visual impairment and blindness when untreated. Genetically, students may inherit total or red-green color-blindness; lack of pigment in albinism causes photosensitivity and vision problems. Accidents or injuries include retinopathy of prematurity from insufficiently regulated incubator oxygen, eyeball punctures, and retinal dislocation or detachment.

Motor or Physical Disabilities

Physical or motor disabilities impair mobility and may also affect coordination, balance, strength, and/or flexibility. Some students are missing one or more limbs, congenitally or through accident, injury, or amputation. They may use prostheses and/or wheelchairs, walkers, canes, crutches or other mobility aids. Students with cerebral palsy have neurological deficits in control and coordination of muscular movements. Impairments range from a slight limp to being in a wheelchair or bed-bound. Cerebral palsy (CP) patients often have dyspraxia or apraxia, i.e., impaired development of their motor coordination. This can affect any body parts, e.g., speech muscles, hand grasp, fine motor skills, walking, etc. with varying degrees of severity. CP also causes spasticity, i.e., excessive muscle tension or rigidity; athetosis, i.e., excessive involuntary body movements; or both combined. Students born with spina bifida may have foot, ankle, or lower-limb weakness to below-waist paralysis, depending on the spinal level of incomplete neural tube closure. Students with severe type 1 diabetes may require amputations when the disease impairs blood circulation, especially in their lower extremities. In addition to assistive and adaptive devices and prostheses, treatments include physical therapy for large muscles, occupational therapy for small muscles, recreational therapy for adapted activities, etc.

Speech or Language Disorders

Speech or language disorders may involve speech only, language only, or both. Speech-only disorders include articulation disorders, the most common of which makes children distort, substitute, or omit certain speech sounds—typically consonants—at ages above typical norms for correct pronunciation. Typical remediation is speech therapy, which can include exercising articulatory muscles, audio feedback, targeting correct articulatory positions, tools (tongue depressors and bite plates), etc. Voice disorders include hypernasality, often secondary to cleft palate; hoarseness secondary to vocal polyps, nodules, or dysarthria (a neurological muscular control disorder); too-high, too-low, or unstable pitch; volume control problems, etc. Treatment depends on causes: nodules and polyps are surgically removed, clefts are repaired, and therapeutic techniques address other problems. Another speech disorder is stuttering, or rate and rhythm disorders. A variety of therapies exists, such as breathing methods, delayed auditory feedback, etc. Some stutterers actually outgrow the condition regardless of therapy. Some become "fluent stutterers." Some benefit greatly from some therapies, some little or none. Language disorders include delayed language development, secondary to intellectual disability or environmental deprivation; aphasia, secondary to neurological damage or deficits, e.g., traumatic brain injury or cerebral palsy, impairing expressive and/or receptive language processing; and language-related learning disabilities, like dyslexia (reading) or dysgraphia (writing). Language disorder therapies include stimulation and practice.

Impacts Sensory Impairments Have on Learning

Students with visual impairments miss a lot of input in our highly visually-oriented society. Orientation and mobility specialists can help them navigate school and other public environments more independently. Blind students may have canes or service dogs to aid mobility; teachers must plan for these and classmate interactions with them. In classrooms, blind and visually impaired students benefit from magnifiers, large-print texts, seating close to the board and teacher, audiobooks, and text-to-speech computer software for adapting texts; speech-to-text software for dictating written compositions; Braille materials or OptaCons for reading; and modified lighting, brighter and/or with less glare depending on the type and degree of impairment. Teachers can also provide materials with bright, solid colors and bold black outlines. Students with hearing impairments are safer in environments that accompany sound-based fire alarms with strobe lights. Teachers and classmates must remember to face or touch them to get their attention; speak face-to-face with students who read lips; include American Sign Language (ASL) interpreters in conversations or lessons for students who have them; and accompany spoken instruction and discussion with supplementary visual information. Speech-to-text software enables deaf and hearing-impaired students to read spoken language. Educators must also respect and teach classmates the importance and strength of deaf culture for students identifying with it.

Behavioral Disorders

Attention deficit hyperactivity disorder (ADHD) is familiar to many: student attention spans are deficiently short; students are too easily distracted; self-regulation deficits cause impulsive

- 30 -

behaviors; students display excessive physical activity and have difficulty sitting still, focusing attention, and persisting in the same activity for extended durations. Medication like Ritalin, Cylert, other stimulants—even caffeine—enable better focusing, but must be accompanied by behavioral therapy. Some students are identified with oppositional defiant disorder (ODD), symptomatized by irritability, aggression, hostility, negativity, and defiance. They frequently lose their tempers, argue with adults, purposely irritate others, blame others for their behaviors and mistakes, express or demonstrate anger and resentment, and act vindictively and spitefully. Roughly half of preschoolers with ODD outgrow it by age 8, a few develop ADHD instead, and some develop comorbid disorders (anxiety, depression). Some develop conduct disorder (CD) in a few years. ODD students tend to have better school performance but worse social skills than CD patients. CD is the severest childhood psychiatric disorder, involving physical aggression to people and animals, bullying, cruelty, property destruction, lying, theft, and serious rule or legal violations. Nearly 20 percent of teens with ODD or CD have antisocial personality disorder (APD)—an extension of CD—in adulthood. Multisystem therapy is most effective; many improve, but few completely recover.

Different disorders can cause similar classroom behaviors. For example, students with intellectual disabilities (ID), autism spectrum disorders (ASD), communication disorders, attention deficit hyperactivity disorder (ADHD), and others can all display disruptive behaviors. The reasons may differ, but the net results are the same. Some inappropriate behaviors are caused by lack of maturity or understanding, as with IDs. Students with ASDs, communication disorders, or ADHD may explode out of frustration over not having their needs met. Students with communication deficits may scream, hit, or throw things in lieu of having the language or speech skills to express what they feel, need, or want. ADHD students unable to sit still or concentrate often disrupt classes with out-of-seat behavior, excessive movements, vocal interruptions, etc. ASD students can have "meltdowns" or tantrums at sensory overload, having to switch activities, etc. Students with IDs or emotional or behavioral disorders often have immature or deficient self-regulation abilities. Attention-seeking behaviors are frequently inadvertently reinforced by the attention of adults trying to address them. While it requires planning and consistent, systematic implementation, behavior modification techniques can successfully resolve many behavioral dilemmas by teaching more acceptable replacement behaviors for communicating, meeting needs, making adjustments, and establishing and reinforcing self-control and social interaction skills.

Learning Style, Gender, Culture, Socioeconomic Status, and Prior Knowledge and Experience

Learning style: student A is nonplused by verbal teacher explanation of a new physics concept, but lights up immediately when shown a drawing of it (visual learning style). Student B does not understand the drawing, but "gets" it exactly when guided by the teacher to act it out physically (kinesthetic learning style). Gender: boys are physically aggressive; girls engage in relational aggression (hurting feelings, undermining self-esteem and reputations). Boys respond positively when educators redirect their aggression to athletic competition; girls when educators redirect their energy to performing services helping others. Culture: students from Asian, Latin, and Native American cultures prefer cooperative over competitive activities; helping others and being part of the group is more important to them than standing out individually. They volunteer to speak in class less not for lack of preparation but to show respect. Socioeconomic status: students in poverty miss school from lacking proper clothing and shoes. Malnutrition impairs ability to concentrate, remember, and perform. Affluent parents can afford private tutoring if their children struggle with academic subjects; poor ones cannot. Prior knowledge and experience: students with marginal literacy cannot write stories but excel at oral storytelling, a strong and familiar tradition in their cultures and families.

Motivation, Self-Confidence, Self-Esteem, Cognitive Development, Maturity, and Language

Motivation: the best-designed and implemented instruction will fail if students are not first motivated. Research finds internal locus of control, wherein students attribute their success or failure to causes within themselves (ability, effort, interest, or ambition, for instance), more motivating for achievement than external locus of control, wherein students attribute their success or failure to outside causes (unfair tests, poor teachers, distracting classmates, classroom conditions). Teachers engage student interest by selecting subjects students want to know about, and offering choices of learning activities and specific subtopics to investigate. Self-confidence: students lacking overall self-confidence hesitate to try anything, anticipating failure. They need encouragement and approval of themselves as persons, plus ample reinforcement of every initial small success. Others only lack self-confidence for specific tasks or subjects; Bandura calls this self-efficacy. Providing alternative learning methods and enabling successful experiences improve self-efficacy. Self-esteem: largely determines self-confidence. Teachers can raise self-esteem by showing and communicating that they value and care about students, entrusting them with responsibilities, and recognizing their accomplishments. Cognitive development: students cognitively ahead of or behind classmates need differentiated instruction appropriate to their cognitive levels for engagement and achievement. Maturity: teachers must consider whether emotional or social maturity differs from physical and/or cognitive maturity and interact appropriately. Language: many teachers mistake ELL deficits for learning disabilities, causing overrepresentation in special education.

Americans with Disabilities Act (ADA)

Signed into law in 1990, the ADA granted the same civil rights protections based on disabilities as previously accorded by the 1964 Civil Rights Act based on race, color, religion, gender, or national origin. The ADA was thus modeled on the Civil Rights Act, and also on the 1973 Rehabilitation Act requiring federally funded programs and activities to provide equal access to persons having disabilities. The terms of the ADA include public buildings, facilities, programs, and activities, which include all public school buildings, facilities, programs, and activities. Hence this law makes it illegal for public schools to prevent students with disabilities from accessing them because of architectural and other barriers. Titles II and III of the ADA include enforceable standards for accessible design and construction of buildings and facilities, barrier removal, alterations, and accessibility. Predating the Individuals with Disabilities Education Act (IDEA), which would more extensively address the rights of children with disabilities to education, the ADA also requires equal opportunities, participation, and benefits from public facilities for individuals with disabilities, "in the most integrated setting appropriate to the needs of the individual." This foreshadowed the IDEA's later emphasis on inclusion. The ADA prohibits discrimination based on disability.

Individuals with Disabilities Education Act (IDEA)

Passed in 1975 and reauthorized a number of times since, IDEA guarantees the right of children with disabilities to a free, appropriate, public education (FAPE) in the least restrictive environment (LRE) possible that meets their educational needs. The right to education of school-aged children is covered in IDEA Part B; Part C, added subsequently, addresses the right to early intervention and early childhood education of babies and toddlers with disabilities. The LRE clause has dual purposes: (1) to prevent segregation of children with disabilities to special schools or classes, and (2) to be interpreted differently according to the needs of every individual student. An important provision of IDEA is that every student to receive special education and related services for an identified, eligible disability must have an Individual Education Plan (IEP). An IEP team including students, teachers, parents, special educators, therapists, and others involved develops the student's IEP, identifying goals the student needs and is able to achieve; related, specific learning objectives; timeframes; and numerical criteria for determining success. The IEP includes any assistive and adaptive devices and equipment and other supports the student requires to achieve identified educational goals.

Section 504 of the Rehabilitation Act of 1973

Section 504 protects the rights of people with disabilities in activities and programs receiving federal funds by prohibiting discrimination against them based on disability. When the US Department of Education (ED) provides financial assistance to public school districts and other local or state education agencies, activities, or programs, it enforces Section 504. ED also has an Office for Civil Rights (OCR), headquartered in Washington, D.C. with 12 enforcement offices, to ensure civil rights laws including Section 504 are followed. Section 504 requires school districts to provide "free, appropriate public education" (FAPE) to each of their qualifying students with disabilities. This law defines an appropriate education as designed to meet disabled students' individual educational needs as well as ensuring that non-disabled students' needs are met; provided together with non-disabled students as much as meets the needs of the student with disabilities; having established evaluation and placement procedures to prevent inappropriate placement or misclassification, and periodic reevaluations; affording due process for parents to receive mandated notices, review their children's records, and challenge identification, evaluation, and placement choices.

Elementary and Secondary Education Act's (ESEA)

The Every Student Succeeds Act (ESSA), replacing the ESEA and NCLB acts, demands fair, rigorous accountability for all school performance levels; meeting diverse learner needs; and more equitable provision of fair opportunities for student success; to ensure opportunity and equity for every student. The reauthorization of ESEA into ESSA requires its programs to offer a wide range of supports and resources enabling students to graduate, attend college, and establish careers. ESSA includes programs for meeting the special educational needs of ELL students, students with disabilities, homeless students, Native American students, migrant workers' children, and delinquent and neglected students. It states the federal government's responsibility for giving assistance to rural school districts, districts sustaining impacts of federal activities and properties, and other high-need areas and regions. The 2010 ESEA reauthorization also proposed to increase support for inclusion and better outcomes for students with disabilities as a supplement to funding for the Individuals with Disabilities Education Act (IDEA). This support includes more appropriate, accurate assessment measures of students with disabilities; better teacher and administrator preparation for meeting diverse learner needs; and better locally and state-determined curricula, incorporating universal design principles, implemented by more districts and schools.

The ESEA's 2010 reauthorization continues formula grants to states and school districts for ELL programs, allowing a variety of program types and ELL teacher professional development. The 2010 reauthorization requires new state criteria for consistent eligibility determination, placement, and program or service duration based on valid, reliable state ELP assessments; and system implementation for evaluating ELL program effectiveness and garnering data on ELL subgroup achievement for driving better district program improvement decisions and effective program selection. This reauthorization also proposed new, competitive grants to states, districts, and nonprofits for innovative program development; best-practice knowledge base building; ELL instructional practice improvement; and funding research, leadership, and partnerships for effective teacher development. Another provision requires states to adopt and implement statewide ELP standards by grade, aligned with state academic content standards for college and career readiness. Strengthening formula grants for meeting migrant student educational needs included updating the funding formula for timelier, accurate data incorporation; and facilitating and reinforcing interstate endeavors for supporting migrant student transitions into local communities and schools. Funds for homeless students were changed from Title I allocation shares to allocations based on student numbers. The administration proposed to remove service obstacles, clarify statutory ambiguities causing service delays, and require grantees to report academic outcomes.

Characteristics of ELL Students as a Population

The ELL student population is widely heterogeneous. Some families speak no English at home, only English, or several languages. They may identify only with American culture, strongly with several cultures, or deeply with one non-American culture. They have been stigmatized for not speaking English, speaking English, or how they speak English. They live in communities sharing common culture, without other ELLs, or have lived in America for generations. They struggle or excel in school—some in specific subjects. They may feel competent or disaffected in school. ELL immigration status, birthplace, socioeconomic status, academic knowledge, language proficiency levels, and expectations of school all vary. ELL student prevalence has extended from a few to all US states. This diversity within and among ELLs requires multiple responses for meeting educational needs. Disabilities are not more prevalent among ELLs: research shows assessments not distinguishing ELL status from disability cause misdiagnoses. Educators should not assume ELL students learn English easily or readily. Also, English oral fluency does not equal mastery: systematic academic assessments are necessary. Differing L1s, previous education, socioeconomic and immigration status mean not all ELLs learn English the same way. Accommodations benefit not only ELLs, but others. Vocabulary is not the sole focus of ELL instruction: structures and meanings are equally important, even with limited ELP.

Instructing ELL Students Effectively

Teachers should give ELLs challenging, meaningful curriculum content, text choices, and authentic reading and writing activities. Placement by academic achievement, not ELP, with high-quality instruction in challenging classes enables greater learning and performance. Technology supports ELL motivation, writing and editing skills development, and class blog and website collaboration. Teacher awareness of ELLs' previous literacy experiences, backgrounds, and L2 learning benefits and challenges enables more effective instruction. ELLs are challenged to understand implicit cultural norms and knowledge; learn to translate and code-switch; develop metalinguistic awareness; negotiate differences between school literacy practices and home or community; and address the social, cultural, and political dimensions of linguistic status issues. Studies show ELL reading comprehension, writer identity development, and peer collaboration are developed through extracurricular composition. Teachers can use these methods to promote ELL investment in school learning, decrease home-school distance, and help students view their home languages and cultures not as obstacles or discards, but educational resources and contributors. Teachers should teach K-12 ELLs academic literacy basics and help them connect school content to their own knowledge.

Classrooms Where All Students Participate and Have Their Educational Needs Met

Establish a classroom climate where students feel safe, secure, and engaged in learning rather than unchallenged or threatened. Discuss how students want the classroom to work and how to maintain the best climate. Promote cooperation, involvement, and a stimulating, inviting, productive, learner-friendly environment with functional, appealing arrangements and displays through a classroom plan, including students in decision-making processes. Organize the classroom to allow movement, stations for long-term involvement and learning, and easy technology and information access. Engage students in the processes of developing, comprehending, and maintaining procedures and routines, with a limited number of positively stated, specific, clear rules; practice and reinforce these throughout the school year. Assign and manage meaningful assignments with purposes, in real-life settings with audiences. Prepare for teaching: active student involvement in planning, preparing, implementing, and assessing learning units reduces behavior and discipline issues. Consider having students create and submit actual proposals to organizations, corporations, or city councils needing new ideas. Consistently communicate and reinforce class procedures and routines. Discuss behavior in class. Discuss adding, removing, or changing procedures. Have students enforce rules. Students' having a voice enables superior classroom functioning. Consistently celebrate success. Evaluate and reflect daily or weekly throughout the year.

Inclusive Practices in Regular Education Classrooms with Special Education Students

According to expert Peter Westwood (2003), research into effective instruction finds that effective teachers keep the focus on academics; give students maximal opportunities for learning; demonstrate good classroom management; use work-oriented, business-like styles; express enthusiasm; communicate high expectations to students of what they can achieve; apply strategies for keeping students motivated, on-task, and productive; introduce new material step-by-step; use explicit and direct instruction techniques; structure all content; give clear explanations and instructions; closely monitor student activities; demonstrate appropriate strategies for approaching tasks; utilize varied resources; adjust instruction to individual student needs; reteach as needed; give students frequent feedback; and spend considerable amounts of time doing whole-class, interactive teaching. In classes including special education students, teachers include: descriptive praise and encouragement, ample guided practice, fast-paced lessons, high engagement and participation levels of all students, careful curriculum content sequencing and control, positive peer assistance and interactions, many practice and application opportunities, modeling of effective school task completion methods, interactive group teaching, and teaching students how best to attempt new learning tasks.

Creating Supportive, Positive Classroom Environments for Student Diversity

(1) Teachers can intentionally teach responsible behaviors. To afford a multidimensional approach for every student, particularly those requiring more intensive intervention, teachers can collaborate with parents, school psychologists, and counselors. General behaviors to teach include communication skills, social skills, character development, anger management, self-control skills, conflict resolution, decision-making skills, taking responsibility for one's actions, and developing emotional intelligence (EQ). (2) Teachers can establish classroom harmony through creating warm, supportive atmospheres wherein every student feels s/he is an important class member. Class meetings, class-building and team-building activities engender senses of a learning community and class ownership. Experts use the acronym "VIABLE": students develop self-respect and respect for authority figures when they feel they are *valued* by teachers and classmates, *included* in classroom activities, *accepted* in their classrooms and schools, have senses of *belonging* to cooperative learning groups, and adults who *listen* to and *encourage* them. (3) Teachers can empower students and promote their sense of class ownership by involving them actively in disciplinary processes. Instead of being part of the problem, students become part of the solution. Activities include arranging study and homework buddies; peer tutors, mediators, and counselors; peer recognition; assigning classroom responsibilities; and student-led conferences.

Invite or involve parents to meet student needs together. The "crucial Cs of parental support" are parent-teacher Communication, Connection, and Collaboration. Invite other teachers and staff— administrators; school psychologists, counselors, social workers, nurses; speech language pathologists (SLPs), occupational therapists (OTs), physical education (PE) teachers, special education teachers, music teachers; ELL or bilingual teachers, etc.—to collaborate in solving learning and discipline problems. Encourage and praise students' positive steps, efforts, strengths, progress, and improvement, not just finished products. Encouragement helps students self-validate and reflect on their own responses to their strengths and accomplishments. Effective praise is informative and appreciative, not evaluative or controlling. Build senses of accomplishment and capability in all students, and particularly in those lacking the following: focus on improvement, not perfection; turn mistakes into learning opportunities; let students struggle and succeed within ability levels; build upon student strengths; analyze past successes, then focus on the present; acknowledge task difficulty; use task analysis; teach positive self-talk; celebrate all students' successes and achievements. Develop positive teacher-student relationships to receive and give respect. Listen to students. Communicate positive expectations. Involve students in class decision-making: use a suggestion box; provide "voice and choice." Show enthusiasm for teaching and learning. Show interest in student interests. Keep communication open. Accept and value diversity and individual differences. Model positive, helpful, and kind behaviors.

Learning Processes and Environments

Facilitating Young Children's Learning Through Play Activities

Adults often observe young children talking about what to play. They should assist this planning by discussing with children who they will be, what will happen, etc.; and encourage children to plan together. If play breaks down, e.g., children wrangle over a toy or object, adults can intervene, pretending to knock on a door, asking if this is a good time to visit—redirecting their attention from distractions, refocusing and extending play time. To engage children in establishing safe environments for play, adults can do more than simply providing them with age-appropriate play materials by involving children in actively developing play rules to help them avoid sustaining or causing injuries and keep them safer. Young children have strong capacities for imitation, imagination, and creativity. Adults should encourage the latter, replacing the former. When children imitate violent or foolish behaviors they have observed, adults can refocus their play on other skills, problem solutions, and roles for accomplishing equal results than derivative actions with narrower scope. Storytelling and painting for younger children, and writing for older elementary-age children, are more controllable ways to work through issues impeding creativity and imagination to access and exercise them.

Processes Whereby Adolescent Students Acquire and Integrate New Knowledge

Younger children have had less time to generate a limited repertoire of schemata about the world and either fit new experiences into these or create new ones. However, older students, having had more time and life experiences, have accumulated more schemata and made more modifications in them to construct more extensive, detailed, and sophisticated knowledge. The first learning process they engage in when encountering new information or experiences is activating their existing knowledge, examining what they already know and believe. When new information or skills are congruent with prior knowledge and extend or supplement without significantly redefining it, older students integrate these into their present belief and value systems. This second process represents assimilation, i.e., acquiring additional knowledge without disequilibrium. When new information and experiences challenge adolescents' fundamental understandings, beliefs, or values, this creates cognitive dissonance, hence disequilibrium. Students then accept or reject the new input, reconstructing or repositioning existing beliefs if needed and resolving dissonance. This third process represents accommodation, i.e., acquiring new knowledge through encountering and resolving disequilibrium, and restoring a new equilibrium informed by new positions or beliefs. Teachers can facilitate ELL access to meaningful learning by relating new concepts taught in English to student L1s, activating their prior or existing knowledge. When teachers pair unfamiliar with familiar language and experience, this facilitates concept understanding and acquisition.

Sources of Academic Difficulty for ELL Students

Some school difficulties for ELL students are directly attributable to teaching and learning environment deficits. These include lack of student access to effective ESL or bilingual instruction, mismatches between middle-class-oriented instruction and low socioeconomic student backgrounds, cultural and linguistic differences that create communication gaps between learners and teachers, etc. Other ELL students may additionally have specific learning disabilities, which require specialized instructional methods to enable successful learning. Experts believe many educators lack expertise to differentiate limited English-language proficiency from true learning disabilities as sources of school failure, evidenced by overrepresentation of ELL students in special education classes. Additional problems include shortages of both assessment instruments and trained assessors that are appropriate and linguistically and culturally relevant, and in special educators trained in concurrently addressing linguistically related as well as disability-related student needs. Factors necessary to ELL success include recognizing the importance of student L1s, collaborative community and school relationships, shared educator knowledge bases of effective instructional methods for ELLs, effective teaching, and academically rich programs that integrate instruction in basic and higher-order cognitive skills in both L1s and English.

Developmentally Appropriate Practices for Kindergarten Environments

According to early childhood education experts, developmentally appropriate practice (DAP) must ensure that classrooms, instructional techniques, and assessment methods for young children consider three main aspects: age, individual growth patterns, and cultural influences. Educators can try various strategies, observing which are effective for different situations and learning goals: acknowledge children's actions and words by commenting, giving positive attention, or sometimes simply observing nearby. Encourage effort and perseverance, not only products and accomplishments. Make feedback specific, e.g., "That didn't reach the basket; try throwing it harder." Model—show, not just tell, approaches to problems and interpersonal behaviors—e.g., saying you must think about why something didn't work or admitting you missed part of a child's message, requesting repetition. Demonstrate correct physical procedures. Add challenge slightly beyond current skills, e.g., once children count objects after subtracting some, hide subtracted ones, requiring strategies other than counting. Decrease challenge as needed, e.g., guide children to touch objects while counting. Ask questions stimulating thought, e.g., "If you couldn't talk, how would you tell classmates what to do?" Give children hints or cues furthering progress, e.g., supply a word rhyming with a child's name, or ask the child for additional words. Directly provide verbal labels, names, facts, and other information. Accompany demonstrations and modeling with clear verbal directions for behaviors and actions.

Teacher Expectations, Teacher Behaviors with Students, and Student Performance

In an experiment, Harvard psychologist Robert Rosenthal (1964) told teachers a standardized IQ test was a "special" test predicting dramatic IQ growth, identifying randomly selected students as about to make significant intellectual gains. In the following two years, teacher expectations became self-fulfilling prophecies: those students' IQs actually did increase. Rosenthal's additional research identified myriad, nearly imperceptible ways teacher expectations influence interactions with students. They consistently smile, nod at, and touch; give more approval; offer more specific feedback; and allow more time for answering questions to students they expect to succeed. Exemplary teachers strive to motivate all of their students to achieve more than they thought they could through high expectations. Dean of University of Virginia's Curry School of Education and researcher Robert Pianta (c. 2012) compared two approaches to changing teacher expectations: talking to convince teachers via information that their beliefs are incorrect, vs. intensive training in new teacher behaviors. The latter shifted teacher beliefs more than the former. For example, a teacher believing boys are disruptive quashes a boy's loud, effusive response, emotionally disengaging and frustrating the student. Contrastingly, a teacher without that belief encourages the student to continue, but while sitting quietly. Different beliefs prompt different interpretations of the same behavior.

Interacting with Students Who Display Problematic Behavior

Experts observe we must change our own behavior to change others' behavior. Educational researchers have found teacher expectations and resulting behaviors subtly yet powerfully influence student behavior. There are several suggestions for teacher behaviors to influence student behaviors. For instance, observe how every student engages, interacts, and what s/he likes doing to comprehend their capabilities. Listen to students, try to understand their goals and motivations, and note their perceptions of classmates, yourself, and assignments you give. Engage with students: ask about and listen to their individual interests without offering opinions or advice. Experiment with different responses to challenging behaviors. Instead of your first impulse, stop and consider the behavior's motivation or function, which could be to connect with you. If or when time permits, interact with students in nonacademic games or activities of their choice; observe student strengths and interests. Assign projects wherein students use preferred media to express, individually and in groups, their extracurricular interests. Consider school through students' eyes. Reflect on your own worst and best teachers, supervisors, and bosses. List five words describing how you felt when interacting with them, and what they did or said specifically to evoke those feelings. List how your students might describe you. Consider parallels between your beliefs and their responses, and how your expectations shape their perceptions of you.

Robert Marzano's Strategies for Improving Teaching Quality and Student Achievement

According to expert Robert Marzano, instructional strategies for effective teaching and learning include: (1) identifying similarities and differences. Students more easily understand, and frequently solve, complex problems through analyzing them more simply by breaking concepts into similar and different characteristics. Teachers may identify these directly and then guide student inquiry and discussion, or have students identify them independently. Research finds the former helps identify specific items, while the latter promotes broader understanding and variation. Venn diagrams and charts are useful visual graphics for showing similarities and dissimilarities. Teachers should also engage student classifications, comparisons, analogies, and metaphors. (2) Summarizing and note-taking. Students comprehend better through analyzing subjects, revealing essential content, and restating it in their own words. Studies find students must be aware of the information's basic structure and delete, retain, and replace some components. Teachers should give students summarizing rules; prepare notes; use consistent note formats, allowing student refinements as needed; have students question, clarify, and predict coming occurrences in texts; and provide time to review and revise notes, often the best test study guides. (3) Reinforcing effort, giving recognition. Connect effort and achievement through success stories and student log-keeping and analysis. Personalize or individualize symbolic, not tangible rewards.

Marzano's strategies include: (1) homework and practice. Students extend learning beyond classrooms. Studies find homework amounts should vary by grade levels, parents should be minimally involved, students should adapt skills as they learn them, and the primary indices of practice effectiveness are speed and accuracy. Teachers should explain homework purposes to students and parents; try to give students feedback on every assignment; vary feedback delivery to maximize effectiveness; inform students whether homework is practice or to prepare for coming units; establish homework policies, advising students to maintain consistent settings, time limits, and schedules; assign timed quiz homework, having students report speed and accuracy; allocate practice time, focusing on difficult concepts. (2) Visual or nonlinguistic representations: studies show knowledge is stored in linguistic and visual forms, and students achieve more using both. Visual representation both stimulates and increases brain activity. Represent information with physical models and movements, relationships with symbolic images and words. (3) Cooperative learning: applied consistently and systematically—not overused—with small groups, cooperative activities enhance learning. Group students by multiple criteria, e.g., common interests or experiences; vary objectives and group sizes; and design projects around core components of individual and group accountability, face-to-face interaction, group processing, appropriate social skills, and positive interdependence.

(1) Objectives and feedback: give student learning direction through setting goals—not overly specific, readily compatible with students' personal goals. Setting each unit's core goal, inviting student personalization identifying areas where they want to know more, helps students consider their own interests and engage actively in goal-setting processes. Define specific student goals and grades they will receive for achieving them through writing contracts. Feedback should be corrective (comparing student achievement to specific knowledge levels as with rubrics), specific, and timely. Invite students to lead feedback sessions. (2) Hypothesis formulation and testing: studies show deductive reasoning—from general principles to specific predictions—most effective. Students must explain hypotheses and conclusions, whether deductive or inductive (from specific observations to generalizations). Ask students to predict what might occur if some aspect of government, transportation, or some other familiar system changed. Have students build things using limited resources, generating inquiries and hypotheses about what might or might not work. (3) Help students apply pre-existing knowledge for additional learning using questions, cues, and advance organizers. Studies find these must focus on important content, be highly analytical, and presented before lessons or activities. Pausing briefly after questions increases students' answer depth. Vary advance organizer styles—graphic images, skimming text, telling stories, etc.—for pre-"learning" exposure.

Learning Activities That Promote Both Critical Thinking Skills and Ownership of Learning

In *Democracy and Education* (1916), John Dewey wrote that true student involvement is stimulated by activities that "give pupils something to do, not something to learn; and the doing is of such a nature as to demand thinking, or the intentional noting of connections; learning naturally results." Thus the same learning activities that promote higher-order thinking, including critical thinking and organizational and time-management skills, also promote student ownership of learning. While interests in community issues fluctuate, students regularly find school-based issues important. Issues—curricular, extracurricular, or leadership-related—must also be relevant, reflecting student identities, interests, and passions; and student roles meaningful, enabling their design, implementation, and evaluative participation for improving student learning and schools. Schools can involve students as planners in designing new buildings, developing classroom behavior guidelines, selecting textbooks, researching careers and planning coursework accordingly, participating in principal or administrator hiring, etc. Students as teachers learn about all curriculum subjects in exchange for instructing teachers how to use technology, enhancing ownership and meaningful involvement. Students as professional development partners collect and analyze data and participate in team development as learning community members. Students as decision-makers in student government influence school climate, policy, and curriculum.

Age-Appropriate Study Skills

Research finds when students must analyze information to identify its most important aspects and then express it in their own terms, they need to know how the information is basically organized, and be able to remove, replace, and preserve elements of it. Thereby they understand it better. These learning processes are included in note-taking and summarizing. Teachers can provide students with rules for summarizing; prepare their own notes for students; and adhere to regular note-taking formats, including necessary student refinements. When teachers prepare their lecture or lesson notes in outline form, students can more easily take notes in outline form. Having students question text, clarify as needed, and make predictions improves their summarizing skills. Allotting time and encouraging students to review and revise their notes frequently enables them to study for tests at their highest potential. Advance organizers help students activate and build on their prior knowledge to learn further. Teachers should introduce analytical advance organizers concentrating on essential subject matter before learning experiences and vary their style, e.g., skim text, tell stories, produce graphic images, etc.

Steps Students Need to Do in School and Libraries in Order to Write Research Papers

(1) Topic: appeal to student curiosity; possible yet somewhat challenging for student skill and learning levels; support grade-level standards so library research matches classwork. Triangulate data, confirming topics in three kinds of available, readable sources; cross-check encyclopedias to broaden or narrow as needed. (2) Subtopics: informed by what students want to know; provide blueprints or outlines for examining topics. Brainstorm for general subtopics, e.g., physical characteristics, habitats, diets, enemies, offspring of specific animal species. "Pre-search" specific subtopics in topic-specific book tables of contents and encyclopedia subheadings. Research time management depends on controlling subtopic number (minimum three) and difficulty. (3) Sources: three kinds minimum, print or non-print; text, images, ideas. Consider student age, ability, topic for primary and secondary sources. Require MLA, APA, Turabian, or other accepted styles to prevent plagiarism and cite sources or use Creative Commons. Teach fair use and copyright regulations. Source evaluation offers lifelong skills. (4) Read, think, select: model, discuss, practice critical reading strategies—scanning, skimming, visual clues, chunking; asking what is important; identifying information supporting subtopics. (5) Note-taking: using subtopics as titles, pre-sort notes; beginners copy facts, phrases, and keywords, citing sources; experienced researchers summarize or paraphrase. (6) Sort notes by subtopic, then into paragraphs. Advanced is logical plan-based, e.g., concepts, timeline, etc. Rereading all notes per section, rearranging into logical order consolidates new information, cementing learning. Number notes consecutively. Write from notes, inserting previous knowledge.

Roles Played by Teachers and Students in Different Instructional Models

In traditional teacher-centered instructional models, the teacher plays the most active role, delivering instruction through lectures and lessons; assigning homework; and creating, administering and grading tests while the students play more passive roles of attending to, absorbing, retaining, and repeating information. In more progressive student-centered instructional models, if the model espouses inquiry and discovery learning, for example, students play more active roles as teachers encourage and guide them to ask their own questions, form their own hypotheses, investigate and test these, and draw their own conclusions. When teachers differentiate instruction for students with diverse needs, teachers may play varying roles of part-time individual tutor; part-time whole-class instructor; and, when teachers include small-group cooperative learning, part-time group facilitator and guide. Teachers providing one-on-one intensive training to students with profound disabilities play highly directive, active roles. At the other end of the spectrum, when students conduct independent projects, teachers may serve only as consultants or occasional advisors until they grade the projects. While some students need explicit instruction, research also finds that while rote memorization works with factual information, active student participation and teaching learning or thinking *skills*, not just information, produces more original thinkers and lifelong learners.

Community, Home, and School Factors with Regard to Teaching and Learning

Community: socioeconomic factors affect learning. For example, students living in more affluent communities have more educational resources and supports like after-school activities, learning and tutoring centers, and educational product stores. Affluent neighborhoods are also populated with more highly educated residents: students are expected to pursue post-secondary educations. In low-income neighborhoods, economic survival often takes precedence over education, or high

- 41 -

school diplomas are primarily for obtaining after-graduation employment. <u>Home</u>: parents with higher incomes can access more educational resources. Frequently more educated, they regard education more highly, have higher educational expectations and goals for children, serve as their role models, and either directly or indirectly educate them. Doctors, lawyers, educators, etc. are more likely have children pursuing similar educations and careers. Conversely, some children with less-educated parents have been motivated to become first in their families to attend college. <u>School</u>: urban schools where riots occur make school unsafe. Students cannot concentrate, so they stop attending. Less dramatic but equally important is classroom environment. Consider true stories of a speech language pathologist (SLP) required to conduct therapy between library shelf "stacks," and a teacher's aide instructing ELL students in school hallways. Such uncomfortable, distracting, and/or noisy settings interfere with teaching and learning.

Characteristics Shared by Effective Learning Groups

Experts find all kinds of effective learning groups share certain common characteristics. For example, their teachers are always involved actively as guides, coaches, questioners, evaluators, and resource people in student group learning processes. Groups are given work to do that is meaningful to students and challenges them. Teachers ensure students clearly understand learning objectives and schedules, and teachers monitor these. Cooperating is more important than competing. All students in each group are actively involved; groups are heterogeneous. Learning group processes enable students to feel comfortable with asking questions and discussing topics and issues. Students in learning groups experience the sense that they are able to achieve more by learning with each other than they could by learning individually. Although learning groups demand adequate social skills and interpersonal interactions, grouping is not primarily for social purposes. Group time is not considered "free time" for either students or teachers. With effective learning groups, teachers can evaluate individual student members, whole groups, or a combination of both. Teachers are able to assess group work through multiple instruments, e.g., presentations, interviews, portfolios, rubrics, quizzes, etc.

Incorporating Different Learning Modalities to Optimize Individual Student Learning

Students need not have sensory or cognitive processing disabilities to learn better through one sensory modality than another. All students have learning styles. Teachers can optimize classroom learning by including multiple and alternative modalities in lessons. For example, some students are auditory learners: they have greater sensitivity, attention, comprehension, and retention for what they hear than what they see or touch. Teachers can provide audiobooks and earphones along with books during reading times. This strategy also benefits students who do have visual impairments. Other students are visual learners: they attend, understand, and remember what they see better than what they hear or touch. Pairing visuals with sounds enhances their learning and other experiences. For example, Walt Disney's classic film *Fantasia* provides visually rich animated sequences accompanying classical music by Tchaikovsky, Grieg, Mussorgsky, etc. Students with haptic learning styles respond to tactile stimuli. Teachers can give younger students materials with varied textures to accompany story reading, assigning older students projects to interpret literature, science lessons, etc. by constructing collages, models, or displays with different textures. Students with kinesthetic styles learn through physical movement. Teachers can let them dance to music and apply exercise and sports movements to physics, mathematical, and other principles, etc.

Benefits of Learning Theory to Education

Behaviorism, or learning theory, has given educators a wealth of tools because it is practical, not only theoretical; applies to all organisms including humans, regardless of cognitive or intellectual level; gives clear procedures and steps to follow; deals only with observable, measurable behaviors, eliminating much ambiguity; follows logical sequences; can change behaviors much faster than other methods; and has undergone much research, yielding specific information about reinforcement schedules and corresponding response rates, effective and ineffective techniques, etc. For example, for students with cognitive or intellectual disabilities (ID) who have difficulty understanding or remembering complex tasks with multiple steps, task analysis derives from behaviorism in its principle of breaking tasks down into smaller, more manageable steps, teaching them separately until mastered, and then connecting them one more at a time. Students with autistic spectrum disorders (ASD) as well as IDs can have horrible trouble making transitions between activities. Behaviorist shaping, via reinforcing successive approximations toward an ultimate target behavior; and chaining, similar to the step-connecting portion of task analysis; are both highly valuable. Students with communication deficits might scream in class to get teacher attention; differential reinforcement of another behavior (DRO) or differential reinforcement of an incompatible behavior (DRI), e.g., raising a hand, waving, touching the teacher's arm, or operating a signal button or switch teaches more acceptable replacement behaviors.

Relationship Between Academic Instruction and Classroom Management

When educators teach and encourage students to take responsibility for their own behaviors rather than taking total responsibility for guiding student behaviors, teachers and students approach and understand content differently. Moreover, when instruction is more demanding (e.g., students address novel problems and/or create products), teachers must make more complex management decisions. This relationship between instructional activity levels and management complexity supports research evidence of the inseparable, complex interrelationship of instructional curriculum and classroom management. Teachers must help students learn to meet concurrent academic demands for comprehending and manipulating content, and social demands for interacting with others to demonstrate that content knowledge effectively. This broader view of classroom management has redirected research from controlling behavior to creating and sustaining learning environments—including furniture arrangements, classroom decorations, developing and communicating rules and routines, and interacting with students. Research shows teachers implementing systematic classroom management approaches when school years begin have students demonstrating higher task engagement and academic achievement. Researchers also identify strategies eliciting low misbehavior and high involvement as communicating awareness of student behavior, overlapping activities, smooth transitions, instructional momentum, and whole-class-focused attention alerting.

Understanding Student Group Dynamics and Managing Their Behavior

Be aware of individual students' group roles, e.g., leader, instigator, conscience, intimidator, enforcer, procurer, or negotiator; develop friendly relationships with the first three, and keep the first two on-task. Know group-required behaviors, conversation topics and interests, and what maintains a group's cooperation and unity. Place a daily "do-now" activity on the board or students' desks to start upon arrival before lessons, preparing students for lessons and continuing ongoing group or team tasks and activities. Greet and converse with students, always respectfully. Pleasantly remind and encourage desired behaviors before classes begin. Engage group leaders in task preparations (equipment setup, writing assignments on boards or overheads, reading assignment directions, handing out worksheets): others follow. Include cooperative learning groups, and allow collaborative team answers. Recognize and reward good behavior. Never embarrass students in front of classmates, which provokes individual and group rebellion. Determine behavior reasons and functions, e.g., boredom, overly easy or difficult assignments, confronting or embarrassing students, favoritism, group leader behavior contagion, pre-existing issues, distracters, etc. Prevent escalation using low-impact interventions: interest in student work, encouragement, good-natured humor, physical proximity, touch, interrupting oneself mid-sentence and using the "teacher glare," reminding classes and groups of times they did well, and changing lesson presentation to become more interesting than any distraction(s).

Productive Classroom Environments for Students at Different Developmental Levels

Teachers must take into account the developmental levels of their students to establish positive classroom environments for them. For example, teachers should not expect young children to begin preschool having already learned to share with other children. Teachers can model sharing and cooperation for them, and encourage and reward their imitating teacher examples as well as spontaneous prosocial behaviors, which researchers have observed in young children. Teachers can also observe whether young students engage in unoccupied behavior; independent or solitary play; onlooker behavior; parallel, associative, or cooperative play; and influencing factors, e.g., how well children know each other, offer matching activities, and introduce experiences at the next higher level. Teachers can offer peer collaboration opportunities to older elementary and middle school students by assigning study buddies, partners for peer tutoring, working together, or think-pair-share and similar activities. Small groups can also be formed for planning, organizing, and implementing team or group learning projects, although teachers must remember that students have typically not developed social interaction skills to the extent of high school students, and so must guide them accordingly. In high school, teachers can extend productive learning environments beyond classrooms to surrounding communities, engaging students' abstract cognitive skills to promote respect, social conscience, and action through service projects.

Respecting Diversity and Promoting the Active Engagement of all Students

Honor student experiences: create safe spaces, enrich curriculum using student experiences, and give students opportunities to learn from each other's perspectives and experiences. View different identity groups from asset-based orientations, let students define their own identities, and avoid or challenge stereotypes. Select texts reflecting demographics of and relevant to specific classes, and assign discussions or reflective writing about reading. Share personal anecdotes inviting student sharing. Student-centered classroom setups should include multicultural decorations or imagery reflecting our society's diversity and student backgrounds. Arrange furniture and materials to support comfort, ownership, dialogue, and collaboration. Structure classrooms for maximal student voice and participation. Involve students in setting norms and expectations, considering gender, language, and cultural and communication differences. Give students daily classroom jobs accommodating different learning styles, innovative student approaches, and real-life responsibility and work skills. Use gender-neutral categories and practices and let students choose group identifications. Build shared inquiry and dialogue through respect, trust, voice, humility, and active listening skills. Revisit participation norms: include and value small-group participation, written and artistic responses, and active listening as well as verbal communication. To create safe climates, actively teach emotional-social skills, work to create positive relationships, build community, prevent or intervene with bullying, focus explicitly on understanding and appreciating differences, practice and teach meaningful conflict resolution, and teach students to challenge exclusion and bias.

Instructional Strategy for Communicating High Expectations

Experts (Marzano, 2010) advise: (1) as early as possible, identify students for whom you have lower expectations. Once formed, negative expectations are hard to admit and change. (2) Identify student similarities. Though teachers resist admitting they automatically form expectations based on student appearance, speech style, or ethnicity, research finds early expectations based on such characteristics. Expectation patterns do not indicate bigotry or racism when people actively work to keep biases from controlling their thoughts and behaviors. (3) Identify your differential behaviors toward low-expectancy students, which are far more important than your expectations. Students observe and make inferences based on teacher behaviors. Affectively, teachers make less eye and physical contact, smile less, and lightly or playfully converse less with low-expectancy students. Academically, they ask them less challenging questions, call on them less frequently, explore their answers in less depth, and reward less rigorous responses from them. (4) Consciously treat high-expectancy and low-expectancy students the same way. Affectively this is relatively easy, but academically more challenging: students habituated to low teacher expectations may experience discomfort when teachers challenge them more. However, ultimately this enables students to ask clarifying questions and risk communicating new ideas.

Responding to All Student Cultural, Linguistic, and Familial Backgrounds and Needs

Students learn more when challenged by high teacher expectations, including open-ended questions and assignments requiring critical thinking skills. Explicitly teaching skills for studying, working with teachers, and completing college applications to students whose parents never attended college fills "cultural capital" gaps, preparing underrepresented students for college. Give students adult responsibilities for collaboratively contributing to planning, coaching, financial activities, etc. Diversity becomes a resource; students learn varied skills. Teacher knowledge and caring about individual students promotes their participation. Understanding student home cultures aids educator understanding of student behavior inside and outside classrooms. Encouraging active parental participation greatly supports student academic success through mutually understanding parent, classroom, and school expectations of teachers and students; helping parents converse to prepare children for classroom communication; helping parents pursue GED or ESL programs; and referring parents to community resources for arts, sports, science programs, and homework help. Eliciting and validating student background experiences, e.g., using semantic webbing to inform lesson planning and increase student engagement. Selecting curriculum for cultural relevance—student ethnic groups' contributions to US history and culture—enhances student self-esteem, makes lesson topics meaningful, and enables authentic, interactive language, literacy, and thinking skills. Culturally compatible social learning organization and communication expectations and norms make teaching and learning more effective.

Developing Student Oral and Written Communication Skills

Oral: the inside-outside circle – students, facing each other in two concentric circles, pair up; take turns speaking and listening; and rotate partners. Choral response – teacher asks a question, gives a signal, allows wait-time, says "Everyone..." and initiates signal, and the students respond in unison. Think-pair-share – students rehearse responses with partners, getting corrective feedback or elaboration help before whole-class sharing. Dialogic reading – teachers read books with individual students or small groups using "CROWD" prompts: sentence *completion*; asking questions requiring student text *recall*; *open-ended* questions about book pictures; *w-questions* (who, what, when, etc.) about pictures; and *distancing* book pictures and words to students' own life experiences. PEER prompts: *prompting* students to talk about text, *evaluating* responses, *expanding* responses, and *repeating* prompts at higher levels. Written: written responses, same answers – teachers ask questions; students write answers on whiteboards; teachers allow wait-time, say "Everyone..." and students hold up written responses. Written responses, varying answers – like same answers, but students check answers with partners, revise as needed; teachers call on individual students. Think-pair-share activities also enable students to get peer feedback about written responses before sharing them with the whole class.

- 45 -

Communicating Expectations to Students

By always behaving fairly and consistently in class, teachers model integrity for students, who understand better what is expected of them by witnessing the teacher meeting his/her own high expectations. Reinforce expectations daily, and repeat continually—sometimes through gentle reminders, other times interrupting instruction to discuss expectations as indicated—to change student attitudes. Support and inform student success through parent-teacher collaboration by communicating to parents your expectations of both students and parents. Prepare "achievement contracts" outlining mutual expectations students sign when the school year begins. Give students time to find answers themselves, only giving hints or ideas, not supplying correct answers immediately. Periodically, have students write about how they think they are doing and suggestions for improving the class. Always speak to students positively, emphasizing their ability to learn your instruction. Let students view you as a real person; get to know them. This attitude motivates some students to work harder to please teachers. However, avoid the trap of being students' friend; maintain authority as their teacher. Tell students exactly what you expect, making activity and assignment standards perfectly clear. Ensure every student knows s/he can earn high grades by working hard enough. Let students revise poorly-graded work, promoting mastery learning.

Good Student-Teacher Interactions and Relationships

Good student-teacher interactions and relationships enhance classroom atmosphere. Research has generated a significant body of literature showing that the quality of teacher-student relationships influences student academic achievement and behavior. Teachers showing students respect and guiding them to respect each other encourage active learners. Learning more about students, interacting and communicating with them, and providing appropriate feedback establish relationships promoting effective teaching and learning. When students have opportunities to communicate with one another, they share responsibility for learning, discuss diverse viewpoints, and shape class direction. Classes with predominant lecture formats are frequently well-organized; teachers typically know content well and clearly present material, but student-student interaction opportunities are lacking. More student-focused classes present small-group, paired, and whole-class discussion opportunities. Tasks having multiple potential solutions or answers can shift lesson direction, generate deeper thought processes, and enhance discussion quality. Small-group discussions particularly enable enough chances to listen, consider others' ideas, and all students to have a voice. Gallery walks, professional communication projects, classroom data explorations, structured academic controversy discussions, open-ended teacher questions, cooperative learning methods, structured jigsaw activities and other discussion exercises, conceptual multiple-choice questions about lesson themes combined with peer instruction, and in-class think-pair-share assignments are all ways to improve classroom interactions.

Teacher Enthusiasm

Numerous studies identify teacher enthusiasm as a behavior which prominently affects student learning. Research also shows that a combination of teacher enthusiasm and constructive feedback enables students to learn more. Investigators find more enthusiastic teachers spend more time on presentation and positive performance feedback. Enthusiastic teacher behaviors include the following: variation in vocal tone, pitch, volume, and pace is important. Teachers with monotonous, droning voices inspire student boredom. Teachers reflect their excitement with teaching and learning through their eyes by making eye contact with students; using their eyes expressively, e.g., raising eyebrows, opening eyes wide, etc.; and using their eyes as well as their ears to listen to students. Judicious teacher use of body language, gestures, and other nonverbal communications also communicate enthusiasm. Effective teachers clap hands, give high-fives, make OK signs, thumbs-up, etc. Sweeping arm motions, energetic body swinging, hand gestures, and facial expressions showing pleasure or displeasure, amusement, disappointment, and approval express enthusiasm. Moving around the classroom not only enables teachers to monitor students, but also makes them less predictable and boring. Nonverbal behaviors also reinforce verbally encouraging students.

Instructional Skills and Practices That Foster Innovation

One expert (Hiam, 2011) identifies "five I's" as components of innovation curriculum: imagination, inquiry, invention, implementation, and initiative. Initiative is the foundation enabling the four others. Although daydreaming is discouraged in classrooms, teachers must learn creative expression skills to encourage student imagination. Master teacher collaboration with invention and creativity experts on curriculum design is one recommended solution. To fuel imagination, educators must connect seemingly unrelated topics, skill-sets, and ideas. Most inventions are innovative combinations of multiple domains. Writing across the curriculum, combining arts and sciences, etc., stimulates imagination. To encourage inquiry, students—not teachers—must ask most of the questions. Students must question, explore, and research curiously to innovate. Teachers can incorporate student question-asking exercises following activities into established curricula. Educators must challenge students to invent new and better ways to solve problems and apply learning to real life more often—weekly, not once or twice throughout school or only through science fairs. Implementation must also be increased: students get insufficient practice putting ideas into action, learning from mistakes, refining plans, and persevering. Initiative is more common in non-hierarchical and individualistic societies. Teachers need preparation for mentoring and coaching students in initiative-based learning; schools must support teachers' guiding students by supplying resources and valuing decentralized activities. Challenge, encouragement, and support develop self-efficacy and agency, promoting invention.

Aspects of How Information and Communication Technology (ICT) Supports Student Learning

Education is socially oriented and greater teacher-student personal contact is associated with quality education; ICT is compatible with and supportive of student-centered learning environments. ICT can have a transformational role in teaching and learning. Student-centered learning incorporates experiential and hands-on learning, self-directed student learning, and flexible learning activities. Students must not simply remember information to understand and apply it; they must question, grapple with ideas, discover things on their own, and construct knowledge, with teachers not being information presenters but facilitators—which also enhance their attention, interest, and motivation. Contrasting with teacher-directed learning, student-centered learning is more congruent with constructivist learning. Researchers conclude that to make complex information their own, students must individually discover and transform it. As facilitators, teachers provide opportunities for students to discover ideas, apply them, and consciously utilize their own learning strategies. Thus curriculum design is shifting from emphasizing informational content to competencies and how information will be used. Teachers use ICT in lesson planning and presentation; students use ICT for exploration, practice, and preparing assignments and presentations; administrators and teachers use ICT to complete administrative tasks more efficiently. Technology-facilitated, student-centered approaches facilitate multimedia presentation, enhancing learning; and encourage student responsibility for learning.

- 47 -

Assistive Communication Technology

Some students have speech and language disorders; some with autism spectrum disorders, cognitive, or other disorders may have limited communication skills or be completely nonverbal. Because academic success depends on communication, assistive communication technology can help students overcome learning obstacles. Visual representation systems are effective for students having difficulty with auditory receptive and verbal expressive, but greater visual processing abilities. augmentative and alternative communication (AAC) systems and devices are assistive technologies facilitating communication. They range from low-technology to high-technology. Low-tech systems and devices are typically easy to use and inexpensive, including dry-erase boards, albums, folders, binders, and other ways of storing and transmitting images. Mid-tech systems and devices include simple, battery-operated or electronic voice output communication aids (VOCAs); overhead projectors; and tape recorders. High-tech systems and devices are more complex and expensive, including computers; software programs, e.g., speech-to-text and text-to-speech software; adaptive keyboards and other hardware; and more complex VOCAs. Special education student Individualized Education Programs (IEPs) must include any kinds of assistive technology required for them to achieve learning objectives and succeed in school. AAC systems and devices enable interactive student-teacher communication, effectively giving voices to students appearing to lack them.

Inclusive Classroom Environments That Promote Equity and Respect for Students

When teachers initiate open dialogues, they engage students in a democratic process and provide opportunities for group decision-making requiring compromise, not competition. Teachers can rearrange classrooms to facilitate group decision-making and student interaction, e.g., sitting in circles, moving all desks to one side, reversing the room's front and back, and letting students learn from their decisions to democratize classroom spaces. They can assign group projects, which should be multidimensional, equally emphasizing textual, graphic, creative, presentation, and other components to address different skills and learning styles. Group projects also require member interdependency for successful completion, and vary in group composition. Rather than the typical forms of talking and writing for classroom sharing, wherein the loudest or fastest student gains the floor, teachers can vary protocols, e.g., visual art; paired and/or small-group sharing; allowing more time for reflecting, organizing their thoughts, and writing; and activities enabling thinkers, talkers, writers, and visual artists to share ideas. During class discussions, creating conflict regarding topics gives students more realistic experiences of complex issues. When students take various views of issues, not for competition or winning but for consensus, it affords experiences that demonstrate the complicated, messy nature of real-life democratic processes.

Organization of Classroom Desks

The classic rows and columns model of student desk placement facilitates a teacher-centered learning environment. All students are facing the teacher who, because of the orientation of student desks, is the fulcrum of every discussion. Eye-contact between dialoguing students in rows and columns of desks may be impractical or impossible. Students can be easily distracted and hard to monitor. Alternatively, teachers might choose to use a U-shaped configuration in which every student has a "front-row" seat. U-configurations are conducive to lively discussion; any student can maintain eye contact with any other student. However, U-configurations may not allow a teacher to reach every student's position. A third option might be pods of three or four. Although pods are not good for lectures and whole class discussions, they are particularly useful for student-centered pedagogy incorporating group projects or collaborative problem solving. Pods will most efficiently allow students to be in close proximity to their neighbors while also allowing a teacher more

- 48 -

efficient access to every student and the opportunity to coach them through difficulties when they arise.

Flipped Classrooms

A "flipped" classroom is a pedagogical model in which the traditional uses of time inside and outside of the classroom are reversed. Traditional time inside the classroom is devoted to teacher-centered (i.e., passive) activities like lecture. In a "flipped" classroom passive learning exercises are reserved for outside of the classroom. Either the teacher will record audio or video segments for students to consume at home or the teacher will make use of pre-existing content (e.g., Mometrix Academy or Khan Academy). Traditionally time outside of the classroom is devoted to more student-centered (i.e., active) experiences such as problem solving. Because traditional homework is generally individual, problems are often less challenging and less instructive. In a "flipped" classroom, problem solving and other traditional homework is done inside the classroom allowing students to collaborate on more challenging problems with additional assistance from the teacher.

In the student-centered "flipped" classroom model, student learning effectiveness is increased because both halves of the reversal facilitate deeper understanding. Students have more time to digest material at home and can pause or replay lectures as often as they like. In the classroom students can solve more challenging and instructive problems through the assistance of classmates and their instructor.

Cooperative Games for Preschoolers

Musical chairs, duck-duck-goose, and similar traditional games exclude children from the fun by emphasizing competition; cooperative games teach preschoolers to listen, follow directions, develop movement and problem-solving skills, and collaborate. "Help": balancing paper napkins on heads, children move about, freezing if napkins fall; touch to unfreeze classmates. "Robots": pairs take turns as robot and commander. Commanders direct robot movements to negotiate obstacles, reaching preset goals. "Balloon keep-up": outdoors or in gyms, children collaborate to keep balloons aloft. "Cooperative musical chairs," or "islands": when music stops, children share, not compete for, remaining chairs or islands. "Roll it": children sitting in a circle, feet touching, roll a ball to others, keeping it steadily moving; as children master rolling, add more balls. The goal is to keep control rolling as many balls as possible. "Cooperative duck-duck-goose": children walk in place in a circle; "it" chooses a goose, who walks, runs, or skips around the circle, chooses another goose, giving everybody a chance. "Cows and ducks" (also known as "frogs and dogs," "cats and snakes," or "chickens and goats"): whisper animal names in children's ears; each moos, quacks, etc., traveling; children making the same sounds group and move together like their animals. "Find it": call a color to moving children; first one finding something that color touches it; second holds the first's hand, etc., until all connect.

Kindergarten Schedules Balancing Active vs. Restful Activities

Kindergarteners apparently have boundless energy, yet fatigue quickly; short attention spans demand change. Teachers therefore must alternate active movement with restful activities to prevent both exhaustion and boredom. Kindergarteners thrive through independently and cooperatively working with small peer groups, conversing, choosing activities, and practicing and applying skills they are learning. Organizing and managing learning environments via learning centers matches kindergartener identities and ways of learning, developing "learning to learn" skills of autonomy, initiative, persistence, creativity, resourcefulness, risk-taking, reasoning, and problem-solving. For example, children decide to create their own board game: they collect materials from learning centers; make a game board, markers, dice, rule book, timer, and (using a computer graphics program) design and print play money; use classroom word walls, charts, or ask the teacher and peers for help writing numbers and words; play their finished game repeatedly, and teach others how. This includes student choice; multiple learning domains; all curriculum areas; teacher guidance; and physical, cognitive, language, emotional, and social development. Skills play develops: literacy is learned through print concepts, reading, writing, linguistic communication, and purposeful writing; mathematics is learned through shapes, number concepts, language, predicting, measuring money, and time; science through exploring materials' physical properties and recycling materials; social studies through collaboratively developing, following rules, geographic thinking and mapping, and money use; arts through drawing and creating; and technology through basic computer use and software navigation.

Establishing and Managing Productive Classroom Learning Environments

For students to take risks, engage effectively in challenging activities, and collaborate, teachers must make classrooms emotionally safe. Establish a rule for students and yourself, e.g., "We do not laugh at others, tell them to shut up, put them down, or insult them." For all students to participate, teachers must make classrooms intellectually safe. Habituate them to starting work whenever you say, "Please begin," starting with easier tasks, ensuring they know more challenging tasks will follow. Make tasks complex and rich, giving diverse students opportunities to excel and assist peers. Accomplished teachers establish active-learning environments—students thinking, speaking on-task, and working collaboratively near 100 percent of the time—and not only closely observe and measure the quantity (number or proportion of students, amount or proportion of time) of on-task behavior, but also the quality (strength, depth) of student attention and engagement. Newer teachers can start developing lessons and skills for creating ongoing active-learning environments by analyzing which activities really engage their students. Make participation inclusive every day by identifying some questions every student can answer simply; have them raise an index finger when ready; when all do, have them whisper answers or signal, e.g., thumbs-up, thumbs-down, or thumbs-sideways.

Facilitating Student Conflict Resolution

Researchers (Crawford and Bodine, 2001) from the National Center for Conflict Resolution Education report most major conflicts escalating into violence begin as more minor incidents, e.g., unprovoked contact, using others' belongings without permission, etc. Few interactions are initially predatory, yet conflicts rapidly escalate. Most conflicts happen between or among acquaintances, either at school or in the home. Violent behaviors commonly share a retribution goal. Violent acts reflect not lack of values, but value systems accepting violence. Based on these findings, experts (Concordia Online Education, 2013) offer four instructional strategies for effective classroom conflict resolution. (1) Role-playing requires viewing behaviors from others' perspectives, teaches empathy, can add humor to resolving conflicts, and enable examining conflicts more objectively for insights about sources. (2) Have students track conflicts they partake in or witness over time, recording observations in journals (keeping identities anonymous), and discuss student reactions pros and cons. (3) Teach good listening behaviors: eye contact, not interrupting, asking questions, avoiding giving suggestions or advice, nodding and smiling as positive reinforcement, and restating messages in one's own words. (4) Have involved students write about conflicts, providing cooling-off or time-out periods and requiring reflection, including how they felt and retrospectively better alternatives. For example, listing three things they would do differently; model and teach using conflicts as learning opportunities.

Student Behavior Management Approaches

To curtail misbehavior by exercising authority while eliciting minimal emotional distress, and additionally model reasonable, respectful use of authority, a "simple authority statement" promptly and authoritatively expresses disapproval as objectively as possible. If it is either unnecessary or unwise to confront students directly, teachers can redirect student energy to other behaviors, e.g., learning activities. This stops or interrupts misbehavior without provoking student hostility. For example, younger students or those with attention deficit hyperactivity disorder (ADHD) may not be intentionally misbehaving, but lack impulse control; redirection can restore on-task behavior without damaging a student's self-esteem or self-image. Reminding students calmly of assigned tasks enhances their understanding of target behaviors without communicating unpleasant emotions or judgments. Telling students what they should do "next time" gives students behavioral correction, but avoids discouraging them by focusing on the future instead of what they did wrong this time. Teachers can prevent responding inappropriately in haste by responding with silence to misbehaviors not significantly disrupting class. Silence also enables teachers to make mental notes and consider later which actions (if any) apply, and gives students opportunities for solving their own problems.

Helping Students Develop and Exercise Accountability, Responsibility, and Self-Regulation

Any time students display careless or unacceptable behaviors, responding with a "check yourself" message advises students to check what they just did, implicitly communicating that by checking, they will realize what they must do to correct their behavior. This reminds students to practice responsible self-management. When students, especially younger ones assigned individual classwork, become restless and off-task, settle them down and increase their concentration powers through a "clock focus" strategy: on the teacher's prearranged cue, students stand and watch the clock's second hand complete full one-minute rotations, choose how many to watch, and then sit down and resume working once the last rotation is complete. This provides scaffolding for students to develop better behavioral self-awareness, self-management, and self-control. Clock-watching, standing, and teacher cues can be gradually eliminated toward independent on-task self-regulation. Placing a student near the teacher in a "visitor's chair," with returning to regular seating allowed whenever the student feels ready to self-manage responsibly, avoids expressing disapproval. When upsetting emotions arise, model honest communication and interpersonal skills without provoking guilt or defensiveness through "I" statements about personal feelings and needs; avoid "you" accusations or comments.

Classroom Transitions Between Activities and Lessons

During transitions, students frequently become distracted, restless, and misbehave because the lessons and activities before and after, and the transitions themselves, are not standardized. Hence teachers must build bridges for students for efficient transitions. Bridges must be totally consistent, using the exact same prompts, cues, and steps in exactly the same way every time, so students can rely on them. This makes activities and events both before and after transitions immaterial because students always know what teachers expect of them. Teachers can design a uniform transition by chaining several mini-routines, which they must model, teach, and practice. (1) Signal for class attention. (2) Once all students are attending and making eye contact, start directions with "In a moment... (e.g., we're going to start another lesson)" to maintain student attention. (3) Give precisely detailed directions, including prearranging cues, e.g., "When I say 'go,' you will put away your materials, clean off your desks, and quietly meet me in the learning center." (4) Ask if anybody does not know what to do. Once everybody understands, use the prearranged cue (e.g., "go") to impel students toward learning objectives. (5) Observe student activity and confirm they are

- 51 -

following directions. Avoid interrupting transitional activity. To address noncompliance, have students repeat the sequence.

Classroom Routines and Procedures

Effective teachers devote school's first few weeks not to teaching content, but to establishing classroom routines and procedures: research finds lacking these causes most behavior problems. Routines and procedures decrease instruction interruptions, increasing smooth class flow. Experts advise handing out copies of routines and procedures to every student on the first day, retaining extra copies for new students arriving later. Do not expect compliance after merely handing out and going over them once. Teach key procedures once or twice daily over several days. Explain reasons for each routine and procedure, model each for students, give students non-examples of compliance, and have one or more students model each. Go over less important routines and procedures, monitor, and reinforce as needed. Consistency is critical: teaching, monitoring, and reinforcing routines and procedures, and firmly establishing these over the first three weeks of school offers enormous benefits; do not give up after a few days. Routines and procedures include entering and exiting; starting work; attendance; lunch counts; announcements; lateness; absence; makeup classwork and tests; out-of-seat; teacher attention signal; assignments; pencil-sharpening; collecting supplies; carrying, handling, or using equipment; forming groups; group, learning center, and independent work; lining up; restrooms; water or snacks; other school locations; submitting homework and papers; exchanging papers; getting help; asking questions; finishing classwork early; classroom visitors; fire drills, codes, and alerts; sudden illness or injury; checking out materials; end-of-day cleanup; organizing materials; changing classes; homework; dismissal.

Theoretically Based Classroom Behavior Management and Monitoring Techniques

Based on behaviorism, functional behavior analysis identifies functions, reasons, and purposes of behaviors, enabling identifying and teaching preferable replacement behaviors meeting the same needs and functions. For example, pay attention to students who raise their hands, but not to students who call out answers. Behavior contracts specify precisely what students agree to do, and for what reward. For example, a first-grader becomes bored with teacher read-aloud story time after three minutes, wandering around the room. An initial two-week contract specifies s/he stay seated and attend for five minutes in return for quietly playing with a toy nearby for the remaining time. Future contracts gradually increase attending durations. Contracts teach students verbal obligation, responsibility, self-control, self-monitoring, negotiation, and compromise. Applying the behaviorist principle that positive reinforcement is more powerful than punishment, and the social learning theory principle of vicarious or observational learning, the "catch them being good" technique involves identifying disruptive and non-disruptive behavior instances. At class beginnings, use a randomized beeper or recording; ignoring disruptive student behaviors (whenever possible) and praising nearby students displaying appropriate behavior. (Use time-outs for severe disruptions.) Instead of a teacher singling out or scolding a student and thereby reinforcing disruptive behaviors, students imitate praised classmates for similar rewards. This teaches students they receive no attention of any kind for disruptive behavior, but favorable attention for appropriate behavior.

Establishing Developmentally Appropriate Behavioral Expectations of Students

Teachers may observe some developmentally unrealistic parental expectations for their children, e.g., expecting them to "do as I say, not as I do" when their own behaviors are not positive models; expecting children to predict how present behaviors will influence future outcomes. While teachers should involve students in behavior changes, teachers cannot expect students to implement changes autonomously. Teachers should consider developmental, not chronological ages of students with cognitive delays or disabilities regarding appropriate expectations. School-aged children and adolescents generally share these cognitive characteristics: they are present-oriented, i.e., they focus on the here and now; usually cannot consider future consequences, which do not seem real to them; have difficulty anticipating consequences of their behaviors beforehand; can understand basic cause-and-effect relationships, provided these are sequenced closely together; have still-developing concepts of time, and difficulty with planning skills. Not standing out as different but fitting in—particularly for adolescents—is a major concern. Expect students to help track goals, not create and track them without reminders; and learn about and select among various choices, not independently make positive choices without concrete rewards and positive parental and adult models.

Promoting Ethical Academic Work Habits

Rather than threatening students with punishment for cheating, teachers can better promote ethical work habits by serving as positive role models; explaining and initiating class discussions about honesty and responsibility, how these are compromised by using others' work without giving credit, etc.; and praising and otherwise rewarding individual student work as examples of ethical academic practices. Research finds that, just as with academic expectations, having behavioral expectations high enough to challenge students, but realistic enough that they can achieve them with effort, is more effective than lowering expectations—including for mainstreamed students with disabilities. Rather than doing all the work for students in monitoring their behavior, teachers can engage students in monitoring processes and procedures, gradually teaching them the skills and responsibilities needed to self-monitor and self-regulate their behaviors. Teaching monitoring skills also supports teaching students about conflict management and resolution skills. Teaching students active listening skills reduces miscommunications, misunderstandings, and thus conflicts. Having them role-play opposing positions teaches empathy, objectivity, and insight; and advances conflict resolution, as does having them reflect and write about actual conflicts and potential alternative responses.

Critical Thinking and Creative Thinking

Critical thinking includes the abilities to question, evaluate, and judge information or material. For example, students should learn to distinguish opinions from facts in what they read and hear; look for evidence supporting author or speaker arguments, or lack thereof; evaluate supporting evidence, e.g., consider whether its source is reputable, proven, accepted by experts in its field, etc.; judge the quality of information or material through comparison, experience, and intuition. Creative thinking includes generating original ideas, coming up with problem-solving alternatives that differ from usual solutions, applying knowledge in novel ways and contexts, and divergent thinking. Traditional academics tend to emphasize and require convergent thinking, wherein multiple concepts, ideas, facts, and information come together or converge to yield the same answer or conclusion. Divergent thinking, by contrast, involves generating concepts, ideas, facts, and information that differ or diverge to yield varying answers or conclusions. For example, some informal assessments of divergent thinking include thinking of as many *different* categories of use for paper clips, or bricks, etc. (Bricks as projectiles represent *one* category, despite different targets and/or projection methods; bricks as building materials, also *one* category despite construction types or methods; using paper clips as fasteners is *one* category regardless of things fastened.)

Questioning, Inductive and Deductive Reasoning, and Problem-Solving

Questioning promotes inquiry learning; gives students purposes for reading; focuses attention on learning targets; fosters active thinking, metacognition, and self-monitoring; augments comprehension; and helps students review new material and connect it to their previous knowledge. Student question generation can help them identify important ideas in learning materials and synthesize information. Teacher and student questions help students clarify meaning, find new information; analyze information by wondering about author intentions, meanings, and choices of content, genres, and formats; and pursue personally interesting topics related to learning material. Inductive reasoning is a bottom-up, specific-to-general process, beginning from accumulating specific observations or information; identifying regularities or patterns; and ultimately drawing general conclusions or principles. Conversely, deductive reasoning is a top-down, general-to-specific process; beginning from a general theory, principle, or field of information; narrowing this down to more specific hypotheses; testing these by collecting observations, information, and data to confirm or refute the theory; and draw a specific conclusion. Problem-solving involves identifying a problem, generating alternative solutions, testing these through implementation, and evaluating their effectiveness. This requires focus for problem identification, divergent thinking to generate alternatives, and critical thinking to evaluate results.

Planning, Memory, and Recall

Planning is an essential cognitive process which many students fail to do before plunging into activities. It requires abstract thinking and imagination to envision the processes of a task before actually performing them. While many higher-order cognitive abilities seem located in the frontal lobe of the cerebral cortex, planning appears to be in the prefrontal lobe. It is high among the higher-order thinking skills. By planning before writing, for example, students are able to organize their compositions in advance, preventing many major problems, failures, and starting over from scratch. Students must plan projects before beginning them to give them organized structures, devote equal or appropriately weighted durations to different parts, stay on schedule, complete them within prescribed timeframes, etc. Moreover, planning academic tasks provides essential practice for planning in everyday life, which facilitates many activities in similar ways on a larger, even more practical scale. Students use working memory to rehearse information in short-term memory and move it into long-term memory for retention. They retrieve information from long-term memory by recalling it directly or recognizing it among provided alternatives. Without memory retention and retrieval, students could not demonstrate, apply, or build upon what they learn.

Direct Instruction vs. Indirect Instruction

Teacher-centered, direct instruction is the oldest, most widely used teaching model. Teachers give explicit, structured instruction using uniform lesson plans. Exploration, discussions, etc. are excluded. Most contemporary K-12 schools use updated versions. Examples include DISTAR, Hooked on Phonics, etc. Some longitudinal research shows Montessori, Waldorf, and other more flexible methods more effective. However, direct instruction is among the few scientifically confirmed ways of improving curriculum. Siegfried Engelmann originated a more specific direct instruction (DI), comparing it with 21 other methods during the federally funded Project Follow Through (1968-1995), meant to extend preschooler education following Head Start programs. Although funding was discontinued when data showed little or no benefit for this purpose, empirical evidence proved DI most effective of 22 methods for teaching reading, language, spelling, arithmetic, and positive self-image—the only one producing positive results consistently. Indirect instruction is student-centered and interactive; teachers facilitate small-group and cooperative learning. Students construct or transform material into new or different, meaningful responses. Encompassing all Bloom's taxonomy levels, it includes reading for meaning, cloze, concept mapping, case studies, inductive and deductive reasoning, content organization, examples and non-examples, questions, student experiences, self-evaluation, and discussion. DI aids learning facts, rules, and sequences; breaking down textbook or workbook material; lower Bloom's taxonomy levels; piquing student interest. Indirect instruction aids learning abstractions, concepts, patterns, inquiry, problem-solving, and discovery learning.

Independent Study

Independent study is not a single instructional method per se, but rather a type of instructional strategy that encompasses a range of different instructional methods. Teachers intentionally provide independent study types of methods for the purposes of developing initiative, self-determination, self-reliance, self-direction, and self-improvement in individual students. In addition to individual students working alone, the definition of independent study can also include paired, partnered, or small-group learning. In each case, the teacher functions as a facilitator and guide rather than directing or controlling the entire activity. Some advantages of independent study include giving students more choices of learning materials, topics, approaches, practices, and more autonomy in completing assignments. These increase student motivation. Another advantage is flexibility: teachers can use it with one, two, or several students and another strategy with the rest of the class; combine it with other strategies; or make it the main whole-class instructional strategy. An additional advantage is freeing teacher time. However, teachers must ensure students have developed skills required for it. Some examples of independent study activities and methods include doing homework, writing reports or essays, learning contracts, correspondence courses and lessons, computer-assisted instruction, research projects, learning activity packages, assigned questions, and learning centers.

Experiential Learning

Experiential learning is a student-centered, activity-oriented instructional strategy whereby students use inductive reasoning to discover information and insights. Process takes precedence over product. Activities involve "hands-on" learning. Rather than passively listening to teachers, only reading text, or viewing video or other visuals, students actively participate in direct experiences. This participation increases student motivation, as does communicating their activities to classmates so that, in effect, they teach one another. Critical components of effective experiential learning include formulating plans to apply learning to other contexts, and reflecting personally about learning experiences. Studies find student comprehension and retention are much higher through experiential learning activities than passive or receptive activities. Examples include administering surveys, building models, taking field trips, making field observations, conducting simulations, playing games, role-playing, synectics, focused imaging, and conducting experiments. Experimental learning involves the scientific method: asking research questions; formulating hypotheses regarding answers; testing hypotheses by experimenting, e.g., qualitative research like surveys and observations, or quantitative like randomly selecting participants, not treating a control group and manipulating independent variables with a treatment group to see if dependent variables are affected or unaffected to support or refute the hypothesis; reporting results; drawing conclusions and communicating these.

Interactive Instruction

Interactive instruction is a teaching strategy that enables a range of different interactive methods and ways of grouping students. It is interactive because it places a major emphasis on having students share and exchange ideas, questions, activities, and tasks, and engage in discussions of their work and learning with classmates. Students in pairs, threes, small groups, or whole classes may participate in interactive discussions, projects, or assignments. Some examples of activities involving interactive instruction include holding debates; participating in student panels; engaging in role-playing exercises, which are also used in experiential learning; discussion, which is also a feature of indirect instruction; group brainstorming to generate ideas; practicing academic skills and tasks with peers; cooperative learning groups, which are always interactive and sometimes also involve independent study; laboratory groups, which can also involve experimental and experiential learning; problem-solving activities; circle of knowledge group activity sessions; tutorial groups, including peer tutoring; and conducting interviews with peers and/or others.

Organizing and Implementing Effective Instruction

First review national and state standards, their course textbooks, supplementary materials, and any test preparation materials required, to ascertain which concepts they must teach. Create a plan of study based on this information. To visualize and organize instruction, make a personal lesson plan calendar. Using the plan of study and calendar, plan instructional units and timelines. Next, write detailed lesson plans for each unit. Effective lesson plans should include learning objectives; student activities; estimates of time needed; materials required; alternative plans for any students absent during lesson activities; and assessment methods, including tests, homework, and classwork. Transfer the general unit plan to a planning book, assembling all unit plans to get an overall picture of the school year, supporting organization, focus, and implementation. Write daily lesson outlines and agendas. Some teachers write detailed information and notes, while others make simple outlines including times. Being organized and making smooth transitions are important to maintain student attention. Collect or create required materials, e.g., lecture notes, overheads, handouts, manipulatives, any planned daily warmups, etc. Request media in advance. Create emergency lesson plans for substitutes and mini-lessons to fill extra or leftover time to plan for the unexpected.

Continuous Monitoring and Charting of Student Performance

Continuous monitoring and charting (1) gives teachers information on student progress with short-term, discrete objectives. They can respond flexibly to student understanding, engagement, lacks thereof, and feedback, adjusting instruction by re-teaching or reviewing skills and concepts immediately instead of only finding students did not learn certain things after having covered several topics; and (2) gives students visual depictions of their learning. Having students chart and graph their own performance can enhance their engagement in learning. Continuous monitoring functions as ongoing evaluation, visual representation, immediate feedback; a diagnostic tool; instructional planning guide; communication mechanism with students, parents, other teachers, and administrators; and an evaluation practice that can motivate and engage students. However, it is not an independent student practice activity. Critical elements are frequently assessing student understanding and performance of discrete skills and concepts; ability to replicate assessment procedures over several days; tally, graph, or chart student responses; and involve students in tracking that progress and setting goals. To implement, select a specific instructional objective; design an assessment sheet students can complete in a few minutes with items reflecting the target skill, and where indicated, concrete, representational, or abstract understanding level; administer and score; have students plot correct or incorrect responses on graphs; discuss; draw goal lines on graphs; repeat.

Scaffolding

Scaffolding, in a metaphorical iteration of literal building construction scaffolding, is temporary support enabling students to complete tasks they cannot accomplish on their own at the time. As students master these tasks, the scaffolding can be gradually withdrawn until students perform the tasks independently without support. During this process, the role of the teacher is shifted from being the dominant expert on academic content to becoming more of a facilitator of learning and a mentor. As students learn how to perform tasks with support and gain increasing proficiency and independence, the responsibility for learning shifts from the teacher to the student. Scaffolded instruction establishes a supportive learning environment wherein students are able to give feedback, ask questions, and support one another in learning new material. Using scaffolding in teaching gives students motivation for adopting more active roles in their learning. Because teachers provide scaffolds for tasks students cannot initially achieve independently, scaffolding requires students to advance past their current knowledge and skill levels, sharing responsibility and taking ownership for teaching and learning.

Scaffolding can be implemented with individual students, small groups, or whole classes. It is useful whenever students cannot understand a certain concept or are not progressing in some aspects of tasks. Step 1: the teacher models how to perform a difficult or unfamiliar task, for example, how to use a graphic organizer when students have never done so. The teacher might prepare an incomplete graphic organizer with some parts completed for handouts and a projection. The teacher describes how the graphic organizer illustrates relationships, asking students to "think aloud" about this. Step 2: teacher and students work together on completing the graphic organizer. Students might suggest information to add. The teacher writes student suggestions on the board or overhead; students complete their copies of the organizer. Step 3: students work in pairs or small groups to complete a blank or partially filled graphic organizer. Teachers may need to provide multiple scaffolds at various times to help students master more complex content. Step 4: students practice independently, demonstrating mastery and gaining speed and automaticity. In each step, teacher and students have different roles and responsibilities.

Instructional Approaches That Emphasize Student Responsibility for Learning

In the inquiry-guided instructional method, students investigate to answer questions, attaining understanding of concepts independently. This not only promotes the development of lifelong research skills, but also places the responsibility for learning with the student. In the learner-centered teaching method, teachers are responsible for facilitating learning, while students take responsibility for learning. This shifts classroom power from teacher to student. In the instructional method of establishing learning communities, every member participates, taking responsibility for accomplishing learning goals. With shared learning, responsibility is collective, not individual. Participants include students, teachers, other educators, staff, administrators, parents, community members, and other stakeholders. Service learning is an instructional approach combining academic content with community service projects. Teachers are responsible for structuring and supervising learning, enabling student reflection. Students learn to take civic responsibility. In team-based learning (TBL), unlike other group activities, students participate as members of permanent teams; group meetings occupy most of class. Students are more responsible for and reliant on each other (interdependent) for learning, and more responsible for arriving to class prepared. Research finds TBL increases both student engagement and responsibility.

Developing Higher-Order Thinking Skills

Align learning goals, objectives, ideas, skills, content, tasks, materials, aids, and assessments. Create organized routines and activities: explain established routines, e.g., starting on time and following planned activity sequences; follow them. Conduct task analysis of a thinking skill to learn: identify the specific skill, prerequisite knowledge and skills, related sub-skills sequence, and student readiness with prerequisites. Prepare examples, sample problems and explanations. Prepare questions transcending simple factual information recall, addressing advanced understanding, e.g., how? How well? Why? Plan strategies for diagnosis, guidance, practice, and remediation. Establish a comfortable, non-threatening atmosphere. Communicate clear expectations, genuine topic interest, enthusiasm, and a businesslike approach combined with warmth. Prepare and organize thoroughly to minimize between-activity transition times. Clearly explain tasks: set goals at beginnings of assignments, and furnish finished product examples. Introduce tasks with clear, simple organizing frameworks like single-paragraph overviews, previews, charts, or diagrams. Introduce key terms and concepts before proceeding. Focus attention on important information using questions. Use written signals, repetition, nonverbal behaviors, and verbal statements for emphasis. Use demonstrations, models, pictures, diagrams, examples, etc. to make ideas vivid. Signal transitions between ideas. Give frequent feedback, including clarifying or correcting incorrect responses.

Student Development of Higher-Order Thinking Skills

Cognitive and learning strategies include organization, elaboration, rehearsal; and metacognition for self-evaluating and self-regulating one's thinking, entailing mnemonics, visualization, diagramming, highlighting; or more complex strategies, e.g., the Multipass reading comprehension procedure. To help students develop critical and creative thinking and learning skills, intentionally design lessons expressly for teaching specific thinking and learning strategies. Teach self-reflection and self-evaluation: give students inexplicable dilemmas, paradoxes, etc., challenging pre-existing beliefs. Guide systematic student inquiry. Encourage reflection and making sense of new information by having students write or discuss in their own words how to integrate it with their existing ideas, approaches, and opinions. Encourage and guide students in forming hypotheses, brainstorming, guessing, speculating about consequences, and discussing how their thought processes have changed their ideas. Monitor inefficient strategies and correct them. Encourage continuous student reflection of beliefs about thinking, thought processes, and evaluating effectiveness. Use advance organizers and cognitive maps to show main parts or steps when approaching various thinking and learning tasks. Teach PQ4R (*preview, question, read, reflect, recite, and review*) with written materials. Instruction in abstraction, analysis, outlining, summarization, and generalization enhances both reading and reasoning skills. Stress broad algorithms, heuristics, and problem-solving strategies; give enough practice to overlearn for effortless, consistent use. Teach specific strategies using modeling, think-alouds, discussion, and practice. Students develop self-confidence from teachers modeling self-confidence in thinking and reasoning processes.

Name and define each cognitive skill for students; ask them for examples and synonyms. Model steps for applying each skill. Explain appropriate and inappropriate skill application contexts. Assign cooperative learning groups to practice skills. To improve comprehension, problem-solving, decision-making; and concept, principle, and procedure application: ask probing questions to diagnose existing student conceptions and misconceptions. Furnish hands-on experiences enabling students to explore generating new explanations or interpreting raw data. Give question stems or examples requiring higher-order thinking; have students answer in groups, pairs, or independently. Give practice in brainstorming, decision-making, experimenting, identifying and solving problems in art, music, and writing as well as math and science. Incorporate individualized options in lesson plans, e.g., assignment choices, modalities for multiple intelligences, varying instruction and application sequences, open-ended participation tasks with multiple alternatives, multi-ability tasks and varied activities accommodating differences in abstraction, language proficiency, and emotional influences. Give opportunities to discover procedural knowledge; explain procedure goals, applicable situations or problems, and corresponding strategies and rationales; demonstrate stepwise procedure application; give students practice selecting and implementing procedures; give performance feedback. Promote internal locus of control by helping students perceive themselves as effective learners.

Integrating Technology into Instruction

Instructional technology integration is effective when it supports curriculum goals. Technology must support four essential learning elements: active student engagement, group participation, frequent interaction and feedback, and connections with real-life experts. In the 1960s, MIT professor Seymour Papert collaborated with cognitive-developmental psychologist Jean Piaget, and then developed Logo, a programming language for children to use without advanced mathematical knowledge. Students using Logo could write and debug programs to control robot movements with minimal instruction. They learned more in-depth geometry concept understanding and programming skills—and were more engaged in learning than in traditional classroom exercises. Papert pointed out the ample overlap of education and fun with computers for promoting all students' internal motivation. Today technology learning tools abound; almost every US public school has Internet connection. When technology is used for more ambitious learning goals than basic skills, studies find it helps students develop creativity, research skills, and higher-order thinking.

Technology can further learning through building local and global communities including students, teachers, administrators, parents, scientists, and others; giving students and teachers more opportunities for reflection, feedback, and revision; offering learning tools and scaffolds, e.g., visualization tools and modeling programs; giving classrooms exciting, real-world problem-based curricula; and expanding teacher learning opportunities. Social media support collaboration, reinforcing learning's social nature. Technology enables learning communities and improves learning cultures. Students learn concepts in ways impossible or impracticable with other instructional methods through social networking, simulations, and digital gaming. Educational technology complements what exemplary teachers naturally do. Experts note that digital games, instead of separating instruction from assessment, constantly assess student problem-solving progress, giving students feedback and further practice. Letting students teach them how they engage with digital media both informs teachers about technology and develops student metacognition. Integration means using technology to learn content and demonstrate content understanding, not simply digital expertise. Students need guided practice and exploration to achieve this.

Computer Mediation

Communicating using computers gives students opportunities to access remote data sources, collaborate with students in other places on group projects, and share their work with other students to obtain their responses or evaluations. Research finds that computer-based instruction (CBI) and computer-assisted instruction (CAI) combined with regular classroom instruction enhances student motivation, academic achievement, and attitudes. Moreover, the increasing prevalence, even requirement, of computers in workplaces demands student preparation; and federal and state standards increasingly require integrating technology into instruction and student computer literacy. Studies have shown that the following computer-mediated communication applications are effective for enhancing student learning of prerequisite skills and higher-order cognitive skills: building skills in logical reasoning, inductive reasoning, deductive reasoning, and making verbal analogies; practicing and drilling procedures that incorporate tests or probes; and practicing problem-solving strategies and skills in making inferences. In addition, interactive learning software programs give students more autonomy in learning, allow them to learn at individual paces, engage student interest, and often make learning more entertaining. Moreover, students need immediate, specific, corrective feedback on their learning progress, which interactive software programs can give more consistently than single teachers with large classes.

Active Teaching and Learning Strategies

Active teaching and learning strategies make students active participants in learning. Rather than passively listening to teachers discuss, read about, or observe others perform skills, students practice skills to gain proficiency. Many students learn best by doing. Hands-on activities take students out of books and sometimes their seats, classrooms, schools, or even familiar thinking habits. In addition to engaging student interest and giving actual practice, they have the benefit of integrating subject-area content with all four language and literacy domains—listening, speaking, reading, and writing. Though research consistently shows students learn better through active content engagement, some teachers avoid active learning. Objections and dilemmas include: concerns they will never cover required content; losing class control by not lecturing; having trouble getting students to work in teams—some doing all the work, others none; students' not knowing how to answer higher-order questions; student resistance to active learning or a preference for habituated listening and note-taking; what to do with ELL or special education students during active learning and group activities. Guidelines include: vary partners and small-group teams via randomization, specific rotation schedules, or other systematic schemes. Vary required team tasks and techniques. Clearly identify team member roles, task purpose, outcome, and time allotted. Prepare all needed materials. Determine how to grade tasks. Start small or brief activities early. Establish a signal for students to stop discussion.

Giving students choices among assignments enables them to decide how to demonstrate their learning. For example, some might choose to write compositions, some to make spoken presentations, some to draw illustrations, and some to construct models to demonstrate the same knowledge. A language strategy is A-Z Taxonomy: small student groups write the alphabet vertically on paper and think of vocabulary terms in the content they are studying that start with each letter. This technique is effective as both pre- and post-instruction. Pairing students to debate some controversial issue related to learning content, having pairs explain pro and con positions to each other and agree to an overall recommendation gives students practice in negotiating and compromising skills, plus listening and speaking opportunities. Brainstorming evokes creativity, originality, and quantity: ask open-ended questions; never criticize ideas. Providing a suitable target number of ideas sometimes helps. Some linguistically diverse students may feel more comfortable responding as members of a small student team or group.

In a "carousel questions" strategy, the teacher writes several questions about a content topic being learned on large posters or paper stations posted around the classroom. Small student groups, each with a different color marker, rotate every few minutes among question sets. At every station, teams add ideas, responses, or answers not already included. Then the class shares all student responses, gaining multiple and varied answers to the questions. In case studies, students are given real-world stories about things that happened to an individual, family, school, or community; students apply their content knowledge and skills to authentic situations. In critical explanation, teachers ask students to consider reasons or factors that might explain some content-related issues or problems. Use "might" and "could," not "why" to avoid implying right, wrong, or only one correct answer. In discussion webs, students consider a content-related issue or problem in small groups, then regroup and share their work and information with classmates from other groups. In field studies, students have opportunities to learn about and study issues in their community related to the content they are learning. Health classes might study community nutrition, disease, safety, environmental issues, consumer health, or healthcare services; earth science classes might collect rock samples, identify them, and determine local distribution patterns; social studies classes might study local landmarks and associated history, etc.

Long-Term Goals, Short-Term Objectives, Instructional Objectives, and Lesson Plan Objectives

Long-term goals typically are mastered over a school year and are stated in very broad, general terms. Goal areas typically correspond to content areas like reading, writing, math, and other subjects. Teachers derive short-term objectives from long-term goals. Short-term objectives can be completed in shorter time periods, ranging from two weeks to three months. Teachers then derive instructional objectives from short-term objectives. Students can generally master instructional objectives within one lesson. From smaller numbers of long-term goals, teachers should be able to generate a larger number of short-term objectives and even larger numbers of instructional objectives from short-term objectives. As an example, if a long-term goal is for students to read at grade level, then related short-term objectives could include recognizing vocabulary sight words; using phonics, context clues, and structural analysis to identify unfamiliar words; and demonstrating text comprehension on literal, inferential, and critical levels. From these, a teacher could break down phonics into rules for short and long vowels, digraphs, initial and final single consonants, and consonant blends to write individual instructional objectives.

Correctly written objectives include: student orientation, behavioral terminology, a criterion, and a condition statement. "Review long and short vowels in one-syllable words" or "teach fire safety" are teacher-oriented. To clarify their significance and use for students, they should be student-oriented: "correctly read aloud words containing long or short vowels"; "identify fire safety rules." Behavioral terminology is observable and measurable. This is why Bloom's taxonomy supplies action verbs for each complexity level in the hierarchy and each domain. Experts remark that while knowledge-level objectives, e.g., to read sight words aloud or recite multiplication tables, are prerequisites for more advanced learning, teachers should still not dwell primarily on these as most easily observable or identifiable, but ensure they give equal time in their lessons to higher-level cognitive skills. Experts also remind teachers not to confine objectives to Bloom's cognitive domain, but include the psychomotor and affective domains as well. Objectives can include all three. For example, an instructional objective for a student to answer comprehension questions orally with 90 percent accuracy after silently reading a passage from a grade-level basal text can include requesting assistance by raising one's hand, using a person's name to get his or her attention, asking a question, and saying "please" or other social amenity.

SWOT

SWOT analysis stands for *strengths*, *weaknesses*, *opportunities*, and *threats*. While frequently used by anyone analyzing market trends, identifying target markets, and/or developing marketing plans (which includes not only salespeople, but also therapists and other practitioners who must promote their services), it is also useful to apply to education. For example, teachers can use it with high school students in career counseling to identify the job-relevant skills they possess (strengths) and those they lack (weaknesses); jobs open, job growth probabilities, and chances for advancement in a student's preferred career field (opportunities); and competition for jobs, dead-end positions, and downsizing probabilities (threats). Accompanying the SWOT analysis, a gap analysis tool identifies employer needs and job requirements; student and candidate knowledge and skills; differences between these, which represent gaps; an action plan to fill gaps; a timeframe to complete the plan; and people who can help. For example, an employer might require knowledge of Excel or other spreadsheet software; the student might only know Word or other word-processing software. The action plan is to learn Excel or other spreadsheet programs through a short community college course, school enrichment program, library-offered class, interactive computer tutorial, etc. Teachers can also use these tools to identify and address other, non-career-related academic gaps.

Hypothetical Situation Wherein a Teacher Identifies and Analyzes Student Knowledge Gaps

Suppose a teacher has designed a unit on a content subject and has taught the class a number of individual one-day lessons within this unit. The teacher's regular practice is to conduct formative assessments, e.g., pop quizzes, oral Q&A sessions, whips (going around the room quickly, having every student answer an open-ended content question), etc. near the end of each day's lesson. So far, each formative assessment has shown 80-100 percent of students grasped main lesson concepts, facts, and points. But on this day, the teacher finds 90 percent of the students fail to demonstrate knowledge or understanding of lesson content. It is highly unlikely 90 percent of students did not pay attention or lacked cognitive ability to comprehend the lesson, and highly likely the lesson was ineffective. Also, the 10 percent displaying knowledge and understanding may have been the most conscientious students and/or had the highest cognitive ability levels; and/or some, most, or all of the 10 percent may already have had existing knowledge of the lesson topic. Therefore the teacher re-teaches this lesson, using different instructional strategies than the first time. This time the formative assessment shows 95 percent of the class knowing and understanding key concepts and information.

Teacher Assessment Literacy, Practices, and Needs

Various research finds teachers viewing learning as memorization assesses student information recall; teachers viewing learning as constructing knowledge and understanding use formative assessment to create continuous information flow about student understanding and adapt instruction to be more effective. Studies also show assessment-literate teachers do not limit assessment to multiple-choice or true-false questions but apply many, varied strategies, selecting those strongest and most relevant for specific learning goals. Pre-service teachers are found having inadequate repertoires of assessment strategies. One study showed the teacher asking the most conceptual questions and having the biggest variety of ways to adapt instruction according to assessment results had the highest student performance level. Also, some researchers (Gottheiner and Seigel, 2012) conclude others frequently overlook how teachers interpret formative assessment data in their studies, and more resources for doing so are needed. Teachers in their study reported that, although student group discussions of questions could contribute to new misconceptions, they also triggered discourse—building on classmate ideas and enabling concept discovery and construction before even learning corresponding terminology.

Addressing Student Conceptions, Misconceptions, and Preconceptions

Multiple teachers agree to the value of having students discuss scientific concepts and struggle to define these on their own before teachers supply them with the scientific terminology. They find this process enables students to construct and own their knowledge. Teachers also observe students from diverse cultural backgrounds may have different ways of making sense of problems, making it important to provide real-life contexts giving them personal relevance to students and accessing prior student knowledge for understanding them. Teachers emphasize structured activities, which afford students chances to develop their thoughts before sharing them; and

- 62 -

allowing each student time to share ideas increases participation. Starting with small groups and progressing to whole-class discussion allows teachers to circulate, monitoring or assessing many more student responses; allows students to exchange and develop ideas in smaller, non-threatening groups; and improves subsequent whole-class discussion levels. Teachers emphasize needing to address previous student knowledge. They realize misconceptions can be based on cultural beliefs and personal experiences, making them resistant to change. Researchers report that, although teachers can often predict common student misconceptions, students frequently give wider response ranges than teachers can predict; and that many teachers propose re-teaching for preconceptions, but more experienced teachers try different instructional strategies.

Differentiated Instruction Practices Effective for Enhancing Student Literacy

Teaching experts advise using common instructional texts for read-alouds to facilitate differentiation. Teachers can use teaching text read-alouds to build background knowledge, demonstrate strategy application to students, introduce issues and invite student journal responses, and assure every student access to the information and skills they need to improve their reading. Researchers find that using multiple texts at varied reading levels—not just one—to teach units enables all students to obtain information from materials they can read best. Rather than teaching "the textbook," teachers need to organize every individual instructional unit around a topic, issue, or genre. This applies whether teachers assign students to small-group work, or use whole-class differentiated instruction approaches. By organizing for instruction this way, teachers can meet all student reading levels. Because students can only become better readers if they understand how to construct meaning while they read, teachers must show them this process by modeling the ways in which they think about texts during read-alouds; work with small reading groups; and one-on-one instructional conferences with individual students. This gives students multiple opportunities to learn how to construct meaning from text.

Expert teachers find discussion particularly important when differentiating reading instruction. Student discussion effectively builds on every individual student's factual knowledge and understanding, and gives students opportunities to build comprehension and clarify meaning. Students deepen recall and understanding when teachers ask them to progress past fact memorization to discussion applying those facts to problems and issues. In-depth small-group or whole-class topic discussions demonstrate how classmates think and reason, build background knowledge, and can make information relevant to students' personal lives. Teachers must never assume every student absorbs the same information from a lesson or demonstration; also, students not having absorbed lesson content can write little or nothing about it because they can only write what they know and understand. Writing strengthens comprehension and enables thinking, exploration, and learning. Teachers can glean insights from reading student journals about student text analysis and inferential thinking skills, supporting intervention planning. Ongoing assessments enable teachers to reveal individual student need areas and successes and target instruction accordingly to support every student. Experts also advise teachers to think through every unit to determine what they want students to learn about genres, issues, and reading strategies; carefully plan units accordingly; and assemble appropriate read-aloud texts, plus reading materials to meet every student's needs.

Culturally Responsive Teaching

Culturally responsive teaching utilizes diverse students' cultural background knowledge, previous experiences, and performance styles, increasing the effectiveness and appropriateness of learning for them by teaching through and to their strengths. Culturally responsive instruction recognizes various ethnic groups' cultural heritages as legitimate—both as legacies influencing student allowing each student time to share ideas increases participation. Starting with small groups and progressing to whole-class discussion allows teachers to circulate, monitoring or assessing many more student responses; allows students to exchange and develop ideas in smaller, non-threatening groups; and improves subsequent whole-class discussion levels. Teachers emphasize needing to address previous student knowledge. They realize misconceptions can be based on cultural beliefs and personal experiences, making them resistant to change. Researchers report that, although teachers can often predict common student misconceptions, students frequently give wider response ranges than teachers can predict; and that many teachers propose re-teaching for preconceptions, but more experienced teachers try different instructional strategies.

Differentiated Instruction Practices Effective for Enhancing Student Literacy

Teaching experts advise using common instructional texts for read-alouds to facilitate differentiation. Teachers can use teaching text read-alouds to build background knowledge, demonstrate strategy application to students, introduce issues and invite student journal responses, and assure every student access to the information and skills they need to improve their reading. Researchers find that using multiple texts at varied reading levels—not just one—to teach units enables all students to obtain information from materials they can read best. Rather than teaching "the textbook," teachers need to organize every individual instructional unit around a topic, issue, or genre. This applies whether teachers assign students to small-group work, or use whole-class differentiated instruction approaches. By organizing for instruction this way, teachers can meet all student reading levels. Because students can only become better readers if they understand how to construct meaning while they read, teachers must show them this process by modeling the ways in which they think about texts during read-alouds; work with small reading groups; and one-on-one instructional conferences with individual students. This gives students multiple opportunities to learn how to construct meaning from text.

Expert teachers find discussion particularly important when differentiating reading instruction. Student discussion effectively builds on every individual student's factual knowledge and understanding, and gives students opportunities to build comprehension and clarify meaning. Students deepen recall and understanding when teachers ask them to progress past fact memorization to discussion applying those facts to problems and issues. In-depth small-group or whole-class topic discussions demonstrate how classmates think and reason, build background knowledge, and can make information relevant to students' personal lives. Teachers must never assume every student absorbs the same information from a lesson or demonstration; also, students not having absorbed lesson content can write little or nothing about it because they can only write what they know and understand. Writing strengthens comprehension and enables thinking, exploration, and learning. Teachers can glean insights from reading student journals about student text analysis and inferential thinking skills, supporting intervention planning. Ongoing assessments enable teachers to reveal individual student need areas and successes and target instruction accordingly to support every student. Experts also advise teachers to think through every unit to determine what they want students to learn about genres, issues, and reading strategies; carefully plan units accordingly; and assemble appropriate read-aloud texts, plus reading materials to meet every student's needs.

Culturally Responsive Teaching

Culturally responsive teaching utilizes diverse students' cultural background knowledge, previous experiences, and performance styles, increasing the effectiveness and appropriateness of learning for them by teaching through and to their strengths. Culturally responsive instruction recognizes various ethnic groups' cultural heritages as legitimate—both as legacies influencing student

- 63 -

attitudes, approaches, and dispositions to learning; and as content worth including in formal curricula. Culturally responsive approaches establish meaningful connections—both between students' school and home experiences, and between abstract academic concepts and the sociocultural realities that they live. It employs a broad range of instructional strategies addressing different student learning styles. It teaches students not only knowledge about their own and others' cultural traditions and heritages, but moreover to praise one another's cultural legacies and practices. Instructional practices that are culturally responsive incorporate multicultural information, materials, and resources in all skills and subjects schools routinely teach. Classroom environment considerations include using literature reflecting various literary genres and ethnic perspectives; incorporating everyday living concepts like jobs, economics, and consumer behaviors of different ethnic groups into math instruction; and activities that reflect a range of visual, auditory, tactile, and other sensory experiences to accommodate different student learning styles.

Culturally responsive teachers maintain cultural identity and heritage as well as academic performance. They teach the whole student, using cultural references to develop cognitive, affective, social, and political learning. Students develop interpersonal relationships, acting as extended family members supporting, encouraging, and helping one another. Group accountability makes individual success everybody's responsibility in academic communities. Teachers satisfy student needs regarding human dignity, sense of belonging, and individual self-concepts. Multidisciplinary teacher teams may collaborate, teaching single cultural concepts; students can actively participate in their own evaluations. Classroom climate, learning context, student-teacher relationships, curriculum content, instructional techniques, and assessments are included in culturally responsive teaching, which is multidimensional. It empowers students as learners and people by sharing teacher and student authority; relating personal growth to public life; developing critical curiosity and inquiry habits as well as strong knowledge and skills; and treating individual development as a social, cooperative, active process wherein students explore society, power, inequality, and change. It uses varied cultural experiences, not traditional practices, as teaching and learning resources. Students learn reflection, decision-making, and effective action—personally, socially, economically, and politically; more humane, caring interpersonal understandings and skills; more insightful, clearer thinking; and continual knowledge criticism, revision, renewal, and sharing.

Cooperative Learning

Cooperative learning requires <u>positive interdependence</u> (students sink-or-swim together): assign assembly line-style and synergistic task completion. Establish collective goals, resources, and rewards; assign group roles; arrange group furniture and environment; have groups compete against each other. <u>Face-to-face interaction</u> entails seating groups in circles or pairs facing each other. Promote <u>individual accountability</u> through checking with random group members, assigning individual tasks, bonus group credit or rewards if all members perform well individually, and having students bring individual work to their groups. <u>Social skills</u> including decision-making, communication, trust-building, leadership, and conflict management must not be assumed but taught. Teachers should record their observations of students on observation forms to provide feedback. Social skills include categories of group formation and assembly, group functioning, and the formulation and fermentation of ideas and knowledge. <u>Group processing</u> can be accomplished orally and/or in writing by small group reflection; teacher provision of feedback to small groups or whole classes; teacher and small group observations; and goal-setting, by students with teacher guidance as needed, for students' next work sessions, e.g., regarding further social skills development.

- 64 -

Promoting Student Use and Refinement of Higher-Order Thinking Skills

To get students to explore ideas from diverse perspectives, plan and ask questions prompting them to use their imaginations. For example, during a lesson on agriculture, ask students what they would think and feel about certain policies and practices if they were, respectively, legislators, corporate executives, factory farmers, small farmers, migrant farm workers, consumers paying for groceries, families eating groceries, etc. In a history lesson, ask students to take the perspectives of Native American tribes and of European settlers; or consider both the viewpoints of American revolutionaries and British colonial governors, etc. To promote problem-solving, instead of telling students how to solve problems—mathematical, scientific, economic, logistical, creative, etc.—ask students how, also promoting inquiry; have them brainstorm to generate many ideas as a group; guide their consideration of alternatives and speculation about potential consequences; and let them practice implementing solutions, analyzing and discussing results. Rather than "yes" or "no" questions, asking open-ended questions allows for many varied responses. To develop research skills, have students form research questions, guiding revision of overly broad or narrow questions; guide them through steps of formulating hypotheses, conducting experiments testing hypotheses; collecting, analyzing, and interpreting data; reporting results; and drawing and communicating conclusions.

Areas of Executive Functioning That Commonly Pose Challenges for Students

Parents frequently identify time management, planning, and organization as challenges for their children. These are three among many areas involving executive function. Executive function skills start developing during infancy, continuing development into adulthood. Considering this duration for full development, children need solid foundations. Executive functioning involves cognitive skills utilized for executing tasks. A single task requires several executive function skills. For example, to get dressed for school, a student must plan ahead for the weather, sustain attention long enough for task completion, manage emotions regarding wanting or not wanting to go to school, and start and finish the task in a timely fashion. Students use executive functioning skills to help them do homework and chores, keep track of belongings, follow rules, save money for things they want, and many other things. Some signs that a student may be experiencing difficulty developing and/or applying executive function skills include: the student has trouble estimating how long it will take to complete a school project, and/or planning the project; telling a story with the details sequenced correctly; or remembering information while performing an activity.

Helping Students Develop Time Management, Planning, and Organizational Skills

Time management: have students color portions of a clock face using dry-erase markers to represent time segments, e.g., five minutes, 15 minutes, etc., helping them visualize elapsed and remaining time; and check in halfway through time allotted. Give students halfway-point questions, e.g., are they halfway finished? Are they still focused on the task's goal? Are any distractions robbing them of on-task time? Must they speed or slow their work pace? Planning: one application is helping students plan homework. Ask them what a given homework assignment would look like; have them sketch it on paper divided into two columns, e.g., with a vocabulary assignment, students write vocabulary words and definitions in the left column, and draw pictures illustrating each definition in the right column. This helps them identify where to start, what they need, and how completed homework will look, promoting more independent work. Post-it note calendars help students visualize longer-term assignment due dates, and divide assignments into more manageable chunks. Organization: workspaces with Post-it notes or baskets labeled "Prepare," "Do," and "Done" support both planning and organization. Dual-pocket folders, one pocket for homework or materials to take home and another for completed homework to turn in, facilitate organization.

Instruction and Assessment

Curriculum Scope and Sequence

In curriculum design, curriculum scope is the breadth and depth in which it covers content in each subject; clearly identified learning objectives reflecting local, state, and national standards; or how coherent curriculum is made through instructing basic concepts across several years of content coverage. Scope includes both how much material teachers must cover on any specified topic, and how much teachers should expect students to accomplish resulting from instruction. Sequence is the order in which scope is taught. If educators fail to structure curriculum scope and sequence deliberately, they risk having students miss significant learning when instruction is delivered without adequate planning. As examples, elementary school teachers might use a curriculum organizer table or chart where they enter titles and descriptions of each learning unit by time period, and the subject focus of each unit (e.g., arranged horizontally in columns). In the first column, before the series of units per time period, they can label cells vertically to enter main ideas, i.e., core student understandings; key concepts and questions to focus learning; teacher focus, i.e., unit goals like language development, group work, a culminating activity, etc.; fundamental content; subject foci, e.g., literacy, math, and respective programs, tasks, texts, and resources to use.

Whereas scope represents breadth and depth of content coverage and learning objectives, sequence represents presenting material in logical order. Sequencing reflects the philosophy that students should be instructed starting with concrete concepts, becoming progressively more abstract throughout successive grade levels. After establishing scope, educators must determine when to teach it. This is important when certain learning is often dependent on previous other knowledge, e.g., understanding certain science or geography concepts requires certain numeracy skills. Even when some learning experiences are not reliant on mastering prerequisite knowledge, curricula may be sequenced instead according to increasing complexity, e.g., in science subjects; logical progression, e.g., from the local environment to the global environment in social studies; or psychological valence, e.g., from immediate to more distant interests in vocational education. Teachers must carefully sequence instruction, both within and across key learning areas (KLAs). For example, "reading effectively" would precede "writing effectively" in a curriculum sequence represented by a curriculum map showing English Language Arts (ELAs) taught by KLA because receptive language like listening and reading develops before expressive language like speaking and writing. Critical text interpretation follows reading and writing. Similarly, understanding and applying numbers precedes selecting and utilizing measures.

The scope of a curriculum refers to all of the content it will include within a specified length of time. The curriculum sequence refers to at which points during the time range specific parts of the scope of learning will occur. In other words, educators must decide which content should be taught during certain grade levels, or to certain classes or student groups. Teachers must also determine sequencing within work units, courses, and school years. Hence scope and sequence support maximal student learning, as well as providing continual opportunities for students to learn. By coordinating the scope of curriculum content and the sequence of curriculum instruction, educators give order to their delivery of curricular content. For teaching and learning to be effective, the important parts of all subjects must be included in scope, and must be delivered in the right order for students to benefit. By mapping curriculum scope, teachers can ensure they integrate the state and district learning standards guiding their curriculum. By mapping sequence, they can ensure they address curricular principles as well as matching knowledge prerequisites, increasing complexity, logical progression, psychological preferences, or other factors influencing temporal order.

Curriculum scope and sequence work together to furnish instruction with an organized structure which enables students to receive the maximum numbers of opportunities to learn and to take advantage of these to learn the most that they can. For educators to overlook important parts of subject content instruction is entirely too easy without the organizing structure of curriculum scope and sequence. It is also much more difficult to deliver instruction depending on previous learning, and avoid repeating material over grade levels, without planning sequence in advance. Most states develop scope and sequence directly from state-level standards. Some school districts design curriculum frameworks, which provide the scope of content and sequence in which to teach it. It is also popular for state education departments and district curriculum departments to divide learning sequences into developmental strands or bands. A common method of organizing a curriculum scope is to divide it into key learning areas (KLAs) or integrated themes used as curriculum organizers. Depending on their size, structure, and sector, different schools approach curriculum scope and sequence development through different processes. Some states define scope and sequence in certain subjects, but leave this to individual districts in others.

Standards-Based Learning

In standards-based education, all grade levels and subjects have clear learning goals; all instruction and assessment are aligned to these because the strongest school-level influence on student achievement is opportunity to learn: students are unlikely to learn specific content without opportunity. Students are given multiple opportunities to demonstrate achievement because reading, math, social studies, and science should be treated like PE and music: poor initial performances do not receive low grades, but rather require repeated practice until students master the skills. Formative assessments, giving feedback and promoting growth, are emphasized because research shows effective feedback is the strongest single classroom instructional change increasing learning and achievement. Rubrics and scoring guides are consistently employed because they enable teachers to give students better, criterion-referenced feedback about specific skill and knowledge levels, not merely norm-referenced feedback via percentage scores. This helps teachers evaluate their learning objectives as well as advance student achievement. Teachers regularly report student progress toward learning goals because specific, formative, more frequent feedback than annual standardized tests critically affects teacher conscientiousness and effectiveness with initiatives developing new reporting practices and forms; with instructing, assessing, and encouraging students; and student success. Instructional activities represent the "how," standards the "what" and "why" of school programs.

The US Department of Education (ED) funds and supports high curriculum standards in public schools, but does not itself develop them; individual state education departments do. ED has given over $350 million in funds to a consortium of the Council of Chief State School Officers and National Governors Association for developing the Common Core State Standards (CCSS). Most US states have voluntarily chosen to adopt these standards. The CCSS has a website with information. Additional sites with information on federal support of other state educational initiatives include a site on the Every Student Succeeds Act (ESSA, replacing No Child Left Behind, or NCLB) flexibility, whereby ED enables states to develop their own accountability systems; sites about the federal Race to the Top initiative and its assessment; and a webpage with US Secretary of Education Arne Duncan's speech about high standards. CCSS are concepts students should know and understand; school districts develop specific curricula, and teachers plan specific lessons, to help students master standards. Districts and schools have traditionally had printed copies of their state standards; today, these are typically also published online, the easiest way for teachers to access them—including any updates, which can be posted electronically more easily and frequently than printed.

While the abundance of federal-level and state-level curriculum standards might seem to facilitate teachers' preparing relevant classroom curricula, it can overwhelm educators trying to design standards-based learning units. However, teachers discover that standards enable more curricular focus, refinement of their previous work, clearer communication of expectations to students, and enhanced learning—provided some model and processes for classroom standards application, many of which are available today. Standards articulate clear expectations for what all students should know and be able to do—regardless of gender, minority status, socioeconomic status, history of academic success (or failure), and previous access or lack thereof to any kinds of educational opportunities—while addressing school constituencies' varying needs. Standards give states common referents for assuring coordinated functioning of educational system components across schools and districts; offer parents, businesses, and community stakeholders a common language for discussing educational processes and communicate shared learning expectations, enabling more effective partnering in education; provide impetus and focus for new school programs and innovations in organizing content, delivering instruction, and planning assessment; make teachers design more intentional, purposeful learning of important content; and for all students, clearly identify performance expectations and means for meeting them; promote more equitable, challenging, and rewarding experiences; and improve performance.

Cognitive, Affective, and Psychomotor Domains

The cognitive domain represents mental skills, i.e., facts, information, ideas, and concepts that one can learn, understand, and apply. Among knowledge, skills, and attitudes that a learner can acquire, the cognitive domain corresponds most to *knowledge*. The affective domain represents emotional *attitudes* that one can develop and apply, with respect to the self and others. The psychomotor domain represents physical *skills* that one can learn and apply. For example, when a student reads some information about physical exercise, understands it, analyzes it, compares it with other information sources, judges it according to established criteria, and writes a paper about it, these activities are in the cognitive domain. When this student finds value in exercise knowledge, demonstrates this by voluntarily participating in athletic events, and becomes an accomplished athlete in a certain sport, these activities are in the affective domain. When this student watches, copies, practices, and perfects the specific physical skills required for his or her preferred sport, these activities are in the psychomotor domain.

Bloom's Taxonomy

Bloom's 1950s taxonomy originally included levels or categories of knowledge, i.e., recalling learned information; comprehension, i.e., grasping, restating, and explaining meaning; application of knowledge to new and different situations; analysis, i.e., separating components of material and showing relationships among components; synthesis, i.e., bringing separate concepts and ideas together to create new wholes and relationships; and evaluation, i.e., judging the value or worth of information according to established criteria. Anderson and Krathwohl's 2001 revision changed these nouns to verbs: remember, understand, apply, analyze, evaluate, and create—also switching the order of evaluate from after synthesis to before create. Instructional objectives should include learning activities that address each of these categories, sequenced correspondingly from remembering to creating to reflect the hierarchy's progressively increasing difficulty. Krathwohl and Bloom's taxonomy in the affective domain covers receiving, or attending to something; responding, or showing new behaviors influenced by experience; valuing, or showing definitive commitment or involvement; organization, or integrating new values into priorities; characterization by value, or behaving consistently with new values. Dave (1970), Simpson (1972), and Harrow (1972)'s psychomotor taxonomies include observing a physical action or event; imitating another's action; practicing repeatedly; and adapting, i.e., fine-tuning performance. In all three domains, these taxonomies progress sequentially from basic to higher levels, as corresponding instructional objectives should.

Observable Behavior

Educational interest in observable behaviors was influenced by behaviorist learning theory, which proposed that because internal mental or emotional states could not be externally observed or measured, the study and modification of behavior should be confined to observable behaviors, i.e., actions or states of being that others could outwardly observe an individual producing. However, because only observable behaviors could be accurately measured, these were the only kind that could be changed through behavior modification techniques based on operant conditioning principles. In applying Bloom's taxonomy to cognitive learning objectives, the same proposition is embraced in that only action verbs are appropriate. For example, under the second category of Understanding, the verb *understand* itself is not found because it is internal, hence impossible to quantify; action verbs under Understand include *describe, differentiate, discuss, cite examples of, demonstrate use of, identify, select, tell*, etc. Thus a good instructional objective would not require a student simply to know or remember something, which requires assuming the student knows or remembers, but rather to *recall, name, list,* or *repeat* it because these demonstrate the student's knowledge and memory in ways that others can observe.

Measurable Outcomes

Learning objectives must be not only observable, meaning teachers and others can see, hear, or otherwise observe evidence a student has learned something; but also measurable, meaning there is some way to quantify the behavior demonstrating learning. Behaviorist learning theory pointed out only observable behaviors can be measured, therefore changed. As a corollary, it has demonstrated that by nature, observable behaviors can nearly always be measured because if people can observe another's behavior, they can also find a way of measuring it. To be measurable, outcomes or results must be specific. For example, "The student will use correct grammar" is not measurable because it is too vague, not specifying what or whether all or some percentage of grammar must be correct, etc. But the objective "The student, given a sentence written in the present or past tense, will be able to rewrite it in future tense with no contradictions (e.g., 'I will see them yesterday') or errors in tense" is a measurable objective, specifying the condition (given a sentence written in present or past tense) and behavior (rewrite it in future tense). These are elements of the ABCD method—*audience, behavior, conditions, degree of mastery* required (e.g. 100 percent, 95 percent, 90 percent, etc.).

Evaluating Technological and Other Instructional Resources

State education departments typically publish guidelines for their districts to evaluate instructional materials according to state criteria, aligned with state content standards and curriculum frameworks for each subject. In some instances, educators tasked with evaluating new instructional materials for certain subject domains (e.g., mathematics or science) and/or grade levels (e.g., preschool, elementary, middle, or high school), after studying various sets of evaluation criteria, found them all inadequate and decided to develop their own criteria instead. Some examples of elements found important to address and overlooked by existing criteria include: need for more authentic assessment practices within the materials evaluated; evaluation criteria focusing on technology's overall role in a specific instructional unit, rather than only criteria for evaluating individual pieces of technology; and criteria for evaluating whether an instructional unit is practical, e.g., whether teachers in schools with typical insufficient funding, overloaded classrooms, long hours, etc. can effectively implement the materials. Educators have consulted resources like standards published by national organizations for their discipline, e.g., the National Council of Teachers of Mathematics, National Council of Teachers of English; research articles and books on subject-specific assessment; local districts; and teacher and researcher experiences.

Learning Resources vs. Learning Materials

Teaching resources include locations and means for finding teaching materials, e.g., websites, libraries, stores, etc.; intangibles, e.g., theories of learning or education, published research articles and books, or support from colleagues; and materials. Teaching materials most often mean concrete objects, e.g., worksheets, workbooks, or manipulatives including tools and games that students can physically handle and interact with to learn new concepts and skills. For example, younger students can use blocks to learn counting. Teaching materials should ideally be customized to the subject content, students in the class, and teacher using them. Students achieve more when their learning is supported by materials. For example, students learning a new skill in class have significant opportunities to practice it using a worksheet. This not only affords necessary repetition, but also enables independent student exploration of knowledge. Learning materials help structure lesson planning and delivery, especially in earlier grades, by guiding teachers and students through regular routines, e.g., having a weekly vocabulary game relieves teachers of pressure while giving students needed practice with new words taught weekly, as well as fun. Materials also facilitate differentiating instruction for individual students. Some teachers make their own; many more are available online, most free.

Thematic Instruction

Thematic instruction reflects a holistic belief that learning is best in the context of a coherent whole, and connected to real life. Teaching thematically organizes curriculum around overarching themes—teaching around experiences, not isolated disciplines. For example, a teacher might design a unit wherein students explore a broad environmental theme including river basins, rain forests, communities, energy use, etc., simultaneously integrating reading, math, science, and social studies into each lesson. Thematic instruction's goal is teaching these cognitive skills within the context of real-world topics, combining both enough broadness to enable creative exploration and enough specificity for practical application. Teachers and students first choose a theme, typically around a broad concept—weather, democracy, etc.; or a large, integrated system such as an ecosystem, city, etc. They then organize their core curriculum's content knowledge and process skills learning objectives around the theme, e.g., with river basins, literature could include Mark Twain or other authors' books involving rivers; science could include floods, weather, etc.; social studies, the characteristics of river communities; math, calculating water volume and flow. Designing instruction includes combining subject hours, adjusting class schedules, inviting outside experts, planning field trips, team-teaching, etc. Teachers also encourage and assign student projects, which are naturally compatible with thematic units.

Interdisciplinary Instruction

Interdisciplinary or cross-curricular instruction applies knowledge, principles, and values to multiple school disciplines and subjects concurrently. Disciplines and subjects are often related through central themes—thematic units have been identified as interdisciplinary teaching's organizational structure—or experiences, processes, topics, problems, and issues. Schools first integrated listening, speaking, reading, writing, and thinking as language arts components, thereafter trending to more widely integrating all curriculum subjects through unifying themes. Cross-curricular instruction is often a remedy to recurring educational problems like instruction in isolated skills and fragmentary learning; and a means of supporting goals like giving students more relevant curricula, teaching reasoning and thinking, and facilitating skills transfer to other contexts. It enables students to apply and integrate knowledge across subjects, which isolated skills instruction does not; raises student motivation and engagement when, through participation, students realize the value of the knowledge; and supplies conditions for effective learning. Subject teachers collaborate, for example, a PE and math teacher may combine math skills of counting and graphing with PE skills of throwing, catching, hitting, and kicking balls, including student practice and teacher assessment of both physical and numerical techniques. Elementary classroom teachers may combine multiple subjects in one thematic unit, e.g., using a bean-growing project to teach science via botany, the life cycle, research questions, and observation; mathematics via counting and measuring; and English-writing reports.

Teachers of different subjects collaborate to plan interdisciplinary instructional units, generating topics, and developing instruction and assessment. For example, math and PE teachers have students count the number of times they can hit paddleballs consecutively, practice graphing them, and practice paddleball skills. Teachers might assess counting skills observationally, assess paddleball skills by observing student demonstrations, and assess graphing skills by reviewing handmade or computer graphing assignments. Elementary-grade teachers integrate English, math, and science, connecting classroom plant study to forest field trips, having students write about these connections. Vocational or technical high school students restored a historic landmark, integrating what they learned in math, journalism, and shop classes—applying learning to a real-life experience. Students also transferred learning, using creative, original thinking: after successfully completing the restoration project, they generated ideas for additional school and community service projects integrating various school subjects, presenting their ideas to teachers. A social sciences and math teacher co-taught students using ancient Egyptian computation techniques, comparing them to modern-day math. Students discussed ancient math in historical context, reflecting on past and present and what "modern" meant. Teachers find students gain more complex understandings of disciplines and their relationships through interdisciplinary instruction.

Lesson Plan That Builds on Prior Student Knowledge

One model (Cunningham, ASCD, 2009) contains eight steps. (1) Introduction: state overall lesson reason or purpose. Introduce main idea, topic, and key concepts. "Hook" student attention with a challenge or a quirky or amazing fact, etc. Explain lesson relevance for extending prior knowledge and promoting future learning. (2) Foundation: confirm prior student knowledge, either by clarifying or double-checking. Connect the lesson to standards. Tell students precisely what they will know and be able to do from the lesson. Include additional information, preparing the main lesson. Introduce essential vocabulary visually, aloud, in reading, and in writing. (3) Brain activation: clarify concepts; add information through probing questions, engaging students and building background. Brainstorm concepts, ideas, and possibilities, enabling students to clarify and expand thinking. Plan activities revealing misconceptions; correct or clarify these. (4) Body of new information: present the main lesson via whole-class lecture, teacher-supervised small-group, or partner activity, including teacher input of new and key points, reading, problem-solving, and active student participation with specific goals. (5) Clarification: check for understanding with sample questions, problems, or situations; guide learning; give practice. (6) Practice and review: supervise practice; work with students. (7) Independent practice: supervise, selecting further strategies for small groups needing them; others work independently. (8) Closure: connect lesson steps and information; summarize; discuss lesson in larger learning context; have students write or explain learning, ideas, questions, and problems.

Eight Step Lesson Plan

Introduction – 5 minutes: teacher writes Lincoln's quotation of the Declaration of Independence's "All men are created equal"; students discuss potential 1860s meaning. Foundation - 5-10 minutes: brief discussion about slavery, men and women, educated and uneducated white men; the goal is explaining the significance of the Gettysburg Address to American history and today's voting rights. Key vocabulary words and phrases include *conceived in liberty; dedicated; proposition; equal.* Brain activation – 5 minutes: ask what the words mean, why Lincoln phrased it thus, what would happen today with this speech, what the speech informs us about 1860s America, how the phrase connects to the American history then and now, and how the first paragraph leads to the ideas in the second and third paragraphs. Body of new information - 10-15 minutes: referring to specified textbook pages and illustrations, discuss the Battle of Gettysburg. Teacher writes key ideas or notes on overhead; students add to history notes. Clarification - 5-10 minutes: students write reflections on text. Practice and review - 5-10 minutes: small-group discussions of the battle's and speech's significance, Lincoln's speaking on the battlefield, and its turning point in the Civil War. Independent practice - 10 minutes: students select and write brief summaries of two or three other key phrases from the speech. Closure - 5 minutes: students share phrases with partners, write favorites with short explanations on "exit passes," and the teacher collects these to assess understanding and inform tomorrow's lesson.

Technology Applications Whereby Teachers Can More Efficiently Complete Tasks

Today, mobile applications abound to save teachers time, effort, and space on administrative tasks, freeing more of their attention for teaching and helping students learn. One example is an app for the iPad called Paperless Teacher (Evon Technologies). It automates and customizes processes of taking attendance, planning lessons, creating rubrics, and entering grades in grade books. It weighs each gradable element, e.g., attendance, participation, assignments, tests, and homework, according to teacher specifications, and then automatically calculates grades. It enables teachers to email these results directly to students and parents. This eliminates the repetition of entering names, calculating numbers, and entering them manually one at a time. Users can easily share common data using this app; hence teachers can exchange student profiles or lesson plans anytime, remotely and effortlessly. The app features an integrated Dropbox framework, preventing data loss and enabling users with various other devices to access data. Its Message User Interface enables exporting and emailing data sharing in format allowing other users to open data directly in their apps. This facilitates notifying students of tests, assignments, schedules, etc. Semester planning and grade setting are customizable for multiple semester plans or grading systems. A protection feature keeps data safe for separate users.

Roles That Special Education Teachers Can Contribute to Collaborative Teaching Activities

Special education teachers have great expertise in how to adapt curriculum and instruction and provide classroom modifications and accommodations for students with various disabilities who receive special education and related services. They can share knowledge with classroom teachers about instructional considerations for each category of disability, individual special education students, and their needs. Since the Individuals with Disabilities Education Act (IDEA) legislation first mandated education in the least restrictive environment possible for students with disabilities, inclusive education has increased and mainstreaming is more prevalent today. This presents challenges to regular classroom teachers, and advantages to collaborating with special education teachers, who can help integrate Individualized Education Program (IEP) goals into daily classroom instruction. In addition to knowing more techniques and strategies for teaching students with special needs, they also are likely familiar with individual special education students at their school to inform classroom teachers from experience about particularly effective and ineffective specific techniques. They can show new teachers how task analysis, chaining, and shaping enable intellectually disabled students to learn complex behaviors; advise newly mainstreaming teachers on practical matters like classroom logistics with wheelchairs and assistive devices, teaching other students device and disability etiquette; and help teachers coordinate varied adaptations, modifications, or accommodations to prevent their interference with each other.

Collaboration Between Library Media Specialists and Classroom Teachers

Library media specialists are experts at locating information and resources, among other things. As information specialists, they contribute skills for accessing and evaluating information resources in different formats for both students and teachers. They function as models for students, showing them strategies for finding, accessing, and evaluating information that is available in their school library media centers and outside them. Due to the impact of technology development on library media center environments, library media specialists also keep up with mastering the newest, continually evolving electronic resources, and pay ongoing attention to the quality, character, and ethical use of information in traditional and electronic formats. They are instructional partners collaborating with teachers, other educators, and administrators. They identify connections among school expectations for student learning, student achievement, school curriculum content, student information needs, and available information resources. They work closely and cooperatively with teachers in designing authentic learning activities and assessments. Collaborating with teachers, they help integrate information and communication skills to meet content standards. They have knowledge of current research literature in teaching and learning, and expertise for its application. They help students find information from multiple sources, evaluate it critically, and use it to support learning, problem-solving, and critical thinking.

Gifted and Talented Teachers

Teachers of the gifted and talented have specialized training in instructing this population. Considering mainstreaming requirements, increasing demographic diversity, school underfunding, staff shortages, and oversized classes, classroom teachers are challenged to meet all student needs in one class. They may have to spend large portions of time on differentiated instruction to students with disabilities, in addition to satisfying whole-class accountability requirements to cover enough required curriculum content and enable every student to perform to standards on high-stakes, large-scale tests to meet Adequate Yearly Progress (AYP). Some teachers having limited or no experience with gifted students may assume they can work more independently and need less teacher attention due to their high IQs and/or special talents. However, advanced students are frequently bored or impatient with the pace of instruction for average student abilities. They can demand more material to learn, at faster rates; more in-depth, extended, or enriched content; answers to their pressing questions; and advice, guidance, and feedback even as they work independently on projects. Teachers specializing in giftedness and creativity can help take some pressure off classroom teachers, by both working directly with these students, and giving teachers ideas for enrichment activities and coordinating these with classroom units and lessons.

Collaboration Between Paraprofessionals and Classroom Teachers

Teachers today not only must differentiate instruction for individual students with a diverse range of needs, they frequently must also do this with excessive class sizes. Teachers' aides and other paraprofessionals provide vital help with these demands. Their collaboration with teachers includes not only concrete assistance like taking attendance; physically setting up activities; helping with adaptive devices, distributing materials, snacks, etc.; but also scoring tests, grading papers;

- 74 -

participating in training they receive from teachers, specialists, therapists, etc.; and then working one-on-one with individual students to deliver differentiated instruction and help students needing individual supervision for classroom tasks. They may be trained by school psychologists to observe students and collect behavioral data, relieving teachers of these additional duties. In mainstreamed classes, teachers cannot always work with all individual students enough. Paraprofessionals are invaluable in making it possible for more students to receive more individualized attention, supervision, and instruction more regularly, for longer time periods, and more often. They can enable more students to achieve their individual educational goals.

Individualized Education Program (IEP) Team Members

Student IEP team members can include any or all the following and more: parents; special education teachers; classroom teachers; audiologists; occupational, physical, speech-language, activity, and/or other therapists; American Sign Language (ASL) interpreters; orientation and mobility specialists; school social workers; school nurses; school psychologists; counselors; advocates, etc. Parents collaborate with teachers, sharing their experience with their children, children's histories, personal preferences, effective behavioral and learning techniques; and may volunteer to help in the classroom and/or at school functions. By advocating, they help teachers meet children's special needs. Special education teachers help address IEP goals by incorporating related instruction and activities into daily classroom lessons and routines; and offer expertise in differentiated instruction, teaching, and behavior management strategies. Audiologists contribute knowledge of hearing loss, hearing aids, classroom accommodations, and modifications. Therapists add expertise in their respective disciplines—physical therapists (PTs) make or adapt devices, provide targeted postural and large-muscle exercises; occupational therapists (OTs), fine-motor, ADL development; speech language pathologists (SLPs) incorporate language development into instruction; ASL interpreters translate between hearing and deaf or hearing-impaired students and families; orientation and mobility (O&M) specialists help blind and visually impaired students navigate classrooms, schools, and communities. Social workers provide student and family histories, coordinate special services, and help families locate and access resources. School nurses help with medications, monitoring diabetic diets and blood checks; school seizures, accidents, and emergencies, etc. Psychologists administer, score, and interpret IQ tests; provide behavior management plans and training; data collection and analysis, etc.

Resources Whereby Teachers and Schools Can Provide Enrichment for Students

The Stanford Mobile Inquiry Learning Environment (SMILE) uses technology innovatively for educational enrichment. This interactive learning model includes mobile software for learning management, plus its own server, which can run on a battery and functions as a Wi-Fi connection, router, and storage device. At schools adopting SMILE, students can exchange questions and ideas with other students worldwide; and teachers can instantaneously collect summaries of learning data analytics. Another American enrichment resource is Students for the Advancement of Global Entrepreneurship (SAGE), a program emphasizing civic responsibility and duty for high school students, who form teams and develop social enterprise businesses (SEBs) or socially responsible businesses (SRBs), which compete in the annual SAGE World Cup. An American remediation resource is Teach for All, a model teaching lifetime educational advocacy and leadership foundations at both local and policy levels, training and developing effective leaders to change education for the most disadvantaged students; and promoting innovation by encouraging best practice sharing. PenPal Schools teach six-week courses about world issues, giving students global partners to share multicultural understandings. Its Pay-What-You-Want policy enables low-income student participation. Many other resources are available in other countries or are shared among the US and other nations.

Vertical Alignment and Horizontal Alignment

Vertical alignment is the process through which courses are sequenced across a curriculum. What a student learns in a 4th grade math course will prepare him or her for what he or she will learn in a vertically aligned 5th grade math course. Horizontal alignment is the process through which different sections of the same course are standardized such that what one student learns in a section of Biology with Ms. Smith is similar (though not exactly the same) as the material learned by a student in a section of Biology with Mr. Johnson. Typically horizontal alignment is addressed locally, perhaps through professional learning communities in coordination with district guidelines for course content. Vertical alignment is often developed on a state or even national level. School districts develop their course outlines in coordination with standards adopted from either the state or national level. Educators at the state level decide the general scope of the schools' curricula and choose yearly statewide assessments for students. Educators at the district level adapt the state course guidelines to fit local communities and teachers implement those curricula in their classrooms. The success of the entire system is dependent on educators at all levels working collaboratively in the best interests of the students.

Cognitive Theory

In cognitive theories, e.g., Piaget's theory of cognitive development, the individual seeks to establish and maintain <u>equilibrium</u> or balance to keep things the same, i.e., homeostasis. When unexpected events occur and/or the individual encounters novel environmental stimuli, these disrupt equilibrium. To restore balance, the individual must adapt. The process of <u>adaptation</u> consists of <u>assimilation</u> and <u>accommodation</u>. In learning to understand the world, Piaget said children form <u>schemata</u>. A scheme is a mental construct about some aspect of the environment—people, things, events, and/or categories of these. A baby might form schemata for "things I can suck on," "things I can shake that make noise," and "people I know," for example. When a child encounters a new stimulus, s/he either assimilates it—fitting it into his/her existing schema for similar things; or accommodates to it—modifying an existing schema to accommodate some different characteristics of the new stimulus; or forming a new schema for it. Thus the process of learning, especially for children, involves frequently forming new schemata and changing existing schemata by adding to, subtracting from, or modifying the characteristics they include as experience and interaction with the environment progress.

Cognitive Information Processing Theory

As computers were developed to function analogously to the human brain in many aspects of receiving, encoding, storing, and retrieving information, so in turn computers were used as concrete models for information processing theory to describe how humans execute and sequence cognitive activities. Information processing theories characterize how people attend to environmental events, encode new information and relate it to existing knowledge, store new information in memory, and retrieve information as needed from storage. According to the computer metaphor, people receive sensory input in the sensory register or sensory memory; attend to it through the process of attention; "chunk" and rehearse it temporarily via working memory in short-term memory; encode it for transferring to long-term memory, where it may be stored indefinitely; and then retrieve it as needed, transferring selected data via working memory from long-term to short-term memory. Encoding includes grouping data into categories, outlining, establishing hierarchies, and developing concept trees as organizational mechanisms. It also uses imagery and mnemonics. Retrieval includes recalling information from memory independently, and recognizing provided information matching remembered information. Cognitive mapping (Tolman,

1948) mentally represents the literal physical and metaphorical environment according to relative importance of features for the individual, enhancing navigation, learning, and recall.

Social Learning Theory

According to Albert Bandura, who originated social learning theory, students need not experience everything directly and personally to learn. Bandura found that children could observe other children engaging in certain behaviors and receiving desirable rewards (reinforcers) for doing so; they would then imitate the other children's behaviors in the hope of receiving similar rewards. Children not only imitate the actions of peers, but also the actions of adults, as all parents have observed. Bandura referred to these examples of behaviors provided by adults as modeling. He thus extended the behaviorist concept that an individual will emit a behavior to get a reward; once it is rewarded, the individual will repeat the behavior to obtain repeated rewards, by showing that because learners also emit behaviors they have observed others emitting, they can learn to produce behaviors based on their observation of others being rewarded for those behaviors. Bandura refers to this process as observational learning or vicarious learning.

Reciprocal Determinism

Albert Bandura concurred with many concepts found in behaviorist learning theory, e.g., that individuals emit responses to environmental stimuli; that desirable consequences immediately following a behavior reinforce or strengthen the probability that an individual will repeat the behavior; and the deterministic nature of behaviorism in its attribution of behaviors to environmental causes. However, whereas behaviorism is sometimes called "learning theory," Bandura calls his theory "*social* learning theory." This name emphasizes a key difference in his theory: his orientation to the social contexts wherein learning occurs. Unlike behaviorists, Bandura finds social interactions vital to learning. This relates to Bandura's concept of reciprocal determinism. By this he means learning is a process involving the individual, the environment, and the behavior. The environment includes other people as well as physical surroundings and stimuli. The individual includes personality; cognitive factors; past experiences with reinforced behaviors; and psychological processes like beliefs, thoughts, expectations, etc. The environment and behavior mutually influence one another. Individual, personal characteristics and social factors reciprocally influence and are influenced by individual behaviors. Bandura identified the conditions of attention (observation), retention (remembering), reproduction (imitating or copying), and motivation (a good reason—past, promised, and/or vicarious rewards) for an individual to learn from a model's behavior.

Constructivism

Constructivist philosophy and psychology view learning as a process whereby the learner actively constructs or builds his/her own knowledge and understanding of the world. Cognitive developmental theorist Jean Piaget was a constructivist. He proposed that children learned by interacting with and acting upon their environments. He likened them to "little scientists" who gathered information about the world, experimented with aspects of the environment by interacting with it, and drew progressively more informed conclusions about the world from observing their results. On the basis of this approach, children need experiences interacting with the environment to learn. Consistently with Piaget's characterization of young learners as scientists, problem-based learning is important to constructivist approaches: like scientists who conduct experiments to answer questions and solve problems, children develop higher cognitive capacities and learn more when they experiment with the environment and learn better trying to solve problems than only for obtaining external rewards or avoiding external punishments. Inquiry and discovery learning involves such active student questioning and inquiry and discovering answers or solutions. Vygotsky's zone of proximal development is the area between where a learner can accomplish something independently vs. with assistance, guidance, or encouragement, illustrating how more knowledgeable others (MKOs) enhance learning. Scaffolding is temporary needed support, gradually withdrawn as learners gain proficiency.

Classical and Operant Conditioning

Pavlov discovered and described classical conditioning when he found he could condition dogs to respond reflexively to a secondary, previously unrelated stimulus by repeatedly pairing it with the stimulus originally producing the reflex. Ringing a bell every time he gave them meat powder, causing them to salivate, eventually enabled the bell alone to stimulate salivation without the meat. Skinner later described what he named operant conditioning. Based on Thorndike's law of effect that a desirable consequence increased the probability of repeating a behavior while an undesirable one decreased that probability, Skinner found through experiments that new behaviors could be established, existing behaviors made much more frequent, and other behaviors made less frequent or extinguished through controlling the antecedents (events or stimuli immediately before) and consequences (events or stimuli immediately after) each behavior. The key difference between classical and operant conditioning is that classical conditioning manipulates reflexive or involuntary behaviors, whereas operant conditioning manipulates conscious or voluntary behaviors. Both contribute to the behaviorist proposition that behaviors can be established, increased, decreased, eliminated, connected, and shaped through manipulating related environmental stimuli. Skinner called classical conditioning "respondent" to differentiate it from operant conditioning, which involves choice.

Internal and External Rewards

According to behaviorist theories of learning, rewarding specific behaviors reinforces or strengthens the probability of their repetition. Rewards can be internal or external. Internal or intrinsic rewards originate within the individual, e.g., feeling gratification at learning or knowing something for the sake of additional knowledge, feeling self-efficacy for being able perform a given task successfully, feeling general competence or self-esteem for acquiring more knowledge or skills, engaging in behaviors congruent with one's self-image, etc. Both traditional and radical behaviorism ignored internal states as not outwardly observable or measurable, but many related theories, e.g., social learning theory, cognitive-behavioral theory, etc. incorporate sources of motivation and loci of control. External or extrinsic rewards are provided by other people or the environment. Research finds internal rewards more powerful for increasing and especially maintaining behaviors than external rewards. Behaviorism defines reinforcement as any consequence strengthening the probability of repeating a behavior. This can be positive reinforcement, i.e., introducing something desirable; or negative reinforcement, i.e. removing something undesirable. Positive punishment, conversely, is introducing something undesirable or aversive consequently to a behavior, making that behavior less likely to recur. Negative punishment is removing something desirable or removing a reinforcer, also decreasing the probability of behavior repetition.

Howard Gardner's Theory of Multiple Intelligences

Gardner outlines eight distinct intelligences that people use in problem solving: namely, linguistic, musical, logical-mathematical, spatial, bodily-kinesthetic, naturalistic, interpersonal and intrapersonal, with a possible ninth: existential. Schools traditionally emphasize linguistic and logical-mathematical. Gardner placed emphasis upon learning skills in context, such as reinforces the crying behavior—not the fall, because the child associates the consequence immediately following with the most recent preceding event. The reinforcement of attention increases the probability the child will cry again next time s/he falls, whether it hurts or not, to reduplicate the attention. This is an example of what Skinner termed operant conditioning. In a related example illustrating Bandura's social learning theory, we have all witnessed a child falling, not feeling significant pain, and looking around at adults to gauge whether to cry or not. Bandura found children can learn by observing others' actions and their consequences (rewards and punishments), and can imitate others' behaviors that they observe.

The behaviorist approach to learning theory is justified in limiting its principles and practices to observable, measurable behaviors in that change cannot be proven nor accurately quantified unless existing behaviors can first be observed and measured to establish baseline rates; and subsequent behaviors following intervention can be measured again for comparison to assess changes from baselines. However, a primary limitation of this approach is that it fails to account for or explain maturational, hormonal, and other changes occurring throughout the human lifespan. For example, puberty, the major experience during adolescence, typically has many outward physical, social, and behavioral manifestations as well as many inward physical, cognitive, and emotional changes. These changes are primarily driven by hormones (though of course societal roles and expectations interact). This internal biological mechanism is not addressed by theories that behaviors are responses to external environmental stimuli. Hence human development has impact on learning theory: finding this theory incomplete, development demands explanation informed by additional biological, psychological, and sociological knowledge about how hormonal maturation, emotions, thinking, and social interactions are interrelated and interdependent, and how they ultimately combine to affect human behavior.

Student Transitions from Elementary to Middle School

Middle school students contend not only with pubertal changes in their bodies and feelings, but also changes from elementary to middle school, e.g., differences in location, learning environments, scheduling, activities, classmates, etc. While early teens become preoccupied and anxious about their appearances, behaviors, and peers' perceptions, they also become more independent, expressing more of their own personalities and interests and making more autonomous choices in friends, school, studying, sports, appearance, etc. Adults must realize this independence prompts greater privacy needs, as well as withdrawing from parents, seeking friends and other adults as role models, identifying their own peer groups, finding groups and friends more important, and experiencing peer pressure. Students' emotional and social development changes their self-perceptions, and educators should adjust instruction accordingly. The adolescent's "imaginary audience" causes self-centered hypersensitivity to others' perceptions; the "personal fable" is the belief their experiences and feelings are unique, and that nobody understands (Elkind). Educators should avoid overreactive discipline interfering with student self-regulation, overwhelming teens; establish safe classroom environments, discussing issues and emotions. Teachers can issue each student a (counterfeit-detecting designed) "leave me alone" pass—not applicable on test or quiz days—to excuse active participation or interaction during class on some days, promoting student empowerment, control, and stress management.

Student Growth Model

A number of states use student growth models to track student progress. These models are statistical methods to gauge student progress on standardized tests, typically from the end of one school year to the end of the next school year. Statistical models allow students to be evaluated more appropriately, based on a dynamic growth measure instead of a static placement measure. A number of background factors (e.g., ELL status, learning differences, or student exceptionalities) may have contributed to low-achieving scores. Growth models incentivize BOTH progress toward proficiency in underachieving students and continued improvement in proficient students. Teachers and schools can be graded based, in part, upon success in facilitating student improvement and are not penalized for having students who begin an assessment cycle with low-achieving scores.

Response to Intervention (RtI) Model

The RtI model is a framework for providing high-quality instruction for all K-12 learners. RtI's three tiers are: 1) research-based **core** classroom instruction, 2) **targeted** instruction for students in need of additional challenge or support, and 3) **intensive** instruction for students whose needs are not accommodated by the first two tiers. The needs of all learners are addressed through the RtI framework with research-based instructional practices, curriculum adaptations responsive to students' individual backgrounds, and appropriate interventions including the extension of the standard curriculum toward greater rigor. The RtI model is data driven. Analysis of student data guides instructional decisions. RtI instructional decisions are made via collaborations of teachers and administrators. No one individual teacher or administrator is capable of implementing RtI. The best interests of the students are served by teachers and administrators teaming to interpret data and decide whether students are in need of additional tiers of (targeted or intensive) instruction.

Universal Design for Learning (UDL)

The Universal Design for Learning is a curriculum implementation/development framework for guiding educational practice that specifically addresses the "what," "how," and "why" of learning. The framework moves away from the "one-size-fits-all" nature of traditional curricula that teaches to the "average" student while overlooking exceptional students. The three principles of UDL are: 1) provide multiple means of representation ("what"), 2) provide multiple means of action and expression ("how"), and 3) provide multiple means of engagement ("why"). UDL embraces learner variability through flexibility in its methods and goals. Learners do not have to start from some predefined point. Rather, teachers are able to differentiate their curriculum implementations, maximize learning opportunities for each student, and empower all students to aim for the most appropriate levels of success.

Ways in Which Individual Student Differences Influence Classroom Communication

Younger students need concrete terms, examples, and materials; older students can handle increasing abstraction. Teachers should give students of all ages concepts and vocabulary slightly above their current levels for challenge and growth. Both student and teacher communication can be influenced by gender, e.g., volunteering, calling out, or waiting to be called on regardless of knowledge and preparation. Teachers may perceive or treat identical student responses differently according to student gender and/or race, e.g., as assertive vs. aggressive or enthusiastic vs. disruptive. ELL and LEP students may know content, but lack English to express it, or feel uncomfortable with their ELP levels. Numerous studies show when teachers communicate high learning expectations for all students, including ELLs and students with disabilities, they perform better. Emotionally engaging anecdotes, examples, and connecting topics to student prior knowledge, experience, interests, value, and utility stimulate student curiosity and interest. To clarify class goals and purposes, focus on major points, letting students find additional information in other activities. Repeat key concepts and ideas, compare and contrast, summarize, use analogies and metaphors to aid student comprehension and emphasize importance. Structure classes logically: present problems, then develop solutions; frame topics as stories; chronologically recount processes and events; show interconnected ideas' relationship to overarching themes; share outlines; explicitly transition between topics using mini-summaries, connections, or verbal signals.

Ensuring Engagement and Understanding of All Students

Verbally, vary vocal speeds and tones to keep speech interesting to students. Vocal projection facilitates student hearing and also demonstrates teachers' confidence in what they say. Pausing strategically gets student attention, emphasizes transitions in topics, and gives students time to process information. Give ELLs and students with hearing, cognitive, learning, and other disabilities more wait time to allow for translating and processing teacher questions and formulating and translating their answers. Nonverbally, stand up straight and maintain eye contact to project confidence. Smiling communicates valuing what you say. While avoiding distracting apparel and excessive gestures, use movement to express enthusiasm, excitement, and energy. To help explain, illustrate, or clarify complex ideas, use media—not to distract from but to enhance instructional communication. Use chalkboards, dry-erase boards and overheads to demonstrate reasoning behind derivations, illustrate processes, and teach dynamically. Use slide presentations to organize varied visual, audio, and animated content, summarize ideas, and emphasize key points. Animations and videos offer sense of scale and illustrate dynamic processes. Audio can illustrate sounds associated with physical processes and introduce new, historical, or remote voices into classrooms. Artifacts can incorporate real-life elements, and print or electronic handouts give students detailed images and information. Redundant and multimodal presentations benefit ELL, exceptional, and all students.

Classroom Question Types to Access Different Levels of Bloom's Taxonomy

Levels, question types: knowledge and comprehension: what are the main points? What happened when...? Why did...? Application: can you think of other words meaning the same thing? Can you use this word in a different context? Can you think of another example of this? Does the same idea apply to...? Analysis: what effect does this achieve? Why do you think the author chose to do this? Does this fit into a pattern? What is suggested by...? How...? Why do you agree or disagree with this? Evaluation: which of these are most effective? What do you think of this? Do you think this works well? What are the strongest and weakest aspects of this? Synthesis: can you create your own version of this? How can you change the audience, features, etc. of this text? Where else can you see examples of this? Student activities, levels: analysis: debate a topic. Create text-based questions. Draw concept maps exploring connections. Mind-map aspects of a topic or text. Synthesis: study pastiche and parody. Analyze authors and writing styles closely; adopt styles. Experiment with genres, audiences, and text type features. Evaluation: devise reader expectation criteria for various text types. Apply assessment criteria to own and others' work.

Active Listening Strategies

Effective, active listening strategies accomplish multiple goals: teachers show students they care about them, demonstrate attention to their concerns, make them feel understood, establish and develop student-teacher relationships, give students emotional connections with school, model effective listening strategies for students to learn and use, and motivate student learning. Research shows student learning motivation requires feeling connected. In active listening, the listener uses verbal and nonverbal signals, asks questions to clarify, and restates main points for the speaker to confirm or correct. Restating in one's own words can also involve interpreting the speaker's message. For example, a student says, "I don't like this school as much as my other school. People aren't nice." The teacher responds, "You're unhappy here?" The student answers, "Yes. I haven't made any friends. Nobody includes me in anything." The teacher responds, "You feel left out here?"

The student confirms, "Yes, I wish I knew more people." Questions, restating, and interpreting clarify factual and emotional message content. When speakers refine listener interpretations, they feel heard, gain insights into their own feelings, and may experience catharsis. Listeners enhance their skills in focusing on speakers and considering implied meanings.

Nonverbal Communication

Open postures communicate receptivity; crossed arms and legs or similar averted body positions communicate the opposite. Ways of walking, sitting, standing, holding one's head, and subtle movements all convey attitudes and feelings. Gestures supplement speech, often unconsciously. Because different cultures assign different meanings to the same gestures, awareness is important to prevent misunderstanding or misinterpretation. Vocal tones and inflections express confidence, affection, anger, and sarcasm; and can even indicate understanding, agreement, and many more. Listeners also attend to speaker loudness, speed, and timing. Eye contact demonstrates interest in our culture; in some other cultures, it is perceived as confrontational and avoiding it shows respect. We communicate affection, attraction, or hostility as well as interest through eye contact; gauge others' responses; and maintain conversational flow. Facial expressions universally show happiness, sadness, anger, fear, surprise, disgust, and other emotions. Personal and social physical space or distance vary by individual, relationship, situation, and culture and can communicate intimacy, dominance, or aggression. Nonverbal communication informs verbal communication by repeating verbal messages; contradicting them; substituting for them; complementing or adding to them, e.g., patting on the back while verbally praising; accenting them; or emphasizing them, e.g., pounding the table, desk, lectern, dais, or pulpit with spoken points.

Problem-Solving Learning Tasks and Learning Project Activities

Technology is an enormous asset to both teachers and students. For example, word processing programs, e.g., Microsoft Word, streamline teachers' work creating instructional documents like learning units, lesson plans, student handouts, worksheets, rubrics, checklists, progress reports, written parent communications, etc. Students can write essays, research reports, papers, short stories, plays, poetry, books, etc. They can type and save preliminary notes and outlines, then easily copy and paste portions into compositions. Students benefit from being able to delete and restore text paragraphs and sections instantly, and easily move paragraphs and sections to other locations as they learn how to organize their writing. Spell-checkers and grammar-checkers, while not substitutes for student knowledge, alert students to typing and mechanical errors for correction. Microsoft Excel and similar spreadsheet programs facilitate organizing numerical data and verbal information. Students can type in figures or lists with little or no editing and Excel displays and prints them in spreadsheet format. Databases give teachers and students large amounts of easily accessible information about specified topics, enabling them to search and sort it. Graphic tools enable students and teachers lacking artistic ability to create colorful, effective, professional-looking visual images to illustrate, organize, and understand information and concepts. Students and teachers can establish, use, and contribute to online communities to communicate and share information remotely, often instantaneously.

Communicating and Publishing Information with Various Technology Tools

Teachers and students alike can use available technology productivity tools to organize, share, and present information in different formats. For example, in preparing a lesson plan, a teacher might create a PowerPoint slide presentation to project while delivering a lesson. By entering summary statements of main ideas, important concepts, major facts, etc. on each slide, teachers call student attention to the most significant aspects of the lesson, reinforcing these even as they provide additional information and details through lectures, discussions, textbooks, etc. Not only are slide presentations good for identifying main points, they also reinforce information presented in other ways (speech, textbooks, handouts), providing the redundancy students need to learn and retain it. In addition to PowerPoints, slide shows are good ways to illustrate lectures, lessons, and student presentations with visual imagery that engages viewers. Teachers can make videos of class for objective feedback and analysis; students can produce videos for class projects. Teachers can create multimedia presentations to access different student learning styles, helping all students benefit from instruction. Teachers can write parent newsletters, and students can create and publish classroom or school newsletters. Students, parents, and school personnel can view documents via websites and programs on monitor screens and/or print copies.

Assessing Learning That Students Demonstrate Through Technological Activities and Projects

Teachers newly integrating technology into student work often wonder how to grade it. Evaluating student processes and actions is the same as with traditional written work, though it differs with the divergent potentials and unique features of each medium. For example, a notebook contains handwritten notes and drawings; a blog can contain hypertext, interactive imagery, embedded video, etc. Teachers must distinguish a technology tool's capabilities from the performance of the student using it. For example, iMovie has built-in, user-friendly professional effects enabling anybody to produce visually impressive video presentations. Hence teachers cannot grade the end product but the process, i.e., the student's research, writing, image selection, and other activities. In this sense, assessment must be more formative than summative to avoid focusing only on flashy end products and observe learning activities throughout the project. Teachers can create assessment rubrics using online generators like Rubistar, Digital Media Scoring Guides, Matrix Rubric with Points, PBL Checklists, Scholastic Rubric Maker, and Common Core Rubric Creator; or use available rubrics designed for general assessment; student blogs, wikis, websites, digital portfolios, social media, effective technology use, videos, digital storytelling, podcasts, graphic organizers, programming, coding, and gaming.

Providing Unique Growth Opportunity for Modern Students

Many technologies (e.g., calculators and iPads) are student-centered. They were developed to provide a one-on-one interactive experience with some form of learning. Research has shown that learning technologies act as cognitive amplifiers. Students can learn more efficiently and effectively with technology. Technology, however, is not a silver bullet. Simple access to technology will not empower students to learn better. Teachers will require training to learn how to properly implement classroom technology (in coordination with pedagogy) and students will have to learn to appropriately and responsibly use technology. In coordination with technology and new pedagogical innovations (e.g., flipped classrooms, collaborative problem solving, or inquiry-based learning), teachers are able to provide their students with engagement opportunities previously unavailable. Students who have access to technology are able to directly engage with concepts and contexts any time of day or night. No longer are teachers the sole facilitators of quality learning. With traditional pedagogies (e.g., lecture), technology may be more distracting and less helpful. Technology is not best utilized as a replacement for old modes of knowledge transfer (e.g., note-taking or board presentation). A professional educator can adapt to both the new devices and new modes of thinking that empower student learning at trajectories not previously attainable.

Incorporating Social Media in the Classroom

Social media is virtually ubiquitous in 21st century America. Our students are immersed in a society dominated by social media and this offers teachers an opportunity to model asynchronous (i.e., outside the time and vicinity constraints of standard class periods) learning processes that help students become lifelong learners. Examples of positive classroom social media outlets include *YouTube* where students can view or develop podcasts directly applicable to classroom topics. Teachers can use *Twitter* to post updates about assignments or deadlines. Teachers and students can blog about classroom experiences and practice academic writing skills. Students can receive more immediate feedback on academic pursuits with *Facebook*. Through all of these social media interactions, teachers can monitor students and model appropriate etiquette for online interactions as they help students become responsible and respectful citizens in a digital world.

Although there are a number of great benefits of social media in the classroom learning environment, these benefits do not come without the possibility of distractions. Students may try to tweet or snapchat with friends during class time. Teachers can always use less common social media tools to provide an opportunity for technologically empowered student engagement without the distraction associated with the most popular social networking platforms. For example, *Edmodo* enables educators to communicate with students, share materials, and distribute assessments in an efficient and non-distracting manner. Teachers and students can share work and gain efficient feedback through shared *Google Docs* that allow limitations on who contributes to social interactions. *Edublogs* allow teachers to share materials, encourage student contributions, incorporate videos, and facilitate online discussions.

Acceptable Use Policies

Like many businesses, most schools have acceptable use policies (AUPs) in place to stipulate the practices and constraints that users must agree to when accessing the Internet or local network. Many schools require students and staff to sign their AUP document before providing them with a network ID to gain access. AUPs are also required by Internet service providers (ISPs) of users when they sign up for the company's Internet access services. Users who sign AUPs agree to comply with such rules as not using the service to contribute to violating any law, not trying to violate any user's or network's security, not posting commercial messages to Usenet groups (sets of collected messages or notes on various topics submitted by users and posted to servers on a global network) unless they have obtained permission in advance, not trying to send spam or junk emails to anybody not wanting to receive it, and not trying to "mail-bomb" websites by flooding their servers with mass numbers of emails.

Electronic Information

To locate information on digital networks, many search engines exist, e.g., Google, Bing, Yahoo, Lycos, Excite, AltaVista, McAfee Secure Search (from the anti-virus program publisher), Trovi, and DuckDuckGo (a "trackless" search engine keeping search history and information private); and search engines offered by websites known as online marketplaces, social media, or information sources like eBay, Amazon, Twitter, Wikipedia, etc. These user-friendly sites create huge databases indexing millions of websites, locating sites relevant to the search terms (words or phrases) that users enter. Software applications enable accessing and manipulating information from remote devices. Similarly to how technical support agents access user devices remotely to resolve technical issues, users with applicable permissions and software can access information remotely. Both software programs and websites commonly include help features: the user clicks a *help* button loading a window, webpage, or website with information like step-by-step instructions, FAQs, and

- 86 -

answers; indexes to look up specific Help topics; interactive tools; and chat windows. To evaluate e-information, first appraise author credentials, publication date, revision and edition, publisher, and journal title. Then critically analyze content, including intended audience, objective reasoning, coverage, writing style, and consult evaluative reviews.

Evaluating Electronic Information Critically

Initial appraisal: what are the author's education, degree(s), experience, publications, and institutional affiliation? Is the institution reputable? Is the source about a topic in the author's expertise area? Look in the source's biographical information and/or *Who's Who* publications. Is the author cited frequently in multiple bibliographies or other sources? What is the publication date? Is the information current? Is the publication a first edition or a revision? Are revision dates given? Who is the publisher? University presses are typically scholarly and reputable. Is a journal scholarly or popular? These differ in complexity levels. Content analysis: read the preface, foreword, or abstract to discern author intent. For a broad overview of covered material, scan tables of contents, indexes, and bibliographies. Read chapters specifically addressing your topic. Is the intended audience general or specialized? Is the source too advanced, technical, or elementary? Or is it suitable for your needs? Is the information fact, opinion, or propaganda? Good writers can convince readers their interpretations are facts. Is information valid and well-researched, or questionable and unsupported? Are assumptions reasonable? Are ideas or arguments fairly consistent with other works on the topic? Is author viewpoint impartial, objective, and unbiased? Does it substantiate, update, or supplement other sources? Are sources primary or secondary? Is the style logical, organized, clear, and readable? Read critical reviews of the publication in online reviewing sources.

Equity Issues Arising from Differences in Technology Access and Use

Although most schools have Internet access and some policies targeting minority, low-income and rural schools have succeeded, recent research still observes "digital divides" between poor and rich countries; differences in access among ethnic groups; unequal distribution of technology across regions and schools by socioeconomic status, minority enrollments, rural and urban vs. suburban schools; more access to computers in schools and homes for boys than girls; and slower Internet connections and unreliable, outdated hardware in poorer schools. Schools often poorly integrate and underuse available technology in classrooms. Even though technology can help students with disabilities access educational content, girls, disabled, rural, urban, poor, and minority students do not receive educational technology's full potential. Most homes have computers, but they are middle-class; in other families, lack of home access exacerbates gaps in school access when students with home access have more technology experience and confidence, dominate school technology, and reap more educational achievement and advancement. Parental support, modeling, and influence are also affected by socioeconomic status, lack of home access, and lack of parental digital knowledge. Girls use Internet and computer technology more confidently and often at home than in school. Even with apparently equal access, boys dominate home equipment, free access, and school computer clubs.

Motivation Theory

Self-determination: student propensity for initiating activities independently, as opposed to only doing what teachers tell them to do. Achievement motivation research finds student motivation to learn and perform is stronger based on internalized motives, e.g., interest in subject matter, self-efficacy, desire to know things, desire to succeed, career ambitions, etc. By comparison, externalized motives, e.g., to gain rewards from teachers, schools, or parents; to avoid punishment; to impress teachers, classmates, friends, parents, etc. are not as effective. Attribution: how and where we assign cause. Students with more internal locus of control attribute their success or failure to personal abilities and actions; students with more external locus of control attribute successes or failures to people, actions, events, or situations outside themselves. Cognitive dissonance: discomfort with contradictory information; we adjust our schemas (mental representations) to reflect new information, form new schemas, or reject the information to restore congruence and resolve the discomfort. Classical conditioning: associating an unrelated stimulus with one that elicits a certain reflexive reaction can condition it to evoke the same reaction. Pavlov repeatedly paired bell-ringing with meat powder to make a dog salivate; eventually bell-ringing alone evoked salivation. Operant conditioning: manipulating antecedents and consequences shapes behavior; positive reinforcement strengthens probability of repeating behavior; punishment weakens it. Negative reinforcement removes a reinforcer or reward, decreasing behavior repetition.

Promoting Student Motivation

Teachers delivering instruction with enthusiasm and energy are role models: demonstrating their motivation and passion motivates students. Teachers showing why they are interested in subject content personalize it for students. Getting to know students, belief in student ability, strong interest in their learning, and personal interest in student backgrounds and concerns inspire personal student loyalty. Many students want to know the application, utility, or real-life relevance of content before further engagement. To do this, use many examples and explain how it prepares them for future opportunities. Design activities directly engaging students in material, offering mastery opportunities: discovery learning requiring reasoning through problems to discover underlying principles independently satisfies students. Positive social pressure makes cooperative learning activities effective. Design assignments with challenges appropriate to student abilities and experiences. Set realistic performance goals; help students set and achieve reasonable goals. Tests and grades should show mastery, not shortcomings. Allow all students opportunities to achieve the highest grades and standards; avoid grading on curves. Make criticism constructive, feedback nonjudgmental. Criticize specific performances, not performers. Seek means of stimulating advancement; emphasize improvement opportunities. Avoid classifying students as leaders or followers. Give students as much choice and control over their learning, assessment, and performance as possible.

Intrinsic Motivation

Students intrinsically motivated to learn are attracted to and fascinated by subjects, recognize their relevance to real life, feel a sense of accomplishment from mastering them, and feel called to them. Their reasons for learning are typically because the content interests them, they find it improves their thinking skills, and/or they find school success rewarding. Advantages include that intrinsic motivation sustains itself and has more longevity than external rewards; teacher efforts to build internal motivation typically involve efforts to further student learning as well, typically focusing not on rewards or punishments but on subject matter. Disadvantages include more specialized preparation, taking longer to produce behavior change, and requiring teachers utilize a variety of approaches in different students. Getting to know individual students and what interests them, connecting student interests to subject content, and strong teacher interest in subject content (and demonstration thereof) support developing intrinsic motivation in students.

According to one model, students offered opportunities to engage in learning activities first decide whether an activity is interesting to them or not. They engage in activities that interest them. If not immediately finding interest in an activity, they then evaluate it according to two criteria: whether or to what extent it is stimulating, i.e., it attracts their curiosity, affords a challenge, and/or appeals to their sense of fantasy; and whether or to what degree it affords them personal control—i.e., it is not too difficult for them to accomplish, and allows them some measure of free choice in the specific topics, learning styles, methods, procedures, materials, and forms of assessment they can use to acquire knowledge and demonstrate understanding. If students perceive an activity as both stimulating and controllable, they consider it potentially interesting or valuable and engage in it. If either or both conditions become inadequate, students disengage unless influenced by some extrinsic motivation. Students are more likely to repeat engagement in activities they find repeatedly stimulating and controllable, and discard those repeatedly not satisfying these criteria. Research finds the more constructive teacher criticism is and the more freely and often teachers praise student efforts, the more encouraged and self-motivated students become.

Including Students in Instructional Decisions

All human beings want some control over their circumstances and activities. This is especially important to K-12 students: as minors, they have less legal and practical power and control over their lives than adults. Students perceiving teachers as having all the control over their instruction are more likely to respond only to external rewards and punishments and less likely to develop internal motivation to learn and achieve academically. When teachers include students in instructional decisions, students feel ownership of the content and their learning. For example, teachers can ask students which aspects and topics within curriculum subjects interest them and let students choose topics they are interested in for papers and projects. They can give students choices among working independently, in pairs, or in small groups for some learning activities. Teachers can offer students options for how to weigh different assignments and assessments to determine their grades. Including papers, projects, tests, presentations, and other varied ways of assessing students allows them more control over how they demonstrate their learning. Participation and control in their instruction increases student motivation for acquiring and demonstrating knowledge.

Internal vs. External Motivation

External motivations include teacher and parent expectations of students; rewards students can earn by demonstrating learning; and grades, which determine passing, promotion, retention, graduation, future opportunities, college admissions, scholarships, etc. Applying external motivators typically requires little preparation or effort, frequently does not require much teacher knowledge about individual students and their interests, and produces more immediate behavior changes. However, designating appropriate rewards and punishments becomes challenging when students become habituated, requiring escalation over time. External rewards frequently distract students from learning subject matter. They are not durable: students lose motivation once rewards and punishments are discontinued. Additionally, multiple experiments (e.g., Lepper, Deci) show external rewards can decrease internal motivation: students of all ages continued to engage in activities without rewards as they found them inherently interesting, whereas those given rewards for engaging in them discontinued engagement when rewards ceased; extrinsic rewards apparently reduced intrinsic interest. Internal motivations, including student interest in subject matter and learning and desire for knowledge and success, require more teacher time and effort and take longer to change behavior, but are durable, not dependent on rewards or punishments. Additional factors affecting student motivation include how stimulating activities are and how much control students have over them.

Contrasting with internal motives that students have for learning and succeeding academically, grades are external motivators. While they provide an index of how a student performed in classroom activities and assessments—which can vary in accuracy—grades by themselves do not give students intrinsic reasons to learn or achieve. Students displaying extrinsic motivation might say they need certain letter or number grades to pass courses and accomplish graduation from high school, to the next grade, receive rewards promised by teachers or parents, or avoid punishment. This differs from students saying that certain grades prove they know, understand, or have mastered subjects. Though some view formative assessment grades as feedback, these often do not inform adjusting performance. In an expert's (Wiggins, 2012) analogy, suppose a student's goal in PE is to run a five-minute mile, already having achieved 5:09. Suppose at the end of the first lap of a mile race, her coach yelled, "B-plus on that lap!" This does not support progress toward the goal. But the coach's yelling individual lap times, feedback, and advice: "You're on pace for 5:15," "You're not swinging your arms," "You need two seconds off the next lap to finish under 5:10—pick it up," provides specific information and advice for progress toward the goal.

Showing Students the Appeal of Instructional Content

Teachers can encourage student interest in subject content by showing its appeal. To show novelty, comment how you have not seen anything quite like a certain topic or activity. To show utility, describe a topic as including valuable ideas you will use later in the course and being a topic they will use over and over in both school and life. To show applicability, point out how relevant certain subject matter is to the course and everyday life. To show anticipation, prompt students to ask themselves while reading what next logical step the text foreshadows. To show surprise, remark that the class has used some subject matter in many different ways, and then whet their interest, saying, "If you think you've seen them all, just wait until our next activity." To show challenge, suggest students will find the upcoming material very interesting and invite them to rise to a challenge. To show feedback, predict that when students try an assigned activity, they will discover whether they really understood the previous lesson or not. To show closure, announce that many students have asked about a topic or phenomenon, telling them they will now finally find out more and why.

Questioning Students

Questions cognitively lower on Bloom's taxonomy—for knowledge and comprehension—are better when imparting or retaining factual knowledge. Open-ended, higher-cognitive questions—for application, analysis, evaluation, and synthesis—should be more than half of those used in higher grades, but elementary-grade students need smaller proportions of these too. Research finds combining higher and lower questions more effective than using either one exclusively. Studies show older students' on-task behavior, response length, number of relevant contributions and questions, peer interactions, complete sentences, and speculative thinking correlate positively with using greater than or equal to 50 percent higher-level questions. Teachers may still need to include explicit instruction, not just many more questions, for complex concepts. Pre-reading questions are effective with older, higher-ability, and interested students, but not with poor readers and younger students, who focus only on material for answering them. Slightly increasing wait-time promotes achievement. Studies find teachers paradoxically allow less wait time for students perceived as poor or slow learners than those perceived more capable. Teachers encourage participation by inviting student responses non-critically, addressing incorrect answers with redirection, and partial answers with probing—both explicit to student answers. Vague feedback, e.g., "Wrong, try again" is ineffective for achievement. Active listening restates student responses, helping clarify student understanding and meaning and encouraging participation.

Teachers ask students questions for varied purposes, e.g., actively involving students in lessons, regardless of questions' cognitive levels. "When did this author live?" "In what period is this work set?" Even low-level knowledge questions involve students as they consider and/or respond. "Why do you think the author did...?" require cognitively higher responses. Teachers might ask "Have you ever...?" or "Do you know anybody who...?" This relates textual events and experiences to students' own lives. Connecting new material to prior knowledge increases motivation and interest. Questions can evaluate preparation and check on assignment completion: in classes with many students not typically hesitant to speak, if nobody answers basic questions about assigned reading, they likely did not do it. Students completing math assignments successfully can likely answer specific questions about the operations they used or solutions they got, while those not doing or understanding it cannot. Questions develop critical thinking skills when requiring students to apply concepts and analyze them, separate inference from fact, evaluate or judge ideas and products, and synthesize components to construct new meaning. Questions help teachers review prior lessons to assess, increase, or refresh student comprehension and retention. They cultivate insights by making students think about topics, assess goal achievement, and stimulate independent learning.

Managerial questions facilitate classroom operations. Rhetorical questions reinforce or emphasize statements and ideas. Closed questions check retention and focus thinking. Open questions promote student discussion and interaction. Probing questions, based on student responses, require students to go beyond first answers. Clarifying: "What do you mean? Can you elaborate?" Increasing critical awareness: "What are you assuming? What are your reasons? What would an opponent say?" Refocusing: "Then what are the implications for...? Can you relate that to...? Let's analyze your answer." Prompting: "What's the square root of 94?" (Student: "I don't know.") "What's the square root of 100?" (Student: "10.") "Of 81?" (Student: "Nine.") "Then what do we know about the square root of 94?" (Student: "It's between nine and 10.") Redirecting to another student: "Do you agree? Can you elaborate on his/her answer?" Factual questions elicit simple information, e.g., "Who wrote this? Who is the main character?" Or they elicit event sequences: "What are the steps for a bill to become law?" "How is hydrochloric acid produced?" "How did Robinson Crusoe react to discovering footprints?" Divergent questions have no right or wrong answer, eliciting exploration of possibilities and both concrete and abstract thinking. For example: "If the Spanish Armada had defeated England in 1588, how would it have changed history?"

Rather than remembering answers, students must figure out answers by higher-order questions, which require generalizing in meaningful patterns relative to facts. Evaluation: requires valuation, judgment, or choice via comparing things and ideas with established standards. Assuming equal resources, would you rate General Ulysses S. Grant or Robert E. Lee more skillful? Why? Which of these two books do you think contributed more to understanding this era? Why? Inference: requires deductive or inductive reasoning. Deductive: if gas temperature remains constant but altitude is increased 4000 feet, what happens to gas pressure? Why? Inductive: considering these world leaders' shared qualities, what can we conclude about required leadership qualities? Why? Comparison: requires discerning similarities, differences, contradictions, and non-relations – How are Social Darwinism and late-19th-century Supreme Court rulings related? How are Pericles' Funeral Oration and Lincoln's Gettysburg Address similar or different? Are clams and mussels the same? Application: requires transferring concepts and principles to different contexts – How did Germany's Weimar Republic demonstrate Gresham's Law? Problem-solving: requires using acquired knowledge, seeing relationships, relating parts to whole – Imagine you grew up thinking dogs were bad, but none bit you; how would you react now? Would the dog's characteristics matter? Explain the idea of prejudice using this example.

Supporting Students in Articulating Ideas

One strategy teachers use to support clear student expression is prompting. Verbal prompting: when a student does not know the answer to the teacher's initial question, the teacher asks additional questions to which the student does know the answers, leading the student to discover more about the answer to the original question. For example, a teacher asks a student a square root s/he does not know; the teacher asks the student two more square roots, one higher and the other lower; the student realizes the unknown answer is between the other two. Nonverbal prompting: nodding or making affirmative sounds and gestures indicating agreement to encourage continuing, pointing at objects or information to give hints, hand-over-hand guidance with manipulatives, etc. Restatement: repeating a student's message in the teacher's own words, either affirming the message or allowing the student to deny or correct the restatement or clarify the message. Student: "This assignment took me all night!" Teacher: "It was too hard?" Reflective listening statements mirror student messages, not just restating them but moreover interpreting implicit meanings. Student: "I will never get this right!" Teacher: "You feel frustrated?" Wait-time enables student processing: understanding questions, recalling information, formulating responses. Research finds three minutes optimal for factual or low-cognitive, and longer for high-cognitive questions.

Methods That Promote Higher Thinking Levels

(1) After assigned reading or video viewing, ask students what they would have done in a fictional character or nonfictional individual's situation. After students complete projects or assignments, have them write (a.) what they could have done differently, (b.) how, (c.) what they will do differently or additionally next time, and (d.) what they learned during the process of the project or assignment. These both require students to reflect on their experiences and articulate insights and thoughts. (2) In class discussion, have students identify a book or movie's main assumption(s). Ask how they know these are true. Have them research for proof or disproof, teaching the habit of questioning and investigating rather than simply accepting others' assumptions. (3) Have students compare similarities and contrast differences between or among books, movies, experiments, natural phenomena, etc., guiding them to find relationships. Have them make cause-and-effect graphics identifying relationships among events or actions in history, fiction, or drama. Ask how fictional characters and historical or current figures influence(d) one another; how chemicals interact, causing reactions; why, etc. (4) Ask students to explain how information relates to current study topics. For examining validity, see (2) above; also have students test claims directly when feasible. (5) Review information identified in lessons and classwork, ask what students conclude based on it, and have them explain the logic leading to conclusions. (6) Assign applying newly-learned skills in other classes, field trips, homes, communities, and workplaces.

Setting the Stage for Effective Classroom Discussions

For teachers to get all students engaged in discussing a topic, they need to make it appealing. One way is connecting topics to existing student experience and knowledge, making them more personally relevant. Ask if they have encountered similar situations or felt similarly in other situations: find some commonality between the topic and every student's life experience. Teachers also need to show respect for all student opinions. Experts note teachers' natural inclinations to evaluate, approve or disapprove, and judge student contributions, increasing student fears against expressing thoughts. To create climates welcoming participation, teachers must suspend judgment; instead of responding with "Right," "Wrong," or "That wasn't what I was thinking about," etc., they can respond, "Tell me more about that," "Thank you for sharing your ideas with us," etc. Asking students to elaborate without judging makes them feel safe to progress in their thinking and share it. This teacher acceptance establishing safety also supports student risk-taking. In safe, non-threatening, non-judgmental atmospheres, teacher acceptance encourages students to express potentially controversial or minority views. Making all students feel safe and invited to participate facilitates collaboration: teachers model respecting others' ideas; students with non-judgmental teachers are less likely to fear classmates' judgment.

Procedural Steps for Teaching That Follow Direct Instruction Principles

(1) <u>Introduction and review</u>: get student attention to introduce new information, or review or build on previously learned information. Identify the lesson's learning goal and relevance or significance. (2) <u>Development</u>: model the skill, knowledge, or behavior students will need to demonstrate. Clearly explain and give sufficient examples of material to be learned. Check for understanding by asking key questions or otherwise eliciting student questions. Use visual aids, multimedia presentations, or other prompts to facilitate successful student information processing. (3) <u>Guided practice</u>: once students respond positively to modeling, explanations, and examples, assign tasks for student practice and monitor them closely. Offer help and additional direct instruction (repeating the second step) to students not having mastered the material yet. (4) <u>Closure</u>: conclude the lesson, recapping what it covered; remind students of the learning goal; prepare them for the next step: (5) <u>Independent practice</u>: assign tasks or activities to students who demonstrated proficiency and competency in step (3) to eliminate any teacher prompts and assess degrees of student mastery. This can include homework. (6) <u>Evaluation</u>: assess progress formatively through classroom assignments, worksheets, etc.; and/or summatively through projects, tests, etc. Determine if learning goals are met or need revisiting in future lessons through evaluation feedback.

Indirect Instruction Strategies

Indirect instruction is student-centered. Students actively discover or construct knowledge through inquiry, hands-on exploration, experimentation, and problem-solving activities. Teachers are facilitators assigning and guiding student activity selection, supervising and supporting work. In inquiry learning, students formulate, ask, and answer questions and solve problems rather than teachers' giving answers or solutions. Students apply content knowledge and skills analyzing and explaining teacher-supplied case studies—detailed, in-depth histories and observations of individual real-life persons, families, groups, schools, communities, etc. Concept mapping facilitates students' visualizing, organizing, and applying learned concepts. Teachers guide student project and assignment preparation, identifying focus, participants, schedules, etc.; idea generation and listing; idea sorting and rating for structure; developing maps using software for multidimensional scaling, cluster analysis, etc.; interpreting; and applying maps. Reading for meaning involves active reading, previewing and predicting before, seeking relevant information during, and reflecting after reading. Students identify explicit textual messages; make logical inferences; identify main themes and ideas; analyze development, connection, interaction of people and characters, events and plot, and ideas; evaluate purpose or viewpoint influences on text content and style; differentiate objective and subjective; integrate and evaluate visual and numerical as well as verbal content; comparatively analyze multiple text topics, themes, approaches, and information. Cloze procedures—requiring student meaning determination from context to supply missing words—teach sequencing awareness, linguistic relationships, searching, prediction, and reconstruction.

Independent instruction promotes individual student autonomy, initiative, self-determination, self-direction, self-reliance, self-improvement, self-confidence, self-efficacy, and self-esteem. Students can pursue individual interests using individual styles and paces. Its applications are highly flexible and adaptable. One caveat is that teachers must ensure students have acquired the skills necessary before beginning. In learning contracts, students agree to complete specified tasks within designated conditions and schedules and sign them, promoting accountability and responsibility. In research projects, students independently develop research questions; locate, access, and consult multiple information sources; use the information to answer research questions; and write reports or papers organizing and communicating results (with teacher guidance as needed). Learning centers are self-contained areas within classrooms containing easily accessible, varied learning materials where students independently engage in self-directed learning activities. They include skill development centers, exploratory and interest centers, and enrichment centers. In computer-mediated instruction, students interact with software programs rather than teachers or classmates, working more autonomously at their own paces. In distance learning, students access information remotely, eliminating restrictions from geographic locations.

Field Trips, Experiments, Simulations, Role-Plays, Games, and Observations

Students generally love field trips for getting them out of classrooms and providing real-world adventures, experiences, and materials. However, they also benefit from applying knowledge and skills acquired in classrooms to real-life situations for authentic, hands-on learning experiences. For example, in a geology lab, rock samples are usually distributed equally; but on field trips, students discover some rock types (e.g., quartz) are far more plentiful; find samples with mixed types; and enjoy independence and excitement in seeking and procuring samples—while additionally interacting with nature. In experiments, instead of reading or hearing about scientific concepts and procedures, students practice these, encountering and solving involved problems and challenges first-hand. They experience direct ownership of their learning. Instead of abstractions, concepts become real to them. Simulations, while not real, are realistic, enabling students to engage in activities not experienced in real life, e.g., developing military strategies, planning battles, and fighting wars; working in various occupations; marrying, raising families; building and managing cities, farms, corporations, etc. Technology makes simulations increasingly accessible, interactive, and vivid. Role-plays enable students to envision different perspectives, developing understanding, empathy, and social interactions. Games apply skills and knowledge in entertaining contexts, structured by rules. Observations develop student perception, detail-orientation, and objectivity.

Interactive Strategies

All interactive strategies promote interpersonal and social skills. Brainstorming eliminates or minimizes student inhibitions and promotes self-expression, originality, and creativity by asking students to generate and express as many different ideas as possible without teacher or classmate criticism, censure, or rejection. Quantity supersedes quality. Students acquire more ideas from classmates than they could produce alone. Cooperative learning groups promote both collective and individual accountability, responsibility, and teamwork. They access and utilize the cooperative, noncompetitive orientations of students from collectivist cultures; and enable ELL and LEP students to ask classmates questions their cultural backgrounds might inhibit their asking teachers. Interviews help students learn about one another, show them they can serve as helpful resources for one another, and develop student communication skills. Discussions let students exchange ideas, information, and opinions; ask and answer questions; consider problems, questions, or ideas classmates propose that did not occur to them; use evidence to support their arguments; learn to disagree civilly; and consider differing perspectives. Peer practice affords classmate support, interaction, and greater comfort levels and identification than individual or teacher-led practice. Debates teach students to apply logic, support arguments with evidence, attend and respond to opponent arguments, take turns, follow rules, and interact formally.

Helping Students Develop Complex Thinking Processes

When students learn concepts, they are not merely memorizing facts, the lowest level of Bloom's taxonomy. They also understand ideas, which is the next level. Problem-solving involves multiple steps: first, students must identify the specific problem, requiring observational and analytical skills. Then they generate multiple possible alternative solutions, requiring understanding relationships between needs and actions, plus independent and divergent thinking. Third, they anticipate various potential consequences of different alternatives, requiring abstraction, imagination, relating hypothetical situations to their own background experiences, and speculation. The next step, implementing solutions, requires active, hands-on, experiential learning. Then students evaluate solution results, requiring analytical thinking, cost-benefit analysis, judging effectiveness, value, etc. Analysis is Bloom's fourth level, evaluation Bloom's fifth. Metacognition involves thinking about one's own thought processes, requiring objectivity, analytical skills, reflection, and application—using metacognitive insights to inform, self-improve, and refine one's own learning strategies and processes for greater effectiveness. Critical thinking requires intellectual standards; discipline; open-mindedness; fairness; empathy, humility, and integrity; distinguishing objective from subjective information; evaluating and judging information and sources for validity and quality; applying logic and reasoning to unfamiliar or new ideas; informing thought with evidence; accuracy, clarity, precision, relevance, consistency, depth, and breadth. Transferring knowledge and skills requires application—Bloom's third level—to different contexts and situations.

The directed reading and thinking activity (DR-TA; Stauffer, 1969) helps students analyze text, determine purpose, question, clarify, and underline predict in all content subjects. Students examine the title to predict text subject matter. Following reading, open-ended questions elicit student predictions, opinions, and opinion-text connections. Comparison-contrast: make students develop questions about similarities and differences, writing them in graphic organizers, e.g., students might ask, "If circles were squares, what would happen?" "How are dogs and cats different and similar?" "How are gloves like hands? How are they not like hands?" Inferring: provide political cartoons or comic strips, and ask students to infer meaning. Student pairs or small groups identify inferences and connections they must make to interpret the cartoonist's point. Categorizing: with younger students, play 20 Questions or "animal, vegetable, mineral"-type games; provide manipulatives, having them sort objects into three different category containers. Give older students a controversial question or statement; have small groups research the topic; sort information into columns headed "Pro," "Con," and "Interesting Facts"; form opinions, and discuss. Summarizing: model first; have student partners or small groups read, stopping regularly to paraphrase; have them summarize key ideas in three or fewer textbook sections in no more than 20 words. Synthesizing: have students contribute to an idea web mural, adding and connecting ideas and comments about a central topic or question.

Modeling, Developing Self-Regulation Skills, Scaffolding, Guided Practice, and Coaching

Modeling: many students learn better from witnessing demonstration than only hearing or reading verbal description, particularly when learning procedures they must execute physically. Modeling also allows teachers to demonstrate correct techniques and sequences. Additionally, modeling helps students develop self-regulation skills including managing emotions, overcoming discomfort, taking turns, listening, demonstrating, and communicating. Teachers modeling appropriate behaviors show students how to perform tasks, and use self-regulation to complete them. They also teach self-regulation through hints, cues, and scaffolding: temporary support students need to complete tasks that are gradually removed as students gain skills. Differentiating instruction: teachers recognize diverse student experience and expertise levels in content knowledge, thinking, problem-solving, listening, speaking, reading, and writing; through ongoing assessments, develop differentiated lessons to meet each student's needs. Having students learn in pairs or small groups promotes meaningful discussion, observation, and learning from each other. Differentiation focuses on concepts and issues, not chapters or books, encouraging students to expand concept understanding and explore so-called "big ideas." Choices of experiences and tasks or projects motivate students. Guided practice: after modeling, explaining, and examples, assign tasks or activities, monitoring closely; offer assistance as needed. Coaching: helps students understand impacts of time management, organization, and disorganization on studies; examine and strengthen study skills, problem-solving, strategic thinking, and effective interaction and collaboration.

Phases of Self-Regulated Learning

One popular model of self-regulated learning defines three phases. (1) <u>Forethought and planning</u>: students analyze learning tasks, setting specific goals for completion. Students learning new or unfamiliar material may not recognize appropriate goals, best task approaches; teachers instruct them about these. (2) <u>Performance monitoring</u>: students apply strategies for task progress, monitoring strategy effectiveness and their motivation to continue. Students may react to discomfort with new strategies by falling back on more familiar, less effective strategies. Teachers help students overcome frustration and gain fluency with new strategies through close monitoring and specific feedback. They also support self-monitoring by having students keep records of how many times they worked on specific tasks, amounts of time working, and strategies they used, enabling students to visualize progress and make needed changes. (3) <u>Reflections on performance</u>: students evaluate strategy effectiveness, their task performance, and manage emotions regarding outcomes. Self-reflections influence subsequent planning and goals. Encouraging setting short-term goals helps students track progress. Goal-setting and planning are complementary: planning includes and supports establishing goals. Teaching students to approach tasks with plans promotes self-regulation and learning. Self-monitoring involves goal-setting and planning. Instructional strategies promoting self-regulation include direct instruction, guided and independent practice, reflective practice, social support, and feedback.

Instructional Grouping Configurations

The whole-class group configuration is the traditional, most widely used model. Teachers deliver lectures or lessons, assign classwork to, ask questions of, and lead discussions with the entire class at once. Small-group instruction, a more recent development, divides classes into groups, usually three to six students each. Each group collaborates, researching and discussing topics. Group members may be assigned different group roles, e.g., leader, facilitator, recorder, summarizer, timekeeper, presenter, errand monitor, etc. Teachers may assign individual tasks to each group member or have everyone contribute to a larger task. Students benefit from sharing, discussing, developing, and preparing their ideas in less threatening smaller groups before doing so in the whole class; and learning and practicing social interaction skills with fewer classmates under more controlled conditions. Small groups can benefit ELL/LEP students culturally intimidated about questioning teachers by enabling questions of classmates, and students with autism spectrum disorders (ASDs) overwhelmed by larger group interactions. Independent learning allows proceeding at students' own paces, using their own learning styles and strategies. One-on-one instruction benefits students needing intensive, direct instruction, remedial intervention, and/or personal student-teacher interactions and relationships. Think-pair-share structures student discussion, limiting off-task thinking and behavior, and builds in accountability through reporting to partners and the class.

Cooperative learning groups are very structured, typically containing three or four students working several days or weeks. Teachers clearly define assignments, goals, and plan of operation, and spend time teaching member roles, e.g., questioner, reporter, recorder, etc. Within designated roles, team members share leadership. All must contribute for team progress: group interdependence dictates groups win or lose together. End products represent whole teams. Cooperation, goal achievement, task completion, and group process awareness are equally important. Highly individualistic or creative students may chafe at restrictions and students preferring whole-class anonymity feel pressured, but learn cooperative teamwork skills.

Collaborative groups feature three to six students working days, weeks, or months on open-ended problems or tasks which can cover much content. Flexible student roles can change throughout assignments and projects. Students help others, observing, evaluating, critiquing, explaining, and suggesting improvements. Team goals, product, and collaborative communication process awareness is constant; meeting goals justifies changing direction. Students honestly discuss ideas, information, resources, procedures, results, their own and/or others' work; multiple approaches and open communication are important. Students needing structure may prefer cooperative teams, but collaborative groups learn flexibility and communication. Homogeneous groups may feel more comfort and commonality than heterogeneous, gender-inclusive and multi-age groups, but lack their exposure to diverse perspectives expanding experience. Multi-age grouping can facilitate helping and mentoring relationships.

Short-Term, Working, and Long-Term Memory

When we temporarily retain information for about three to 20 seconds, this involves short-term memory—a receptacle for visual and auditory information we rehearse, consider, analyze, interpret, or otherwise manipulate using working memory. For example, repeating a phone number to oneself silently or under one's breath until dialing or telling it to someone is in short-term memory. When we encode or consolidate and transfer information from short-term memory to long-term memory, that information is stored for an indefinite time period. Depending on individual cognitive characteristics, relative importance and meaningfulness of information, its affective impacts and associations, whether and how often one accesses the information, etc., long-term memories can last a lifetime, years, or less. Via top-down processing, prior knowledge in long-term memory strongly influences sensory perceptions; expectations about sensory experiences influence their interpretation, contributing to bias. Instructional design implications include making information sufficiently meaningful and relevant for transfer to long-term memory; and dividing information into chunks to facilitate transfer. Chunking enables the brain to automatically group some items for better retention and learning. Long-term memory, organized into interrelated schema networks, enables recalling relevant knowledge and relating new information to existing knowledge, which teachers activate using curiosity-piquing questions, graphic organizers, video, etc.

Teachable Moment

Teachable moments, unlike instruction teachers plan in advance, are unplanned situations arising in classrooms, offering teachers ideal opportunities to impart some understanding or insight to students regarding some concept or topic. Teachers cannot design or plan for teachable moments. They occur momentarily; therefore, teachers must be observant, notice them, and seize the opportunity to take advantage of them. Because they are unexpected, making use of teachable moments can insert temporary detours into a teacher's original lesson plan in order to explain some idea which has aroused collective student curiosity and/or captured their interest. As an example, a teacher describes a morning class meeting wherein one student asked why the previous day had been a school holiday to observe Veterans Day. The teacher took advantage of this question as a teachable moment to discuss military service personnel's historical and current sacrifices on behalf of our country. Students were so fascinated with this topic, they discussed neighbors, relatives, and friends serving and the meaning of the military to the country's future for 20 minutes. The benefit of following such tangents is their maximal impact on students through their natural timing. Teachable moments can ultimately develop into complete lesson plans or instructional units.

Useful Feedback

Useful feedback must be consistent, formative, timely, and ongoing to enable student performance adjustments. It must be user-friendly: students must understand feedback to apply it, so it must be age-appropriate or developmentally appropriate, not containing excessive or overly technical information for students to handle. Expert educators communicate observation of one important behavior, which changing can produce noticeable improvement immediately, not offering advice until ensuring students understand the significance of observations. Effective feedback is actionable: grades, "wrong," and "good job" are not feedback. Inferences from data without presenting data are not descriptive enough. For example, "Many students were bored in your class" is judgment, not observation. "Twelve of 25 students texted or passed notes during your lecture; only one did during the small-group activity" is less arguable, more neutral and useful. Feedback must include explicit goals and tangible, goal-related results. Students can be too occupied with performing to attend to results: video recordings help. Most school district "formative" test grades refer to recently taught objectives, not final performance standards. Evaluating fall and winter performance against spring standards, measuring progress using more pre- and post-assessments, and using item analysis to identify individual student performance improvement needs are more effective.

Diverse Student Backgrounds and Needs

Today's classroom diversity includes students with different native languages, cultural backgrounds, previous educational and personal experiences, and knowledge. Disabilities are also a possibility. Regardless of background, gender, or other characteristics, all students need teachers to behave and communicate in considerate ways. Teachers who consider how peers and faculty may misjudge some students and how this affects them, and are aware of stereotypes and their consequences, can develop true awareness of others' perspectives. Using language, examples, and behaviors to treat students with interest and consideration and encourage others to follow suit facilitates establishing welcoming environments where students feel comfortable participating, enabling their success. Even though teachers may have student records, they need to inform themselves of individual students' background knowledge. They can begin school years surveying student knowledge prerequisite to their subject or class; give students lists of basic content-area vocabulary they expect students to understand, asking them to identify unfamiliar or problematic words; consult Individualized Education Program (IEP) information, special educators, and parents about how student disabilities can affect attendance and participation; and ask students, parents, school social workers, and/or others about student religion, family obligations, and other unique factors to consider.

Statistical Reliability and Validity

Reliability: whether a test gets consistent results over repeated administrations. Test-retest reliability retests the same respondents with the same test, e.g., two weeks or a month later. Difficulties include having to write different questions on the same material, etc., to control for memory and practice effects. Internal consistency reliability compares two versions of a test concurrently, evaluating whether they correlate or measure the same construct. Validity: whether a test measures what it purports or intends to measure. Criterion validity: whether a test reflects certain abilities. One type is concurrent validity: whether a test correlates with benchmark or criterion tests. Another type is predictive validity: how well a test predicts abilities by testing respondents for a given construct, then comparing future results. Content validity: whether a test represents all of a given construct. Construct validity: whether a test measures its identified construct and not others—e.g., depression, not stress or anxiety. Convergent validity: whether constructs we believe are related are actually related. Divergent or discriminant validity: whether constructs we believe unrelated are unrelated. Bias: subjective slant toward expected results. Example: IQ test item "cup and (a.) saucer, (b.) fork, (c.) table," presumed student familiarity with cup-and-saucer sets; but low-income students chose "table," having experience only with cups on tables, not cups in saucers.

Formal and Informal Assessments

Standardized tests are a primary example of formal assessments. They have been used to test large numbers of students; data from results are mathematically calculated and summarized; standard scores, percentiles, or stanines are provided. Statistical analyses support conclusions based on test results, e.g., a certain score range is the average for representative samples of the student population in a given grade, hence other scores can be defined as above or below average and by how much. These are typically norm-referenced tests. Informal assessments are performance- and content-driven, not data-driven. For example, a running record of how well a student is reading a particular book is an informal assessment. Typical scores are most rubric scores; percentage of words read correctly; 15 correct answers out of 20 questions, etc. These are typically criterion-referenced or performance-based tests. To compare students to peers their own age, compare student strengths and weaknesses with those of peers, or assess overall achievement, formal assessments suit these purposes. To inform and improve ongoing instruction, as in formative assessment, informal assessments meet those purposes. Formal tests, statistically proven, are good for summative, not formative assessment and generalized data, not individualized data. Informal tests, more individualized, are good for ongoing assessment but less objective or statistically supported.

Formal assessments all include standardized methods for their administration, scoring, and interpretation of the scores. Some examples of formal assessments include all standardized achievement tests, which are often national or statewide; so-called high-stakes examinations; standardized intelligence or IQ tests; many standardized screening tests; and many standardized diagnostic measures. Standardized testing instruments have been statistically proven valid, i.e., they test what they are meant to test; and reliable, i.e., they yield consistent results across repeated administrations. Their manuals include statistical methods for scoring and interpreting the scores, and tables or charts showing the average scores of samples of students that represent the test-taking population, plus other scores and how many standard deviations these are from the average. Quizzes and exercises at the ends of educational textbook chapters, sections, and units are also examples of formal assessments. Informal assessments do not typically include standardized instruments, though some exist, e.g., standardized reading fluency measures. Teacher observations, class or student question-and-answer sessions, running reports, student projects, presentations, and experiments, student portfolios, and performance assessments are examples of informal assessment measures. Some find peer teaching and debates informal assessments as well.

Formal assessments provide quantitative data because they are standardized and report standard scores. Informal assessments provide qualitative data because they are not standardized, so the results reported by teachers using them are more subjective. Formal assessments enable comparison of individual students with peer groups, but typically not specific details about individual students. Informal assessments can give more detail about an individual student's strengths, needs, and performance; but less objective comparison of individual student performance with age, grade, or peer performance. Formal assessments are norm-referenced tests comparing student performance to norms for their developmental level, age, or grade. Informal assessments are typically criterion-referenced tests comparing student performance to pre-established criteria students are expected or intended to achieve and teachers are expected or intended to teach. Some students experience significant test anxiety when standardized formal tests are administered in whole-class or group settings. Some students also experience significant anxiety, even panic, when teachers single them out to answer questions in class as informal assessment. Hence it is important that teachers obtain sufficient results from both formal and informal assessment, and multiple forms of each, to develop more comprehensive pictures of student abilities and achievements.

Student scores from standardized intelligence scales and standardized scales of adaptive functioning are often used to inform student placements into specific schools, grades, and types of classes most compatible with their educational strengths and needs. While tracking is generally unpopular these days, educators seek to place students into groups where ability levels are similar and teachers can offer material (even if via differentiated instruction) that is sufficiently challenging, neither impossibly, inappropriately, or overwhelmingly difficult nor overly easy or boring. For students with certain disabilities, e.g., autism spectrum disorders (ASDs), many formal assessments exist to inform educators where a student is on the spectrum; intellectual and adaptive functioning levels; individual interests, difficulty areas, and specific behaviors, which can be both typical of the disorder and vary widely individually. Formal assessments are given at ends of school years to measure student achievement. These results are used for purposes of individual student grade promotions; to compare year-end student performance to baseline scores to assess student progress toward instructional objectives; and school accountability, to compare school effectiveness by comparing rates and percentages of student achievement to those of other schools, inform school improvement plans, and secure or continue government school funding.

One of the most valuable and prevalent uses of informal assessment findings is to inform ongoing instruction. While teachers plan instruction based on initial student assessments, during implementation they may find some students are not responding to their methods or having difficulty learning new material. With new students and large classes, teachers can discover new individual student characteristics throughout the school year. For example, by using informal measures regularly as formative assessments, teachers may find early on a student(s) not progressing at the rate(s) projected. They can then either (1) change the timeframe when the student is expected to achieve certain objectives; (2) change objectives to represent smaller increments, amounts, or lower levels to achieve within the timeframe; or (3) change the instructional approach, techniques, or strategies to be more compatible or effective with particular students. Conversely, when students progress much faster than anticipated, teachers can adjust instruction to provide higher difficulty, enriched content, etc. Formative assessments also monitor and document on-target student progress. In addition to formative assessment, informal measures afford alternative ways of evaluating student performance that formal standardized tests cannot measure, e.g., performances, portfolios, creative projects, etc. Some students cannot respond to objective examinations but demonstrate their competencies in different formats.

Essay Questions vs. Selected Response Questions and Written Tests vs. Performance Measures

Essay questions have one obvious advantage of testing composition and writing skills as well as subject content knowledge when testing subjects other than English composition. They also enable students to go into depth and detail about topics, showing the extent of their knowledge. Essays afford students choices of subtopics, points they make, examples they use, how much they emphasize certain subtopics and points, how they organize their essays; allow them to persuade or convince readers through argumentation; require recall, not recognition; and showcase student higher-order thinking skills. Disadvantages include being more time-consuming to administer and write; requiring writing skills, which if deficient can obscure a student's other subject knowledge;

and requiring far more time and subjective judgment to grade. Selected-choice questions are much faster to administer; can cover larger numbers of smaller points; allow teachers and testers more control of subject matter; are easier for students, requiring recognition, not recall; have more clear-cut right and wrong answers; are graded more objectively, and far faster, even electronically or automatically. Disadvantages include less information about individual students' overall knowledge; lacking elaboration or depth; and enabling some correct answers from sheer guesswork through probability. Written tests can be more objective; performance measures enable students to show what they can actually do, an advantage for those who do not write well.

Portfolio Assessments

Portfolio assessments involve reviewing a collection of student work products gathered cumulatively over a period of time, e.g., a semester or school year. One of their advantages is that they can provide clear evidence of student progress, growth, and other longitudinal changes that a written test or single term paper will not show as clearly. Another is that products may be artworks, models, and other concrete objects, not just test answers, written essays, or papers. These are more individualized, demonstrating more student skills than tests or papers, including nonverbal skills like artistic ability, creativity, divergent thinking, spatial awareness, mechanical ability, nonlinguistic organization, etc. Students with different learning styles, who may not use the linear thinking needed for objective tests and/or lack organizational, language processing, and/or verbal skills for writing, but excel in other areas, can produce evidence of those strengths in portfolios. Another advantage is avoiding test anxiety for many students. Students also have less time pressure and can devote more total time to creating things more gradually. Portfolios can be used for both formative and summative assessment. Some disadvantages include more subjective teacher grading, time required to accumulate portfolio products, teacher time and effort to match products with learning objectives, and lack of standardization.

Considerations for Selecting Assessment Formats and Instruments

When choosing assessment instruments, educators and testers should first always remember that any comprehensive assessment must include multiple and varied methods, instruments, tools, and (when feasible) formats. They should never rely on a single test. One test might be most indicated for assessing a very specific skill, but even for single domains, e.g., language or adaptive functioning, multiple tests are better, as responses and scores can differ and some reveal abilities others overlooked. Age-appropriateness is important. For example, to use Wechsler's IQ scales with a young child, one would administer the Wechsler Preschool and Primary Scales of Intelligence (WPPSI), not the Wechsler Intelligence Scales for Children (WISC) or Wechsler Adult Intelligence Scales (WAIS). (If a gifted child exceeded WPPSI's top levels, administering the WISC would be interesting, though other giftedness instruments would also be indicated.) Students who are nonverbal—e.g., some with autism spectrum disorder (ASD), cerebral palsy (CP), intellectual disability (ID), or other disorders—can be evaluated using the Leiter, Raven's Progressive Matrices, UNIT, etc. Young and/or disabled students with receptive language understanding but absent or limited expression can respond to the Peabody Picture Vocabulary and other receptive tests.

A student's age or grade level are not the only factors to consider for selecting assessments. The educational context is also a key to format and instrument choice. For example, while intelligence scales give an idea of a child's intellectual capacity for purposes of educational placement, curricular and instructional design, individualized or differentiated instructional planning, etc., intelligence testing is not necessarily relevant or even significant to define adaptive functioning levels. Some children, due to innate characteristics, life experience, and training, function significantly higher in daily living and social skills than intellectually. Other children function adaptively much lower than their intellectual capacities would suggest due to behavior disorders like attention deficit hyperactivity disorder (ADHD), autism spectrum disorders (ASDs), learning disabilities (LDs), major mental disorders, etc. To ascertain daily living activities a child can perform compared to age peers and inform instructional design for developing adaptive skills, tests like the Vineland Adaptive Behavior Scales are indicated. When developmental delay is suspected in young children, tests like the Bayley Scales of Infant and Toddler Development help evaluate developmental levels. Because many school districts model their goals on their state education department's standards, the best way to align assessment with campus and district goals is often to administer standardized tests provided by statewide assessment systems.

Aligning Instructional Design and Goals with Statewide Assessments

Teachers need not view the process of aligning their instruction with assessment as "teaching to the test." Instead, they first need to read the standards on which the statewide assessments are based. As an example, many states are now basing their statewide assessments on the Common Core State Standards (CCSS). This means that what students in the state are expected to learn to know and do via the instruction they receive is encapsulated within the CCSS. A teacher whose students will be taking a test based on the CCSS would need to first review the standards and align their teaching to ensure that everything included in those standards is also included in their planned curriculum for the year. Because the state tests are written to align exactly with the standards on which they are based, teachers can be assured that students who are adequately instructed in the knowledge and skills outlined in the standards will be measured appropriately by the exam, without the need for focusing on the test itself.

Monitoring Student Understanding and Guide Instruction

Rather than teach an entire unit and administer an end-of-unit test, only to discover most or all students did not understand key or major points the teacher wanted to convey, it is more useful to monitor student understanding early and often. For example, at any grade level, after a teacher makes introductory statements in a lesson, s/he can stop and ask the class questions whose answers should reflect whether they heard and remember the few main points, whether they can repeat one or a few key definitions the teacher gave, whether they understood the concepts communicated, etc. Seeing few or no volunteers or many students looking perplexed indicates a need to reteach and/or explain or demonstrate concepts differently. Quizzes at ends of lessons within units also monitor student understanding of shorter segments. When teachers assign small-group projects, they may have a member of each group orally report current group or project status and progress to the teacher or class periodically. Teachers can offer time-management strategies if they are falling behind schedule or advise reducing project scope, information amounts, etc. Teachers who find the majority of students not understanding or learning need to revisit and revise their instructional levels, approaches, methods, and/or techniques.

Formative and Summative Assessment

Formative assessments are conducted during instruction. Teachers use them to obtain feedback that they and their students can both utilize for improving the teaching and learning that will occur as it continues. For example, after giving a lecture, a teacher might ask middle or high school students to write down a sentence or two that identify the lecture's main point(s). Similarly, kindergarten and first-grade teachers can review an orally taught lesson by asking students to repeat one or two key vocabulary terms included, and/or one or two main points. When a teacher has told older students they will be assigned a paper as part of a unit, once the class has completed enough reading, teacher lessons, lectures, classwork, discussions, etc., the teacher can have students write and turn in outlines for the papers they will write. Summative assessments are conducted after instruction. They may evaluate learning from a unit, semester, or school year. Teachers use these to determine course grades, student grade promotion, and evaluate class, grade, and school achievement compared to those of other schools for accountability purposes. For example, grading final exams, critiquing senior music recitals or art projects, etc. help determine final course grades.

Research finds that formative assessment reduces learning gaps. It also helps teachers design instruction targeting specific learning goals; supporting student learning; monitoring student progress; identifying strengths, needs, learning gains; differentiating instruction; evaluating instructional effectiveness; informing and adjusting ongoing instruction; promoting effective teaching practices; enhancing learning for struggling students, ELLs, and students with disabilities; improving all student learning outcomes; augmenting coherence through alignment or connection with state comprehensive assessment systems; and reforming curricula. Hence federal legislation like the Every Student Succeeds Act (ESSA), replacements for the ESEA and NCLB Acts, the Individuals with Disabilities Education Act (IDEA), and state policies promote using formative assessment to narrow learning gaps. Researchers find: (1) to identify learning gaps, educators must understand differences between what students know and need to know to design instructional support enabling student progress toward learning goals. (2) Teachers must give clear, detailed feedback designed to close instructional gaps. Reciprocal teacher-student feedback informs student learning status and next instructional steps. (3) Active student involvement in learning and assessments, and student-teacher collaboration to develop shared knowledge regarding current learning status and actions needed for progress develop student skills for self-monitoring and knowing when they need help. (4) Teachers must break down major learning goals into smaller learning progression components to locate students on the skill set continuum required for mastering learning standards.

Diagnostic Assessment

Whereas formative assessment is conducted during instruction and summative assessment is conducted after instruction, diagnostic assessment is conducted before instruction. Also called pre-assessments, these frequently focus upon one domain or area. Administering diagnostic assessments can give educators information about previous knowledge each student has about a subject. This informs teachers where to begin their instruction for all students in the same class to access it without experiencing either significant knowledge gaps or significant repetition of things they already know. Pre-assessments also inform teachers of existing student misconceptions to correct during instruction. And they establish student knowledge baselines to compare knowledge following instruction to assess learning and instructional effectiveness. Teachers can use diagnostic assessment results to inform their development of lesson plans, and also differentiated instruction for individual students within classes to meet their specific needs best. Pre-assessments also gauge student preparation during sequential learning, e.g., after teaching the Coriolis effect, teachers might determine student concept retention through diagnostic pre-assessment; and refresh or reteach as needed, before they proceed to begin teaching a unit about ocean currents.

Multiple-Choice Tests and Oral Questioning

Multiple-choice tests have stems—usually questions, sometimes statements—and several answer choices. One answer is correct, others incorrect; in some formats, there is more than one correct answer. These are efficiently, easily administered to large classes. They can be scored by teaching assistants, machines, or computer programs. These are effective to measure memory, knowledge, convergent thinking, and problem-solving in convergent subjects; but not when "correct" answers are equivocal, ambiguous, or disputable. Writing wrong answers reflecting common misconceptions or errors enables diagnostic value from wrong-answer pattern analyses. However, students cannot elaborate on topics. High-quality tests are harder to write than some teachers realize. Overuse can lead students to memorize separate pieces of information instead of developing overall subject understanding. Oral questioning is the most common classroom assessment. Teachers can use hypotheticals ("What would you have done if...?"), get explanations and reasons for specific student practices, challenge practices, and check understanding of underlying concepts or principles not directly observed. Not requiring reading and writing is often more inclusive and less discriminatory. It applies highly to assessing spoken, not written language. It is more valid than reliable, and time-intensive, indicating standard questions for summative assessments or multiple assessors. Recording is required for permanent documentation, which has its own considerations. Experts advise asking students' opinions of lessons and activities before questioning, for highest information quantity and quality.

Different Assessment Formats

For making preschool and kindergarten placement decisions, developmental scales are useful for assessing their developmental levels in various domains. These tests are also helpful in comparing developmental levels to age norms for diagnosing developmental delays. Developmental scale results then also become useful for designing instructional objectives whereby teachers can help children with developmental delays to reach or approximate normal development. When assessing students with significant disabilities, it is important to assess their adaptive well as intellectual functioning, as these sometimes differ widely. This also informs the levels, types, and weights of instruction for each. When older students are new to a school, diagnostic pre-assessments help educators evaluate their prior knowledge to determine classroom placement and where to begin instruction. When educational records are incomplete or unavailable, new assessments help determine intelligence, literacy levels, strengths and difficulties in specific academic subjects, etc. Standardized tests like ACT and SAT differentiate student verbal vs. quantitative abilities. For example, when a student more verbally than numerically gifted used a 166-point gap between verbal and quantitative SAT scores to justify her math struggles, her guidance counselor responded that her quantitative score nevertheless indicated she should be performing better in math.

Student Self-Assessment

Self-assessment promotes student reflective and metacognitive skills development, critical thinking in analyzing and judging effectiveness of teacher instructional practices and student learning strategies, and helps teachers identify and understand individual student differences to make their instruction more responsive to student needs. Having students create or contribute to rubrics defining success in group discussions, multimodal presentations, reading response tasks, etc. augments learning levels. Having students create and agree to learning contracts when beginning units engages students in defining learning goals, agreed activities, and products as evidence of learning. Teachers have students revisit contracts frequently during units to document new learning, identify points needing clarification, and obtain teacher or classmate feedback. Teachers can designate a classroom area for "muddy points," questions, or topics that students want the class to revisit. Teachers can build student learning ownership by periodically asking students to choose an item from this board. In the "nameless voice" method, teachers have students submit work samples anonymously for class sharing and discussion of similarities and differences with their understandings. Having students write end-of-unit letters to future students explaining what they learned, tips for learning, working with difficult texts, etc. This promotes both reflection and feedback on student thinking and learning.

Because student needs vary widely, educators must differentiate content, processes, and products of learning for individual student readiness, learning styles, and interests. Also, because of this student diversity, more than one record and voice are needed to recognize and report student growth, development, and learning needs. Moreover, research finds both conducting ongoing assessment and engaging students as partners in their learning and assessment vital. When students must analyze their own thinking and learning critically, they become more motivated to learn; they develop metacognitive skills, enhancing their engagement across subject areas and supporting lifelong learning motivation. When ongoing assessment is used to inform and adjust ongoing instruction, both students and teachers reap benefits of additional knowledge about what students do and do not understand from student feedback. However, students commonly lack the experience, training, and expertise to conduct assessments as teachers can. They obviously are less objective than others when assessing themselves. Individual student differences cause corresponding self-assessment differences, whereas one teacher's assessments of all students may be more uniform. Teacher assessments must accompany self-assessments, to standardize evaluation across students and mitigate self-interested, self-destructive, or overly subjective results.

Peer Assessment

Constructivist and active learning theories provide foundations and support for peer assessment. By assigning peer assessment, teachers can empower students to take responsibility for and manage their own learning. They can help students learn assessment techniques and develop lifelong assessment skills. Peer assessment leads to exchanges of ideas and diffusion of knowledge among students, enhancing all individual students' learning. Teachers can also motivate students to engage in more depth with course materials by having them assess one another's learning. Teachers can incorporate peer assessment by identifying activities and assignments wherein peer feedback could benefit students. They can include peer assessment opportunities at different stages of larger assignments, e.g., an outline, first draft, second draft, etc. of a paper. Teachers should create rubrics or guidelines defining tasks clearly for students conducting peer reviews; and use learning exercises to introduce rubrics to assure student abilities for effective rubric applications. Peer reviews can be in-class, homework, online, etc.; teachers should determine these. Teachers must also model constructive criticism, appropriateness, and descriptive feedback in their own responses to inform peer assessment. Including small-group feedback sessions enables recipients to question, and peer reviewers to explain, written comments to recipients.

Before assigning peer assessment, teachers should explain to students the benefits and expectations of the peer review process. One disadvantage is that student relationships and interactions can influence peer review to be personal or subjective. Teachers can keep student work anonymous for peer review, making feedback more objective. Students inexperienced with peer assessment may not know what kinds of feedback are or are not useful and why or why not. Teachers can address this by giving students feedback on their feedback to classmates. They can also give examples to students of feedback with different levels of quality, and discuss with students which are more or less useful and the reasons why. To impart structure, norms, and appropriateness, teachers should provide time limits and clear direction for in-class peer review, and define deadlines for homework peer review assignments. Peer assessments are more valid when students are more familiar with and take more ownership of criteria, so teachers should engage students in discussing designated criteria. Teachers should offer necessary input and guidance during group feedback discussions. Peer assessment is better assigned for academic tasks that students have experience with, not professional tasks. To encourage more individual responsibility, avoid letting multiple students assess identical tasks.

Interpreting Student Assessment Scores

In general, a student's raw score on a statewide assessment equals the number of items that a student answered correctly. Raw scores can only be meaningfully interpreted relative to both the total number of items on the assessment and the raw scores of other students in the same grade. Raw scores must not be compared among different test administrations since minor variations in the test can result in widely varying average performances. With the limitations of the raw score, many assessments use a horizontal scale score allowing score comparison by adjusting for varying test form difficulty in different administrations. Using the horizontal scale score, educators can compare student cohorts (age and grade groups) taking the same subject or grade assessment in different years, compare individual students taking the same subject or grade assessment, and identify satisfactory or advanced performance. A vertical scale score, meanwhile, allows educators to measure student progress across subjects or grades.

Communicating Assessment Results to Students and Parents

Experts recommend two steps in reporting assessment results to students: an initial briefing for the whole class or group tested; and then follow-up meetings with individual students, focusing on how teachers will meet their needs. Briefings should include an overview of the assessment program and instruments; how teachers, school, and districts use test results; the process for reviewing results with individual students; which results students receive; and any plans for recognizing outstanding assessment performance. Follow-up meetings should include assessed student strengths and needs, how these relate to other student information from other tests and/or teacher observations, and the plan of action recommended for addressing individual student needs. Teachers and school administrators should jointly report results to parents to build active partnerships for student learning. Individual parent-teacher conferences are ideal for explaining individual student results, reporting school-wide performance, answering parent questions, and explaining instructional improvement initiatives. If these are impossible, teachers can provide written reports carefully describing assessment processes and procedures, explaining how to interpret results, and including contact information for questions. Parent group meetings are alternatives if individual meetings are impossible. Parent newsletter articles describing assessment, scoring, overall school placement, improvement initiatives, FAQs, etc. are additional communication options.

Getting Students Engaged in Class Activities and Increasing Their On-Task Times

Seating arrangements appropriate to the specific activity enhance engagement and on-task time. Choosing course materials relevant to students, and emphasizing how they can apply the learning in real life, enables students to connect activities with prior knowledge and their lives. Students view schoolwork meaningful to them as more valuable, important, and worth the effort. Giving students some control and choice in learning, e.g., self-monitoring and self-evaluating progress or choice of paired or individual work, increases sense of autonomy, hence engagement. Assigning achievable yet challenging tasks for all students, including those with disabilities, at-risk, remedial, etc. enable students to feel successful, and to believe that they earned their success. Repetitive, rote tasks and seemingly impossible ones both discourage engagement. "Mystery" approaches give students partial or contradictory information and require they develop hypotheses based on available evidence, piquing their curiosity. This also fulfills needs for autonomy, competence, self-directed inquiry, and independent discovery. Assignments only teachers will read are unilateral: teachers typically do not need the information that students submit. Contrastingly, designing cooperative learning and other projects enabling students to share new knowledge with peers promotes reciprocal relationships, making learning activities more engaging.

- 106 -

Unanticipated Learning Opportunities

According to some experts, effective early childhood development programs combine adult-guided and child-guided educational activities. Adult-guided activities include active, significant roles for children; child-guided activities include intentional adult roles in which adults take advantage of both learning experiences they planned, and unexpected opportunities for learning. For example, consider the preschool teacher whose class collected acorns outdoors and brought them back into the classroom. The teacher observes two children playing with the acorns. One child divides the acorns into two halves. She spreads her half out into a long row and clusters the other child's half into a pile. The second child becomes upset that she has more acorns than he has. The teacher asks the children how they could find out whether they each have the same number of acorns. Prompted by this intentional question, the second child gets the idea of counting both groups of acorns. The teacher observes, gives supportive comments, and asks thoughtful questions. The children discover they have the same number of acorns despite their arrangements and appearances. This teacher used an unexpected opportunity, helping two children normally in Piaget's preoperational stage of cognitive development to achieve an insight associated with Piaget's later concrete operations stage.

Progress Maps

When teachers find traditional test results do not give students the feedback they need to understand and correct their errors, they can design classroom assessments to help students organize their learning goals. This involves establishing benchmarks to use as criteria in rubrics; identifying transfer levels as referents for rubric expertise levels; making individual student progress maps, plotting their scores over time, and giving them feedback customized according to their developmental or expertise levels; plotting collective student scores on aggregate progress maps, and planning future learning opportunities in response to score clusters and deviations; and informing student self-reflection and personal goal-setting by embedding these progress maps into students' electronic portfolios. Progress maps describe knowledge, skills, and understandings in their typical developmental sequence, depicting longitudinal improvement in specific subjects and domains by organizing longitudinal assessment data according to subject knowledge and skill continua. They include initial baseline assessment data, e.g., at the beginning of a school year, relative to associated standards; and subsequent formative assessments throughout the year according to developmental benchmark criteria. Their visual nature enables quick, easy appraisal of student progress toward subject content standards. Technology makes data collection, organization, and storage most efficient.

Integrating Technology

Examining patterns of teacher and student use of technology can show whether and/or to what degree technology is integrated into their teaching and learning environment. For example, an indication related to teacher activity is use patterns, e.g., the percentage of teachers using computer technologies for a variety of instructional and instruction-related tasks, including locating instructional resources; accessing resources and libraries online; downloading curriculum materials; communicating and networking with colleagues and other professionals; using computers to create instructional tasks, visuals, and/or materials; collaborating with remote teachers and classrooms on projects; communicating with parents; and publishing instructional materials online. Student use patterns, e.g., the percentage of students using computer technologies for various learning and instruction-related tasks, is another indicator of technology integration in the learning environment. Student instruction-related tasks include performing calculations; gathering information from varied sources; information organization and storage; collecting experimental or investigational data; making measurements; analyzing, interpreting, or manipulating data and information to draw conclusions, generate questions, discover relationships; reporting or communicating results, information, or conclusions; creating visual information or data displays; interacting or communicating with classmates, schoolmates, and others outside school; producing audiovisual presentations; composing, editing, and publishing text; creating original art, music, or graphics; publishing materials or projects remotely; and developing understanding of abstract or complex concepts and materials.

Rubrics and Analytical Checklists

A rubric defines in advance a specific behavior(s), skill(s), or task(s) to perform. It supplies basic guidelines for performing task components and criteria for successful performance of each component. Rubrics also typically define general performance ranges and levels, e.g., unsatisfactory, satisfactory, or excellent, briefly describing each level's characteristics. Teachers and/or students can create rubrics or select from existing ones. The teacher should first go over the rubric with students, explaining what each part means, demonstrating when necessary. Then the teacher directs students to follow the rubric as a guide in performing the task. Finally, the teacher uses the rubric's criteria to assess student work. Advantages include combining learning objectives, associated tasks, performance guidance, and task evaluation criteria; and brevity, conciseness, and clarity. Disadvantages include assigning performance levels, not more precise grades or percentages; and perhaps not lending themselves to more detailed assignments. Analytical checklists pre-define certain behaviors, skills, and tasks; teachers check observation of their presence or absence. Advantages include saving time and effort by pre-listing tasks, behaviors, and skills, enabling quick and easy assessment; and making assessment uniform across students in terms of tasks and components. Disadvantages include not identifying additional valuable accomplishments observed (without additional notes); and sometimes limiting assessment to Yes/No formats, though some checklists do incorporate performance levels like rubrics.

Scoring Guides, Anecdotal Notes, and Continua

Scoring guides are typically issued by authors of specific standardized assessment instruments to help teachers and testers score their tests. An obvious advantage of such a scoring guide is that it instructs scorers to follow procedures and interpretations designed by the authors, minimizing chances that scoring will be inaccurate, inappropriate, or interpreted incorrectly. Also, scoring guides do not force assigning specific responses specific scores, but allow some flexibility to use judgment according to individual student responses and test conditions within a reasonable range. Disadvantages include guideline misinterpretation or misapplication by users lacking experience or good judgment. Anecdotal notes have advantages of recording teacher observations of individual student behaviors often not included in standard checklists or test instruments; and collecting information outside of as well as during assessment, which can contribute to valuable insights. Disadvantages include lack of standardization, norms, or criteria for comparison unless a recording teacher includes these; and often, lack of supporting context. Continua offer the advantages of avoiding the limitations of discrete grades, percentages, and numbers, enabling more precise and individualized evaluative description; and more realistic, accurate performance ranges than exact numbers or cutoff scores. Disadvantages include difficulty comparing scores within or among students, classes, and schools without exact numbers, making continua more applicable to individualized than standardized assessment.

Standardized Tests of Ability and of Achievement

Some standardized tests measure abilities, such as intelligence quotient (IQ) tests, which are the most prominent examples; tests of creativity, of divergent thinking (considered a key element of creativity); and more domain-specific abilities, e.g., verbal, numerical, quantitative, spatial abilities, memory, etc., which are often included as subscales on standardized IQ tests. Ability tests do not indicate or necessarily even predict student school grades. They only indicate what a student is capable of, i.e., they gauge competence, not performance. In addition to abilities, some tests measure levels of mental health constructs, e.g., Beck's Depression Inventory and Anxiety Inventory. In contrast to ability and competence or mental and emotional states, standardized achievement tests measure what students actually achieve rather than what they are capable of achieving. Standardized achievement tests are summative evaluations typically given at the ends of school years, not formative evaluations made during instruction. They test what students have learned and can demonstrate knowing and doing. This allows educators to compare individual student progress across years, compare students to peers, and compare their school to others.

Standardized Aptitude Tests

One thing that most standardized aptitude tests share in common with most standardized ability tests is that both types of instruments measure potential rather than accomplishment. For example, IQ tests measure intellectual ability in various cognitive domains, but not how students perform academically—i.e., what grades they actually get in school. Similarly, aptitude tests measure student interest and ability for certain subject areas and domains—not specifically IQ or cognitive levels, but how inclined a student is toward certain activities or areas of interest. Some tests evaluate broader domain aptitudes, e.g., for numerical or mathematical thinking and activities, verbal or literary thinking and activities, etc. Others evaluate interest and ability for more specific activities, e.g., preference tests often used in career counseling with high school students. While these identify discrete interest areas, when some tests combine responses, they may produce strange results not accurately reflecting the whole person or even applicable career directions, e.g., a student whose responses indicated liking books and nature received results recommending careers of librarian or forest ranger—neither was appropriate. Aptitude and preference tests, like IQ tests, differ from achievement tests by testing competence, ability, and interests; achievement tests evaluate learning a student has achieved and can demonstrate.

Norm-Referenced Tests

Norm-referenced tests are standardized tests that provide pre-established norms for student scores on given tests. Before publishing or marketing standardized tests, e.g., national or statewide achievement tests, test authors typically administer their test to groups of students they have selected as samples representative of the larger intended test-taking student population. They then conduct and publish statistical analyses of the scores received by students in the sample groups. These show what the average score or range of scores is, the proportion of students receiving this average, and the distribution of all other scores on the test. Once a test is statistically proven valid and reliable and is published, educators who administer it can compare their students' scores to the established norms supplied with the instrument. This enables school administrators and teachers to compare their students' average and individual performance on the achievement test to the performance of the students in the norm samples. Because the sample students were selected as representative of the national or statewide student population, their scores provide norms against which educators can compare their students' performance. Such comparisons are typically used to satisfy federal and state legal accountability requirements for all schools receiving federal funds to educate their students adequately.

Criterion-Referenced Tests

Whereas norm-referenced tests provide established norms in the form of average scores, all scores, and score distribution of students selected as samples representative of the larger student population, to which educators can compare their own students' scores, criterion-referenced tests do not compare student results to norms or other students. Instead, they compare student results to some pre-established criterion or criteria. Test authors have selected criteria to indicate successful student performance on each item tested. Criteria can include minimum percentage or number out of a total of correct items; minimum number of attributes included in responses; descriptions of required detail, clarity, and/or other features which responses must match or approximate; in some tests, rates of speed, e.g., assessments of oral reading or speaking fluency; or other criteria specific to the skills or learning being evaluated. Student result data from criterion-referenced tests can be used for formative assessment to monitor student progress, evaluate instructional effectiveness and adjust instruction; and/or as parts of summative assessment to demonstrate students have achieved pre-defined learning objectives, in addition to norm-referenced measures.

Validity, Reliability, Raw Scores, and Scaled Scores

Validity in testing means that a test instrument measures what it intends and/or claims to measure. For example, a test validated for educational diagnosis and/or placement could be completely invalid for determining high school graduation. However, the same test might be used for both purposes on the condition that the test has been validated for both. Reliability is consistency, i.e., whether a test yields similar results over repeated administrations. Internal consistency is reliability determined by administering two forms of the same test concurrently and finding they correlate. If one such form is given to students and the other form to the same students a month later—eliminating practice and memory effects from giving the same form both times—and they achieve similar scores in both administrations, this establishes test-retest reliability. Tests can be valid but not reliable, or reliable but not valid. Raw scores are students' actual scores on test scales, e.g., number or percentage correct. Scaled scores convert raw scores to common scales permitting numerical comparison, of individual student progress across semesters and years, among students in subject areas, etc. Scaled scores typically vary within tests among different content-area subscales.

Standard Deviation, Mean, Median, Mode, Grade-Equivalent Scores, and Age-Equivalent Score

Percentile is a statistical ranking method indicating a score or value below which a specified percentage of scores falls within a group. For example, if a student's test score is in the 90th percentile, this means s/he scored higher than 90 percent of other students in the group tested. Standard deviation (SD or σ) is the "mean of the mean," measuring score, data dispersion, variance, or spread. Numerically, SD equals the square root of variance. SDs nearer to 0 indicate all data points clustered close to the average; higher SDs indicate wider distribution. The mean is the average of a data set or score distribution. The median is the middle score in a distribution. The mode is the value or number occurring most frequently in a distribution. Grade-equivalent (GE) scores indicate where on a continuum a student's test score falls. For example, if a 9th-grade student scores a 10.5 GE, this represents the raw score typical of a student in the fifth month of 10th grade. Age-equivalent (AE) scores are based on student age, not grade. For example, for a student aged 7.5 years, a 6 AE score indicates performance typical of a 6-year-old. GE and AE scores should only be used as comparative or relative, not absolute assessment measures.

- 110 -

Analytic Scoring

Analytic scoring separately evaluates and scores discrete writing features, e.g., concise concept expression, creativity, grammar, punctuation, etc. Teachers may average these scores, but more often weigh them by relative importance. Analytic scoring helps teachers consider all writing elements, preventing them from, for example, giving too low a grade because of poor mechanics to an essay with excellent concept expression or problem analysis. By enabling final score breakdowns and teacher comments, it diagnoses areas needing improvement to guide further student efforts. Disadvantages include being time-intensive for teachers, not all students reading their teacher comments, and not using those teacher comments to benefit future assignments. Also, negative feedback, particularly combined with unclear or confrontational comments, can be counterproductive to student development. Written analytic scales define grading criteria and expectations for students. Teachers should weigh criteria by importance, e.g., if an assignment's goal is learning course information, then ideas, organization, and/or logic outweigh grammar and mechanics. Comments should balance challenge with support. Teachers should avoid confrontational practices like sarcastic comments; crossing, scribbling, or blocking out student work; etc.

Holistic Scoring

When teachers have many essays to grade, holistic scoring is less time-consuming than analytic scoring, which divides writing into various components to score separately, deriving the composite score by weighing components according to assignment goals and purposes. Holistic scoring also enables multi-grader scoring. The original teacher chooses at least three student essays which, according to the teacher's criteria based on the learning objectives for the assignment, represent average, high, or low achievement. Using these as models, the teacher and other graders assess many essays written by a class (or classes) of students. Holistic scoring is found highly reliable and consistent as a method of scoring student writing. Because it takes so much less time than analytic scoring, holistic scoring is more efficient. Disadvantages include that, although scores are reliable, individual students are not necessarily informed of specific reasons for their grades. Most teachers write some final comment to give students some idea why their essays were worse, better, or similar to model essays. However, detailed comments throughout as formative feedback for student improvement are not provided as with analytic scoring. Holistic scoring is also most useful for two or more graders and can be impracticable for single instructors.

Explaining Tests and Results to Parents and Students

A common parental question is why their children were tested. Educators can explain to parents that standardized tests can identify their child's school strengths as well as areas where their child may need to improve. They can also evaluate and improve their child's school and the entire school district to provide better education. Educators should also tell parents their children are never evaluated based on a single test, and any assessment program is one among multiple tools evaluating student performance. Some parents are bewildered by scores like percentiles, stanines, grade-equivalent scores, etc. Teachers can help clarify these. For example, "stanine" refers to "standard nine," meaning that on a scale from 1-9, a score of 1-3 is below average, 4-6 is average, and 7-9 is above average. Percentiles tell what percentage of students scored below that percentile. Teachers should explain to parents that a score in the 75th percentile does not mean their child got 75 percent of test items correct; rather, it means their child scored higher than 75 percent of other students in the test group. If a student gets an 8th-grade-equivalent score on a 5th-grade reading achievement test, parents may think their child is ready for 8th-grade material; however, teachers should explain this means their child reads 5th-grade material as well as a typical 8th-grader.

When educators explain the meanings of scores like stanines, percentiles, and grade-level equivalents to parents, they should also explain that these are derived by comparing their child's scores with those of a comparison group, which may be a sample of students representative of the national population or the other students in the school district who took the test at the same time. Discussing a student's test scores relative to other students' scores makes test results most meaningful for parents: teachers can tell them how their child is different and/or similar to others in the group. Parents most often want to know what test scores mean. Teachers should compare student test scores with daily classwork before parent conferences to ensure scores match. Differences can be attributable to subscale scores. For example, a student's overall reading test score may seem adequate in the 75th percentile; but the student's subscale score in comprehension might be in the 85th percentile but in the 65th percentile for vocabulary, indicating need for vocabulary improvement. To track progress, teachers should compare students' present to past scores with parents whenever possible.

When explaining test results to younger students, teachers should avoid technical terms that the students will not understand. They can simplify while preserving general accuracy. For example, rather than telling a young child s/he scored in the 95th percentile, a teacher can say s/he did better than most of the other students. Even among parents, audiences vary, influencing how teachers should communicate test results. For example, if a parent is an educator and/or psychometrist, the teacher can likely give percentiles, stanines, grade-level and age-level equivalents without having to explain them. Such knowledgeable parents may only want to know which comparison group was used; or how their child's score compares to a larger, national comparison group, etc. However, for parents with completely unrelated backgrounds, occupations, or little formal schooling, teachers may omit technical terms entirely or give parents concise, clear definitions of them; either way, be prepared to offer a common-sense equivalent, e.g., their child is doing similarly, better, much better, or worse than most other students in the class, group, or school.

Some parents' cultures and/or countries view education as more unilateral and authoritarian than in America. They may punish children for low test scores; and/or avoid helping children with homework, studying, or getting involved in school, viewing these as inappropriately challenging school and teacher authority. In some cultures, students typically receive few years of formal education; parents from these cultures may have lower expectations for children's educational achievement. Regarding English language proficiency test results, some immigrant families want to abandon their native languages as soon as possible to acquire English, discouraging children from using L1s. When these children are still too young for verbal fluency, this can hinder their proficiency in either language. Educators can explain how L1 proficiency contributes to L2 acquisition. Some parental attitudes positively influence English learning. Parents in communities lacking opportunities for independent English learning have positive attitudes toward English acquisition. Most immigrants, viewing literacy positively as key to succeeding in America, want to learn how to help their children in school. While preserving native cultures and languages, many parents also want to participate in mainstream US culture. Many cultural family structures are stronger and more involved than in America; collective commitment to family exceeds individual motivations.

Professional Environment

Partnering with Students' Families to Support Education

Family involvement improves student attitudes, test scores, grades, post-secondary enrollment, self-esteem, attendance, and behavior. Research finds teacher practices and school policies predict parents' educational involvement more than race, marital status, or education levels. Avoid preconceptions or judgments about families; respect and make them allies in helping students. Contacting and building rapport with families at the beginning of the year, communicating the importance of their contributions and partnership—not meeting only if or when problems arise—sets an inviting tone. Give all families information about ways of creating positive home learning environments, e.g., limiting TV, creating homework spaces, scheduling homework times, and making homework-checking plans. Contacting families at the first signs for concern shows teachers care and respect family contributions. Regular communication—via newsletters, phone calls, meetings, individual and mass emails, etc.—sustains partnerships. Ask about family expectations for children, how they currently support them with schoolwork, how you and the school can help, if hardships are emotionally affecting students, and sibling childcare or other student home responsibilities. Encourage family questions about students, classroom practices, and contacting you. Include families and students in goal-setting, problem-solving, and creating student consequences and rewards. Focus not on inadequate-appearing family involvement, but helping students succeed. Encourage collaboration among parents and families, particularly considering time constraints.

Helping Students, Teachers, and Families with Educational Processes

Guidance counselors can help parents and families by interpreting student scores on standardized tests, identify individual student strengths and needs, counsel students on school programs and career paths, collaborate with teachers on programs supporting student career interests, listen to student academic and social problems and concerns, and make suggestions to improve and support student study habits and social interactions. IEP team members can offer ways to incorporate classroom activities enabling students to address IEP goals and objectives, contributing expertise from their respective disciplines and knowledge about individual students. Special education teachers provide ways of adapting and modifying curriculum and instruction to accommodate special student needs, strategies for inclusive and differentiated instruction, and knowledge about assistive devices. Speech-language therapists can inform teachers of student therapy goals, therapeutic techniques, and how to integrate or connect these with classroom instruction. Physical therapists inform teachers of exercises for gross motor skills development, and make or adapt devices. Occupational therapists inform teachers of fine motor skill development and daily living skills activities. Library media specialists help students and teachers locate, access, and evaluate information resources in various formats, and keep them technologically current. Teachers of the gifted and talented provide accelerated and enrichment activities and compressed and streamlined curricula. Para-educators can complete many routine classroom duties and work one-on-one with individual students.

Factors That Impede School-Home Communication and Parent and Family Participation

Collaborating with families makes teachers' jobs easier and raises student odds of succeeding. Higher family involvement in children's education correlates with higher student achievement. Teachers impede communication when they only tell parents and families what to do; they facilitate communication when they spend equal time listening to families, share teacher and parent or

- 113 -

family expertise equally, and brainstorm together for strategies that best support each student. Diverse family member educational backgrounds can impede communication and participation when parents and families had poor school experiences, feel ineffectual due to their own histories as unsuccessful students, feel alienated from school processes by differing cultural or linguistic backgrounds, and/or experience language barriers to communicating. Parental availability and participation can be affected by family dynamics including number of children, work schedules, transportation, custody arrangements, etc. Teachers who collaborate non-judgmentally can address such constraints with appropriate solutions. Teachers should initiate positive parent and family communication when school years start, not wait for problem-related contact; not wait for problem escalation to contact parents; give every family suggestions for establishing positive learning environments at home; maintain regular communication using phone calls, conferences, meetings, emails, and newsletters; inquire about home conditions and parent and family expectations; encourage family questions; and collaborate on student goals, effective reinforcers, and consequences.

Strategies for Effective Parent-Teacher Conferences

Experienced teachers advise always starting with some positive student aspect, working into needed improvements, and sandwiching criticisms between positives. Some teachers send conference invitations with forms requesting parents write and return questions or concerns before meeting; and include lists of major topics covered and expectations for each student, so parents are prepared for collaborating during conferences on plans to help students. Keeping student work samples handy for conferences is another strategy. Some teachers design games and ideas parents can use at home with their children. Some write pre-conference notes on student strengths and needs. Teachers emphasize the importance of thanking parents for attending conferences and listening to parents. Administrators also encourage teacher conference preparation, including having specific suggestions prepared for parents asking how they can help. Teachers advise reviewing two or three things students can improve, and asking parents to contact them in the weeks following conferences to report whether students have improved. Tactful phrasing prevents antagonizing parents and students. Some teachers include students in parent conferences. Some agree on one or two goals with students and parents early, then stay in communication throughout the year about goal progress and future plans. Some include student-led conferences about report cards, portfolios, etc.

Benefits of Teacher Participation in School and District Committees and Activities

By participating in school functions and projects, teachers access opportunities to work with professional colleagues. Collaborating on committees enables teachers to solve problems for both their students and themselves. Committees work both during school days and during extracurricular events and activities, e.g., PTA (or PTO) nights and school open houses. Teacher participation in such events and committees enables both communication with parents and demonstration to students their interest and support for them beyond academics. Whether students have extracurricular activities frequently depends on teacher support. Numbers and types of committees available for teacher participation expand opportunities for professional development; keep teachers engaged in school activities; and benefit those with whom teachers share their time, individual expertise, and special interests. In addition to traditional department, faculty, staff, and PTA meetings, teachers help other committees decide school rules; disciplinary actions; furnish leadership for athletic and intramural events, concerts, recitals, plays, musicals, book fairs, carnivals, field trips, talent shows, awards, hospitality, holiday programs, and fundraising; safety maintenance and crisis management, child abuse prevention, gang and/or drug awareness and prevention; multicultural awareness; tutoring; new teacher mentoring; technology;

school spirit; special population admission, review, and dismissal; instructional continuity; curriculum design, textbook identification and adoption; needs assessments; and faculty professional development and individual content-area training.

Teacher Appraisal Systems

Experts maintain that reflective teachers fear neither self-evaluation nor evaluation by others, but seek experienced other educators' opinions to inform their self-improvement to serve students best. Teacher performance appraisals are typically conducted annually by trained administrators who observe individual teachers throughout the school year and apply established criteria for identifying acceptable performance. Appraisal systems evaluate teachers in areas including: student-centered instruction; successful, active student participation in learning; student progress evaluation and feedback; time, material, instructional strategy, and student discipline management; professional communication; professional development; requirement, policy, and operating procedure compliance; and improvement of all students' academic performance. Administrators evaluate and score teachers separately in each area. In addition to scores and teacher observations, documents and procedures can include teacher self-reports, annual printed summative appraisal reports (which administrators share with teachers), and annual summative conferences. Typical rules include not making classroom observations right before holidays or at the very beginning or end of the school year, time limits for assessors to provide feedback following observations, and time limits for teachers to dispute assessments in writing. Teachers receiving unsatisfactory ratings typically must follow growth or improvement plans. Teachers can prepare by requesting mentor observation and feedback, and planning lessons according to prescribed formats aligned with appraisal systems.

Working with Mentors

Mentors provide newer teachers insights, resources, and strategies developed through years of experience, reassurance regarding challenges, and non-judgmental support. In student relationships and classroom management, they help teachers identify ineffective and inconsistent responses to student misbehavior, arrange classrooms for lesson activities, and organize material distribution and collection. They help with gaps in subject-area content knowledge, specialized vocabulary, information-accessing resources, and content-area emphasis decisions. They also help with unit planning addressing performance standards; incorporating lifelong learning skills; connecting lessons coherently; and including varied challenges, activities, and experiences for extending and applying text and teacher information. Mentors help teachers understand appropriate per-lesson material amounts and student need for clear directions, spiraling material, and regular review; include techniques activating and building on existing student knowledge and relating content to student experiences and interests; activities related to real-world experiences that apply learning; challenges with gradually increasing difficulty requiring individual and cooperative student discovery and work; and questions requiring higher-order cognitive skills. They help teachers implement lesson plans effectively by timing activities properly, anticipating and incorporating student responses into additional questions and discussions, and determining when to diverge from plans regarding student responses; and design, select, and refine and manage assessments. They help teachers contact and interact with supervisors, school staff, and parents; meet supervisor expectations; self-evaluate and pursue professional development.

Findings About the Benefits of Teacher Collaboration

Evidence is mounting of positive correlations between teacher collaboration and student achievement. Researchers have found lower rates of turnover among new teachers at schools providing support through induction and mentoring programs. Teachers report strong collegial relationships, decision-making involvement, and self-efficacy beliefs afford greater personal satisfaction. Though all teachers' sharing responsibility for all students' success and support for new teachers enhance teacher satisfaction and retention, this occurs at the minority of schools. In the majority, teachers plan and teach alone; even in states that fund mentoring programs, new teachers are not guaranteed the support they need or want. Experts recommend school leaders earmark resources for supporting collaboration in classroom observations, planning, and mentoring; engage experienced teachers in both professional development and inducting and mentoring new teachers; and cultivate shared responsibility. Studies find teacher collaboration often dramatically turns around student achievement at chronically low-performing schools within a few years. Case studies find teachers collaborate by meeting to review student work relative to standards and target instructional improvements, form teams for aligning lessons across grade levels and self-plan professional development, receive regular lead teacher and coach support, access data guiding instructional decisions and planning, and share planning time.

Teacher Roles in Shaping Policy and Advocating for the Teaching Profession

Teachers play important roles in nurturing and preparing not only students, but also the next generation of teachers. Secretary of Education Arne Duncan stated public education for coming decades will be shaped by attracting and retaining "the best talent... to elevate and strengthen the teaching profession," which he said would require "massive cultural change" but have "extraordinary" long-term impacts. The US Department of Education (ED), in efforts to enlist this next teacher generation, started the TEACH.org project, subsequently reforming it as a public-private partnership with Microsoft. ED's related Project RESPECT (Recognizing Educational Success, Professional Excellence and Collaborative Teaching) temporarily employs active classroom teachers for input about federal budget proposals, widespread teaching reform efforts, and redefining teaching in the global economy. Elements include attracting and preparing diverse, high-performing talent; creating a professional career continuum with competitive compensation; creating conditions for success; supporting and evaluating teacher and leader development and success; providing highest-need students with the best educators; and transitioning to a more effective educational system beyond the project grant. Duncan identified RESPECT goals as elevating teacher voices in federal, state, and local education policy; collaborating with educators to rebuild teaching; and making teaching "not only America's most important... but most respected profession."

Benefits, Characteristics, and Elements of School Partnerships with Community Members

Schools' broad-based community involvement, and development and implementation of strategies promoting effective partnerships strengthen schools, families and communities and improve all students' learning. When schools share responsibility for student learning with families and communities, students can see how school curriculum and skills required in the real world are connected. They have more opportunities for engaged, meaningful learning. Schools can use meetings, interviews, and surveys to identify not perceived, but true family and community strengths and needs to develop policies and programs for involvement and partnership. Community needs assessments help school action teams develop involvement program goals leading to full policies reflecting supported involvement levels and types, school priorities for formal partnerships with community businesses and agencies, outreach approaches, and developing parent education and support programs. Some partnerships include learning compacts ensuring shared stakeholder responsibility for education and defining school, parent, family, and community goals, expectations, and responsibilities. Local needs, resources, and interests determine each specific community's most applicable strategies. Important elements include

- 116 -

identifying varied means of community member involvement; activities mutually valuable and meaningful to students, schools, and community; emphasizing two-way communication; school outreach soliciting community constituencies' involvement and support; and redefining schools as community learning centers.

Research vs. Practice

Educational researchers and educators alike agree that the gap between research and practice, while varied and complex, requires more cooperation between researchers and practitioners. Some researchers propose professional learning communities, and/or design-based research models (rather than only research-based design) as solutions. Some, distinguishing research-based knowledge published in journals vs. classroom teachers' pedagogical knowledge, perceive researcher-practitioner tension attributable to researchers' seeking new knowledge vs. practitioners' seeking new solutions to operational problems. Others distinguish fundamental gaps, i.e., disagreements about vocabulary, reward systems, and the nature of theory and knowledge; from practical gaps, i.e., different time and resource allocations, authority issues, and lack of cross-organizational collaboration. From literature reviews, some researchers have identified four interrelated issues characterizing research-practice gaps. (1) Education research yields insufficient valid, reliable, or conclusive results. (2) Education research has limited practical applications. (3) Teachers find educational research not meaningful, conclusive, or practical. (4) Teachers either lack the skills to apply research findings, or seldom apply it appropriately. Proposed solutions include more researcher-educator cooperation and collaboration; more educator involvement in research processes; including research training in educator preparation; and replacing top-down, linear models of disseminating research knowledge and developing and disseminating educational innovations with mutual, two-way, circular models.

Interpreting the Results, Data, and Conclusions of Research

Authors of educational journal articles, speakers at teacher education conventions, and others frequently cite research in support of opinions about learning and teaching. However, as researchers themselves point out (e.g., Ediger, 2000), apparently those citing or even quoting research do not necessarily determine a particular study's quality. For example, a study may examine teaching practices and student outcomes in only one school district, county, or state, but not nationwide. If a study references a conclusion "according to" a specific standardized test, the conclusion stated by that instrument was contextual; different instruments could reach different conclusions. Hence to interpret educational research, teachers should consider researchers clearly state their study's purpose without pre-study opinions or vague assertions. They must remember study participants vary in intelligence, motivation, reasons for learning, achievement capabilities, socioeconomic levels, etc.; researchers cannot always control for all variables. Hypotheses must also be stated clearly. Teachers may need to accept statistical formulas, e.g., for determining significance levels, on faith as these are often too difficult for non-statisticians to understand. Experimental study averages, such as those of student scores, do not reflect individual high and low extremes. Student scores on specific tests and in studies may contradict their typical performance.

Purposes, Characteristics and Benefits, and Teacher Uses of Educational Research

Purposes: research informs educational policy and practices; supports high-quality instruction for all students; and stimulates discussions among educators, parents, business leaders, legislators and other stakeholders. Characteristics and benefits: teachers do not passively receive research findings; they actively decide its implications for classroom practice, give researchers guidance, and conduct their own classroom-based research. Research explicitly describes its guiding beliefs and assumptions, enabling teachers to inform instructional practices with varied theoretical orientations and viewpoints, e.g., research into writing as an individual cognitive process and a social process, respectively. Research also explicitly describes its methodology and explains how methods address classroom realities, enabling teacher insights. Research benefiting teaching and learning is trustworthy and plausible via utilizing methods appropriate to research questions and applying those methods rigorously enough. Such research must also be ethical. Teacher uses: teachers study research to inform instruction, critique research by asking evaluative questions, strategically select research most promising for enhancing teaching and learning based on their knowledge about theory and the relationship of theory and research, apply research to their own classroom practice, and conduct research to answer their own classroom questions and concerns systematically.

Teacher Self-Assessment Model

One teacher self-assessment model (Silver Strong & Associates, 2011) synthesizing much of the best instructional design research from constructivist perspectives has nine dimensions, resulting from combining two main component categories: (I) Instructional Design and Delivery, containing five elements; and (II) Four Cornerstones of Effective Teaching, containing four elements. The five elements for category (I) are: (1) preparing students for new learning (knowledge anticipation), (2) presenting new learning (knowledge acquisition), (3) deepening learning (practicing and processing new knowledge), (4) helping students reflect on and celebrate learning (reflecting on new knowledge), and (5) applying learning (knowledge application). The four elements for category (II) are: (1) organization, rules, and procedures; (2) positive relationships; (3) a culture of thinking and learning; and (4) engagement and enjoyment. Teachers rate themselves on each dimension using a four-point scale of (1) novice, (2) developing, (3) proficient, or (4) expert (or "NA" for self-assessment questions not applicable to an individual teacher's work). The model includes checklists of student behaviors indicating teacher effectiveness in each dimension. For example, for category (II), element (1), organization, rules and procedures, student behaviors include demonstrating respect for the classroom and one another, understanding and following rules and procedures, access to needed resources, using time well, self-direction, responsibility for learning, positive attitudes, and conflict-resolution techniques. Teachers also write ideas for improvement.

School and Community

No single person educates a child. Everyone in a child's community (both inside and outside of school) helps that child develop into the citizen he or she will be as an adult. Although schools have the primary responsibility of educating children, community engagement is a vital aspect of any truly successful school. Teachers can always use additional classroom resources to improve the effectiveness of education inside of the classroom. That might entail borrowing a book from a local library or bringing in a professional guest speaker from the community. In a large number of ways, community resources contribute to the development of students each year. One characteristic of a successful teacher is his or her ability to build and maintain positive partnerships with members of the community. Effective school-community partnerships are marked by a sense of ownership and pride of a school, its students, and its successes. A supportive community will come out to support its school at athletic contests, musical/theatre performances, and other events throughout the year. An involved school can give back to its community through service and volunteer projects in coordination with local institutions (e.g., hospitals, nursing homes, shelters, and soup kitchens).

Professional Organizations

In addition to research, mentors, supervisors, and colleagues, professional development resources for educators include professional organizations. Discipline-specific and other organizations enhance educator knowledge, expertise, and skills through conventions, conferences, workshops, trainings, publications, online courses, networking, local chapters, etc. Organizations include: the American Association of School Administrators, National Association of Elementary School Principals, National Art Education Association, American Counseling Association, American School Counselors Association, National Association for the Education of Young Children, American Library Association, International Reading Association, National Council of Teachers of English, American Council on the Teaching of Foreign Languages, Teachers of English to Speakers of Other Languages, Council for Exceptional Education, National Association for Gifted Children, National Council of Teachers of Mathematics, American Association of Physics Teachers, National Association of Biology Teachers, National Science Teachers Association, National Council for the Social Studies, Council for Exceptional Education, National Association for Sport and Physical Education, American Educational Research Association, Association for Educational Communication and Technology, American Federation of Teachers (AFL-CIO union), National Education Association (union), Association for Childhood Education International, Association for Supervision and Curriculum Development, National Middle School Association, National PTA, National School Boards Association, and National Staff Development Council.

Determining Professional Development Goals

US states typically certify or license college graduates to teach in public schools for two years or similar periods with the expectation they will attain master's degrees or some other additional certification during that time. Teachers meeting state-established goals earn more advanced licensure. Even teachers with advanced graduate degrees must continue throughout their careers to set and achieve goals. Mentor teachers help new teachers set personal goals, develop personal development plans (PDPs), and document ongoing professional activities. Goals can include reading professional literature, attending educational conferences and seminars, etc., as well as taking college and graduate courses, accruing continuing education units (CEUs), etc. School district professional development committees (PDCs) work with new teachers and mentors to assure goals meet established district guidelines, sometimes paying workshop tuition. Teacher PDP approval by PDCs gives state licensure boards documentation of new teacher efforts to meet state requirements. PDCs and district administrators collaboratively set district-wide professional teacher goals, both subject-specific and interdisciplinary—e.g., aligning curricula with state standards and raising standardized test scores. PDCs offer all teachers training that targets district goals. Teacher, mentor, and PDC goal-setting must meet state education department standards. Goals should also be SMART—*specific, measurable, attainable, relevant/result-oriented*, and *time-limited*.

Professional Development Resources

Educational research studies often evaluate the effectiveness of various instructional practices. Educators benefit from many available literature reviews, meta-analyses, compilations, or other syntheses identifying consensus on effective practices to implement. Federal and state education departments, boards, and local school districts frequently adopt research-based instructional practices for individual teachers to follow. Professional organizations also disseminate research findings and provide courses, workshops, and conferences where members can learn additional information, insights, skills, and techniques to improve their teaching and student learning. A common route for teachers to improve knowledge and practical expertise is through graduate courses. Some teachers begin with bachelor's degrees, then complete master's degrees while working, obtaining more advanced knowledge of pedagogy and specific subject-area content, higher-level teaching certification, and salaries. Some certified in general education subsequently complete graduate courses in educational specialties. Some get degrees or certificates in additional subjects and specialties, e.g., math plus science, multiple languages, English plus ESL, special education plus early childhood education, etc. Mentors personally and individually advance PD, helping educators with PD plans; observing and providing feedback; sharing their knowledge, experience, and expertise; and providing reassurance, encouragement, and support. Pre-service internships provide closely supervised on-the-job practice and experience. Study groups and learning communities enable information sharing; learning communities also allow workshop and presentation collaborations, etc.

Helping Educators Utilize and Integrate Technology into Instructional Design and Delivery

Contemporary technology not only greatly facilitates and enhances instruction, learning, and education overall, but integrating technology into instruction has become a necessity now that society depends on and requires its use so heavily. Among many available resources, one is the International Society for Technology in Education (ISTE), offering consulting services and helping educators develop customized PD learning programs. Workshops include one providing in-depth examination of worldwide educational initiatives using technology. Another, for teachers and educational leaders with advanced technology skills, teaches ISTE Standards and how to teach others these in schools or through peer coaching. A virtual workshop gives lead teachers hands-on experiences in designing learning activities embedding ISTE Standards, measuring activity effectiveness, and working district-wide with faculty teams to integrate these standards across the curriculum. A three-day onsite leadership academy provides in-depth PD knowledge and understanding of ISTE Standards; and instruction from experts in these standards regarding the conditions essential to implementing them at district, school, and classroom levels. ISTE mobile learning support services help educators and stakeholders apply prevalent (and popular with students) mobile technology for learning. ISTE's classroom observation tool measures effective classroom technology integration. ISTE offers school administrators and principals digital citizenship, technology leadership institutes, a standards readiness workshop, and essential conditions readiness Survey.

Reflection

Reflection enables teachers to gain some distance and objectivity to analyze their instructional practices and interactions with students, which in turn enables them to identify, plan, and implement measures to improve these for improved student learning. To track their effectiveness in the classroom, teachers should establish baselines early in the school year. They can keep journals, writing their reflections about classroom interactions as often as possible. Selecting one high-achieving and one low-achieving student in a class and charting how the teacher's professional relationship with each student develops can often accurately reflect learning opportunities the teacher provides for all students. Writing honestly and rereading previous entries regularly help teachers change their behaviors to improve student-teacher relationships, hence learning. Many pre-designed self-assessment checklists, questionnaires, and tools help teachers evaluate their practices systematically and use their responses to reinforce or expand teaching strengths and address weaknesses. Through peer assessment, teachers have colleagues observe and provide feedback on their instruction: others often see behaviors and omissions we cannot, and/or provide alternate perspectives. The "critical friend" method is similar. Systematic incident analysis enables teacher insights into student behaviors and teacher-student interactions and how changing teacher behaviors can change student behaviors. Portfolios enable teachers to review work development and changes longitudinally.

Reflection Questions That a Teacher Might Ask Him or Herself After a Classroom Activity

1. What were the learning objectives for this experience? Did I expect too much or too little of the students?
2. Did this experience work well? Did the students react positively or negatively? What data do I have that this experience was (un)successful?
3. What can I change about this lesson? Is it possible to better prepare my students for this lesson next year?
4. What questions should I have asked before the experience? Which questions should I have asked after the experience?
5. What student behavior was most notable? Did any circumstances from outside the classroom affect this behavior?
6. How do my students learn? Would my students learn better in some different way?
7. Were all my students actively participating in this experience? How can I adapt my lesson to make it more student-centered?
8. What data do I need to make an informed decision about this activity's effectiveness? What plans should I make to get this data in the future?
9. What do my data tell me? How can I adjust my expectations and my activity based upon the data I got?
10. Can my students meet the objectives in a more efficient manner? Does this activity need less time or more time? How can I adjust for next year?

Practices That Apply Research Data Finding Them Effective for Instructing Students

Cognitive research studies have established that comparing, contrasting, and classifying help students understand complex concepts. Teaching students to identify idea similarities and differences applies these findings. Research shows students' higher-order cognitive skills for analysis and synthesis, in-depth analysis, and reading comprehension improve through effectively summarizing information and note-taking. Teaching students how and assigning them to summarize and take notes efficiently applies research to improve instruction and achievement. Educational achievement motivation research demonstrates the impact of recognition for reinforcing and monitoring student effort, e.g., symbolic or abstract recognition is more effective than concrete rewards; rewards contingent on meeting some performance standard are most effective; 8-year-olds' learning strategies differ radically from 12-year-olds' and adults' strategies; and 8-year-olds learn mainly from positive feedback, not negative. Teachers raise student achievement by recognizing, rewarding, and praising specific goal achievements. Studies show learning occurs linguistically and non-linguistically; visual or other non-linguistic representations help students understand, retain, retrieve, connect, and apply knowledge; and the more students combine linguistic and non-linguistic systems, the better they learn and think. Teachers apply these findings using multimodal instruction. Additional research-based effective teaching practices include practice, homework, objectives, feedback, generating hypotheses, testing hypotheses, advance organizers, questions, cues, cooperative learning, and teaching and assigning nonfictional writing.

Feedback

Teachers receive feedback from a number of sources (e.g., students, parents, colleagues, department leaders, and school administrators). Some (but not all) of the feedback will be useful. Feedback like "I don't like your class" does not give a teacher the opportunity to improve his or her classroom practice. Other feedback like, "Try to allow more wait time between asking a question and calling upon a student to answer" is more specific and teachers can act on this. Helpful feedback and less helpful feedback both provide a teacher with the opportunity to initiate a conversation on his or her pedagogy. In response to non-anonymous feedback, a teacher can ask follow-up questions to clear up any vagueness. Feedback can be something to talk over with a mentor, an invitation to initiate a discussion within a professional learning community, or even a starting point at which to begin a process of action research in the classroom. Unfortunately the feedback a teacher receives (particularly from students) is not always helpful and in some cases can be hurtful. A beginning teacher must remember not to take feedback personally. A professional teacher is only expected to do the best that he or she can to improve based upon the appropriate feedback he or she receives.

Characteristics Associated with Helpful Feedback (TOTAL)

1. **Targeted**: Feedback should be targeted towards a goal and allow the subject of the feedback to adjust his or her actions in an effort to improve. Vague or imprecise feedback is not only unhelpful but can also be misleading.
2. **Ongoing**: For feedback to be useful, individuals must have the ongoing opportunity to improve.
3. **Timely**: Feedback must be timely. Late arriving feedback deprives an individual of the opportunity to improve recent behavior or efficiently affect better results.
4. **Actionable**: "Great Work" or "This is not right" are not examples of good feedback. Both lack the specificity necessary to be useful. Good feedback can be acted upon. Adjustments can be made in response to specific and useful suggestions on how to improve.
5. **Level-Headed**: Feedback must be genuine, trustworthy, and not overly ambitious. Improvement in any endeavor is an incremental process that is best accomplished slowly, in short increments over long intervals of time. A feedback recipient must be able to trust that a critique is both sensible and prudent.

Resources Available to Help Professional Development and Enhance Effectiveness

Every educator in the world (at universities, colleges, and schools of every type) is a part of a professional learning community, in the broadest sense of that phrase. The growth of the internet and data resources have made teacher professional development more available than it has ever been before. Websites like *Edutopia* can help a teacher stay current with the latest technology or innovative pedagogy. National organizations (e.g., NCTE, NCTM, NCSS, and NSTA) offer memberships for teachers in every field and each offers publications and web based resources. National and state-based organizations organize conferences at which educators come together to share and collaborate. Numerous research journals are published regularly and are searchable via indexing services (e.g., ERIC and JSTOR). Journals regularly publish peer-reviewed articles featuring the best new ideas in teaching and learning in their fields. A virtually innumerable amount of resources is available for every teacher who wishes to stay current. A modern professional teacher is one that is open to new ideas and is willing to put forth the effort to learn about new pedagogical methods. A modern professional teacher is willing to try to implement new classroom methods based upon new learning about the best practices.

Implicit Teacher Bias

Implicit teacher biases are stereotypes or attitudes that are manifested unconsciously in the classroom. In some cases these biases may adversely affect student learning. One pervasive stereotype is that girls are not able to do mathematics as well as boys. A math teacher may subconsciously call on boys more often or praise girls less often. Boys may do better in this math class because they are given more opportunities or praise, which may not be available to girls

- 122 -

because of a stereotype. As a teacher, awareness of potential biases is the first step in overcoming them. Teachers should reflect on their teaching practice and collect/analyze classroom evidence (data) to determine if biases are present. In order for each student to have a fair chance to succeed, teachers must recognize each as an individual, rather than a member of some stereotypical group (e.g., athletic team, ethnic group, gender, or those with past behavioral issues).

Mentors as a Resource for Strengthening Teacher Knowledge, Skills, and Effectiveness

Collegial collaboration is the basis of quality educational practice. No individual can reach every student or solve every problem. In recent years, a number of school systems have begun formal programs to help train veteran teachers to serve as mentors for younger teachers. A mentor is a veteran teacher who is accepting of a new teacher, is effective in a variety of different interpersonal contexts, and adept at providing instructional support. A mentor is empathetic, optimistic, and open to development in new aspects of the teaching profession. A mentor is a resource who can provide insight into the culture of a school, share tips and tricks that he or she has picked up over the years, and talk about how to resolve challenging circumstances. A mentor is a colleague who can put issues into their proper perspective and reassure a new teacher who may feel isolated or overwhelmed.

Professional Learning Community (PLC)

Although the phrase "professional learning community" can have multiple meanings, PLCs are most often small groups of educators who meet on a regular basis to discuss and collaborate to improve teaching skills and student academic performance. Professional learning communities might discuss the creation or editing of class materials, completed student work as exemplars of student learning, data from student assessments, or professional literature pertinent to classroom experience. The focus of professional learning communities is learning: student learning and teacher learning about student learning. Professional learning communities can offer an opportunity for teachers to engage in reflection on teaching practice and cycles of action research or other evidence-based adaptations of classroom activities/assessments towards better student performance.

Professional Versatility

Education has never been and will never be a one-size-fits-all endeavor. No two learners are exactly the same and no two classes are exactly the same. What works for one student or class may not work for another. Given the diversity of students in the classroom, open-mindedness and a willingness to adapt are arguably the most important characteristics of successful teachers. Both as an individual in the classroom and as a part of a professional learning community outside of the classroom, an openness to the possibility of a new approach allows a teacher to persevere through the most challenging of circumstances. Challenges encountered might arise due to: behavioral problems, learning differences, student exceptionalities, technology, and any of a number of possible distractions originating inside or outside the classroom. A versatile teacher open to collaboration with colleagues, creative problem solving, and trying new methods can overcome almost any challenge.

Action Research

Action research is a process of reflective classroom inquiry performed by the teacher. Action research is a technique through which a teacher might refine his or her teaching practice by using available data to inform new methods or mechanisms of student learning. The four generic stages for action research are: Plan, Act, Observe, and Reflect. A teacher plans a learning experience for his or her students and then puts that plan into action. The teacher observes his or her students' reactions during the experience and the learning results (positive or negative) through either formative or summative assessment. After analyzing the available quantitative and/or qualitative data, the teacher formulates a new plan of action for future student learning experiences and the action research process begins again. Action-based research is the most natural mechanism of classroom study for the teacher. The teacher is using the evidence available in a scientific process to improve his or her educational practice. Action research is one example of the evidence-based educational practice advocated by the standards.

Investigating a Problem Using a Mixed Methods Study

Quantitative methodologies are adept at answering "if" questions. Numerical-based methods can help answer questions regarding whether there is evidence that a particular pattern is occurring. For example, a study of test scores will tell you **if** your students understand a given concept. Qualitative (text-based) methods are adept at answering "how" or "why" questions. For example, qualitative (text-based) methods would be required to determine **why** students have not learned a given concept well. Mixed method inquiry (including both quantitative and qualitative aspects) can greatly benefit an educator seeking to grow as a professional by providing both direct verdicts and indirect contexts to questions of pedagogical effectiveness.

Quantitative and Qualitative Research Methods

Quantitative methods are deductive in nature. Quantitative investigators will collect and analyze numerical data with mathematical and statistical tools. An example of a quantitative method would be to compare the results of a pre-test (before a lesson) and a post-test (after a lesson) to determine **if** a lesson was effective. Quantitative methods are commonly applied in scientific fields in which numerical data is available (e.g., biology and physics).

Qualitative methods are inductive in nature. Qualitative investigators will collect and analyze textual data collected from interviews, observations, or conversations. An example of a qualitative method would be to discuss a lesson (after the fact) and ask the students for their perceptions about the effectiveness of the lesson. Qualitative methods will help determine **why** students were or were not successful on a given assessment. Qualitative methods are commonly applied in fields studying human behavior (e.g., marketing and sociology).

Pros and cons of quantitative and qualitative research methods:

- Quantitative methods are number-based. Qualitative methods are text-based. Numerical methods can determine **if** students are learning about a particular concept. Qualitative methods would be required if a teacher wished to understand **why** students were not learning a given concept.
- Quantitative methods are more objective; numerical data is gathered using unbiased measurements. Qualitative methods are more subjective. Researchers must interpret the results of interviews or discussions and can be susceptible to implicit or explicit biases.
- Quantitative methods tend to require more planning time before implementation while qualitative measures require more time after the implementation. Numerical data are more straightforward to analyze but more difficult to collect. Textual data are more challenging to analyze but less cumbersome to collect.

- Quantitative methods are stricter in their design; collected responses must be numerical. Qualitative methods are more open-ended in their design; a greater variety of responses can be accepted and analyzed.
- Both quantitative and qualitative methods can be shown as valid and reliable.

Legal Rights and Responsibilities of Teachers, Students, and Parents

Teachers have Fourteenth Amendment rights to due process receiving termination notice; protection from discrimination based on race, gender, and nationality; privacy; setting student behavior rules and directions, training students to follow rules, requesting support with student behavior; First Amendment academic freedom of expression, limited by student age and grade level, teacher experience, subject content—specifically prohibiting political or personal class discussions; rights and responsibilities to correct, guide, or punish students to meet educational objectives; student custodial responsibilities; training students in moral values and civilized citizenship. Federal rights include for students with disabilities to free, appropriate public education in the least restrictive environment under the Individuals with Disabilities Education Act (IDEA), which gives parents due process rights to advance notice and refusal of identification, evaluation, and placement for special education and related services; to appeal school decisions about their children, etc. Other student rights and responsibilities vary by state and district. An example (Fairfax County Public Schools, Virginia) includes rights to attend safe, welcoming schools; property safety; fairness, respect, and courtesy from school staff and other students; freedom of expression; advocacy for change in laws, regulations, and policies; complaint and response; expulsion and suspension disputes; responsibilities for timely attendance, dress, rule-following; respecting others' rights, property, beliefs, and differences; staff authority; peaceful dispute resolution; not bullying, hurting others, or using violent, obscene, disruptive, or disrespectful words, gestures, and images; and reporting dangerous behavior to staff.

Teacher Roles at Progressive Levels of Qualification, Experience, and Expertise

While specific districts and schools must determine teacher roles and responsibilities, ED provides an example: resident teachers are beginners—not teachers of record, but paid; not student teachers, but completing a (typically 1-year) Master teacher-supervised residency or practicum. Novice teachers are certified, but still developing; paired with master teachers; not tenured, but may receive tenure; typically promoted after two to five years, possibly after two consecutive years' of effective ratings. Professional teachers are tenured, lifelong learner exemplars, academic coaches and advocates. Many teachers spend whole careers at the professional level. Master teachers, key school leadership team members, work in classrooms, lead school teams, and are teaching resources for the whole professional team, modeling effective teaching practices for resident and novice teachers, teaching both students and colleagues—sometimes dividing hours between classrooms and faculty support. They typically have worked at least five years in classrooms, being rated highly effective at least three years. Teacher leaders also divide time between classrooms and working with leadership teams and principals, e.g., sharing distributed leadership, designing peer evaluation and review systems, and developing communities of practice. They have at least five classroom years, demonstrating effectiveness at least three consecutive years. Each level earns more. With development, master teachers and teacher leaders may become principals.

Instructing Special-Needs Students

With legal mandates for inclusive education and mainstreaming being today's prevalent trend, special education students frequently end up in regular education classrooms, whose teachers are required to instruct them. This can happen even when students are found eligible for special

- 125 -

education and related services, assigned a special education teacher, educational specialist, various therapists, other service personnel based on individual student needs, or Individual Education Plans (IEPs) and learning goals. Teachers collaborate with special educators, who provide knowledge and expertise about classroom accommodations and modifications, differentiated instruction, etc. However, teachers are still responsible for special-needs students' instruction unless student IEPs specify otherwise. Diverse student needs including disabilities; ELL or LEP status; and varied cultural, racial, ethnic, and socioeconomic backgrounds require teachers to ensure all students receive educational equity by making curricular, instructional, and classroom environmental modifications and/or accommodations, including selecting or adapting materials to reflect multicultural perspectives; differentiating instruction; consciously avoiding bias, offering equal opportunities, and treating all students fairly. Teachers are both legally and ethically required to keep student records confidential and protect their personal information's privacy. By copyright law, teachers must also request and obtain author or publisher permission to use copyrighted materials as teaching resources.

Family Educational Rights and Privacy Act (FERPA)

FERPA applies to all schools receiving federal funds under applicable ED programs. Parents and eligible students (aged 18 or attending post-secondary school) have rights to inspect and review schools' student education records; to request school corrections of misleading or inaccurate records; to formal hearings if schools refuse to amend records; and if schools still refuse following hearings, to file statements contesting information with records. Schools must generally obtain written parent or eligible student permission to release information from student education records. However, records disclosure without consent is allowed by FERPA to these parties or under these conditions: school officials having valid educational interests, schools where students transfer, specified auditing and evaluating officials, appropriate student financial aid-related personnel, accrediting associations, those conducting certain studies on school behalf, by legal subpoena or judicial order, appropriate personnel in safety and health emergencies, and by specific state laws and local juvenile justice system authorities. FERPA allows schools to disclose student names, addresses, phone numbers, birthdates, birthplaces, attendance dates, honors, awards and other "directory" information without consent. However, schools are first required to inform parents or eligible students and allow them enough time to request non-disclosure. FERPA requires schools to notify parents or eligible students annually of their FERPA rights.

Equal Access Act (1984)

The federal Equal Access Act (1984) prohibits discrimination against student religious groups in public high schools receiving federal funds. Such schools having at least one non-curriculum, student-led club meeting outside class hours ("limited open forum") must allow organization of additional such clubs and equal access to school meeting places and publications. Groups interfering with orderly school activities are exceptions. Technically, schools can prohibit all non-curriculum clubs to "opt out" of this law. In *Westside Community Schools v. Mergens* (1990), the Supreme Court declared this law constitutional, ordering the school let a Christian student group meet. It has been invoked in lawsuits against school administrations denying Gay-Straight Alliance assembly and privileges. State Supreme Courts have always ruled in favor of these alliances, saying schools must either allow them or ban all non-curriculum group assembly. Two major legislative acts governing privacy and confidentiality of student education records in schools are the Family Educational Rights and Privacy Act (FERPA, 1974) and Individuals with Disabilities Education Act (IDEA, formerly PL 94-142, 1975). Both grant similar rights to parents and eligible students (aged 18 or attending post-secondary schools) to review or inspect records, request correction, have formal hearings, document contested information, and advance notice and non-disclosure of directory information.

American Association of Educators (AAE) Code of Ethics for Educators

Principle I: Ethical Conduct toward Students – Educators interact justly, considerately with every student, resolving disciplinary and other problems by school policy and law; eschew intentionally exposing students to disparagement; protect student information confidentiality unless laws require otherwise; constructively endeavor to protect students from conditions harming safety, health, or learning; and seek to present facts without bias, personal prejudice, or distortion. Principle II: Ethical Conduct toward Practices and Performance – Educators meet appointment or contract terms and apply for, accept, and assign positions and responsibilities based on professional qualifications; maintain physical and mental health and social judgment to perform professional duties; continue professional growth; follow laws, regulations, and school policies; avoid intentionally misrepresenting official school or educational organization policies; distinguish these from personal opinions; account for all funds in their charge; and never use professional or institutional privileges for partisan or personal advantages. Principle III: Ethical Conduct toward Professional Colleagues – Educators protect colleague information confidentiality except required by law, make no willful false statements about colleagues or school systems, do not interfere with colleague free choice, and fight coercion violating professional integrity. Principle IV: Ethical Conduct toward Parents and Community – Educators work to communicate to parents all information in student interests; respect diverse cultural values and traditions in classrooms and communities; and take active, positive roles in school and community relations.

Suspension or Revocation an Educator's Certificate

The Education Practices Commission may suspend an educator certificate for up to five years, or revoke it for up to 10 years or permanently for: fraudulent certificate pursuit or acquisition; knowingly not reporting suspected or actual child abuse, alleged administrator or instructional staff misconduct affecting student safety, health, or welfare; proven incompetence to teach or perform duties in public school or teach in or operate private school; acts of moral turpitude or gross immorality; suspension, revocation, or surrender of certification in another state; conviction or guilty plea to a felony, misdemeanor, or any criminal charge except minor traffic violations; being found guilty of personal conduct seriously decreasing district school board employee effectiveness; breach of contract; Department of Revenue notice or court order of certificate suspension due to noncompliance with a written agreement, subpoena, or order to show cause or child support order; violation of Principles of Professional Conduct for the Education Profession according to State Board of Education rules; other law provision violations penalized by certificate revocation; violation of any Education Practices Commission order; plea agreement or court order in any jurisdiction requiring permanent certificate surrender or relinquishment, pursuant to commissioner probable cause finding; or disqualification from educator certification under any of the felony or misdemeanor offenses prohibited under any section of the statute on disqualification from employment (s. 1012.315). There are six additional provisions, three with two, three, and two respective subsections.

Provisions Included in Most School District Policies for Using Technology in Schools

Individual school districts establish policies for technology use. For example, district policies may include Internet safety terms like software filters blocking access to material that is pornographic, obscene, harmful to children, otherwise inappropriate, or disrupts the educational process. Typical disclaimers include that filtering software may block access to other materials, may not succeed in blocking access to all inappropriate or disruptive materials, and does not cancel user obligations not to access such materials. Terms and conditions of use for curriculum and instruction include using district technological and telecommunications resources consistently with district curriculum and diverse student developmental levels, abilities, instructional needs, and learning styles; adhering to selection criteria for instructional and library media center materials; and permission for school staff to use technology and Internet resources throughout the curriculum, consistently with district guidelines and goals. Terms and conditions may define district electronic resources as part of curriculum, not a general-use public forum; stipulate that staff give students developmentally appropriate guidance in using digital information resources for district curriculum-related study and research; and inform students of their network user rights and responsibilities before giving them access. Acceptable use prescriptions and proscriptions, including regarding copyright laws and software licensing agreements, are typically parts of these policies.

Use and Maintenance of Student Records and Information

Permanent, cumulative student records—physical or electronic—can vary by school district in kinds of information they contain. Student records include student information, curriculum information, annual standardized test scores, Individualized Education Program (IEP) records, ELP levels, academic background, recent report cards, conference information, teacher comments, and other pertinent information. Teachers should check their school's policy and procedures regarding student records; check cumulative records first when they have questions about individual students; open and update cumulative records when school years start; update IEPs, ELP level changes, and conference information throughout the year; add final attendance, curriculum covered, report cards, comments, and close records at years' ends. Every student cumulative record is a confidential, legal record. Parents and students aged 18+ can request access to their records in writing. Otherwise, only school officials whose professional responsibilities require it can legally view cumulative records. Keep all information safe, intact, and confidential. When working on secure or shared computers, always log out after accessing electronic cumulative records to protect their security. Paper cumulative records should always be kept in school fireproof cabinets unless staff is directly working with them. Replace checked-out cumulative records nightly, never taking them home or leaving them in classrooms.

Ethical Responsibilities for a Classroom Teacher (CAPTAIN)

1. **Confidentiality**: A teacher must not reveal confidential information regarding a student, unless for a professional purpose or as required by law.
2. **Advantage**: A teacher must not use professional relationships with students for private advantage.
3. **Protection**: A teacher must protect a student from harm to his or her health, safety, or welfare. A teacher's duty includes reporting any suspicion of abuse or neglect and taking the proper care not to expose a child to inappropriate disparagement or embarrassment.
4. **Truth**: A teacher must faithfully render reports regarding either students or colleagues. A teacher must never knowingly make false or malicious statements about a student or a colleague.
5. **Authenticity**: A teacher must not distort or suppress elements of his or her subject matter. A teacher must not deny a student's access to different viewpoints and must not impede a student's independent action in pursuit of learning.
6. **Integrity**: A teacher must not misrepresent his or her educational credentials or those of another person.

- 128 -

7. **Non-Discrimination**: A teacher must not unfairly deny benefits from (or grant benefits to) a student on the basis of race, gender, personal beliefs, family, cultural background, or sexual orientation.

Role of the Education System in a Democratic Society

American education systems arose, in part, as a mechanism to prepare students to become responsible citizens in a democratic society. Historically, decisions regarding schools were made in deference to the common good. The school system is open to every student and every student is entitled to an education that will allow him or her to have a fair opportunity to become a successful adult. As a cornerstone of the American democratic society, schools have sometimes been at the center of controversial social questions. For example, 1954's *Brown vs. Board* Supreme Court decision forbidding segregated schools was a crucial part of the larger civil rights movement. Since 1954, Congress has passed legislation (such as 1973's Individuals with Disabilities Education Act) promising each student a free and appropriate public education. This phrase is particularly meaningful for exceptional students who may not be served well by standard educational offerings. Exceptional students may be entitled to an Individual Educational Program (IEP) that provides access to the general curriculum otherwise unavailable due to disability. Educators at every level (national, state, and local) work in collaboration so that every student can have access to a quality education and the promises of a democratic society.

Suspicion of Abuse or Neglect of a Student

The exact guidelines regarding the reporting of child abuse or child neglect will vary by state. In many states teachers who suspect abuse or neglect are required by law to report the suspicion to local authorities within a set timeframe (e.g., 48 hours). Reports of suspected abuse are most likely confidential and educators who make a report of suspected abuse in good faith are typically immune from criminal or civil repercussions. Although you may wish to talk about the situation with a mentor or administrator, reporting to an educational superior will not satisfy a teacher's legal reporting requirement. All reports must be made to the proper local authorities (e.g., Child Protective Services).

Classroom Fair Use of Copyrighted Images, Sounds, and Videos Found on the Internet

Images found on the internet may be used for in-classroom purposes by a teacher or student. Images found on the internet may not be reposted to the web without permission. No more than 15 images or 10% (whichever is less) of a given collection may be used. Up to 10% (up to a maximum of 30 seconds) of a copyrighted musical composition may be used by educators or students as part of a multimedia presentation. Videos may be used in the classroom for instructional purposes and may not be used for entertainment. No more than 10% of a video or three minutes (whichever is less) may be used.

Indiana Core Practice Test

1. In the process of determining the rationale of an objective, the teacher should ask all of the following except:

    a. Does this objective have an important learning outcome?
    b. Will this objective fit my planned activity?
    c. Will my students be able to use this knowledge in the future?
    d. Are the prior knowledge and skill levels of my students sufficient to achieve this objective?

2. Which of the following is the strongest signal for getting students' attention before starting a lesson?

    a. Say "Good morning."
    b. Say "Let's get started."
    c. Ring a bell.
    d. Use a hand signal for silence.

3. Besides signaling for attention, a teacher should set-up and open a lesson by:

    a. Stating behavioral expectations during the lesson.
    b. Helping the students to focus by explaining the objective of the lesson.
    c. Discussing ways the students can connect to the lesson through their personal experiences.
    d. All of the above.

4. Which of the following is *not* part of the process of closing a lesson?

    a. Extended practice.
    b. Review of key points.
    c. Preview of future lessons.
    d. Demonstration of student work.

5. All of the following statements are true about the evaluation component of a lesson except:

    a. Evaluation may be group-wide instead of individual.
    b. Evaluation must occur in some form with every lesson.
    c. Evaluation may occur on an on-going basis.
    d. Evaluation may occur again; for example, during a unit test.

6. In regard to the process of writing a lesson plan, which of the following is true?

    a. The steps of writing the plan may vary with the teaching model.
    b. Experienced teachers won't need to write down as much as new teachers because some actions become automatic with time.
    c. The lesson's opening, body, and closing should be written in order.
    d. Only the parts of the lesson to be presented to the students need to be written down, not necessarily the pre-planning and editing tasks.

7. There are differences among planned activities that are necessary classroom routines, activities that are fun and provide a break, and activities that are directly related to the curriculum. Of the following, which is an activity for taking a break?

    a. Singing a song.
    b. Packing up to go home.
    c. Playing math games.
    d. Taking a field trip.

8. Activity planning and lesson planning are the same in which of the following:

    a. The plans include an opening that motivates students.
    b. The plans provide students a chance to apply previously-learned skills.
    c. The plans can be designed for a whole unit.
    d. The plans ask for skills from different subject areas.

9. For teachers to be comfortable with student diversity and to help students to be comfortable with diversity, teachers should:

    a. Review the stereotypes they have learned and find ways to bring reality to these views.
    b. Study the cultures they encounter among their students.
    c. Encourage students and parents to share about their cultures.
    d. All of the above.

10. Ms. Brown has a diverse set of family situations and cultures in her classroom. Which of the following actions would *not* be sensitive to these families?

    a. On the class information form, ask "What is the primary language in the family?"
    b. On the class information form, ask for information using the labels "Mother," "Father," and "Siblings."
    c. Write materials to be sent home in the language of the home.
    d. On the class information form, ask for information using the labels "Adults in the Home," and "Children in the Home."

11. A teacher wanting to show items from various cultures to the children in her classroom asks a child of Chinese heritage to bring a coolie hat to school. The family is insulted by the teacher's assumption that all Chinese are/were coolies. What is the best response for the teacher once she has realized her mistake?

    a. Apologize and let the issue drop.
    b. Rescind the request to other families for cultural items to avoid more problems.
    c. Ask the family to send whatever it feels appropriate.
    d. Have the child make a coolie hat in class since one was not available at home.

12. Of the following, which is often the resolution to parent/teacher cultural conflicts?

    a. The conflict is resolved through compromise; i.e., both teacher and parents making accommodations.
    b. The conflict is resolved when the teacher changes her actions to address the parents' concerns.
    c. The conflict is resolved through parent education about American cultural practices.
    d. The conflict is not resolved and parents/teacher continue their own practices.

13. When teaching children from non-English speaking families, it is correct to assume that:

    a. Children will give up their previous language/culture in order to adopt that of the American majority.
    b. Proficiency in one language can help in learning a second, so language skills will improve if children are encouraged to be bilingual.
    c. Nothing is lost when the child's language and culture are not reinforced at school because they will be maintained at home.
    d. Linguistically different children are educationally delayed.

14. For classroom teachers, awareness of issues in the family situations of their students is important. Which of the following is *not* true about children of divorce?

a. Children are almost always more traumatized than their parents.
b. Of children from divorced parents, 75-80% do not have serious problems.
c. Children from non-divorced parents have no fewer problems than children from divorced parents.
d. Pre-school children are usually the most afraid and symptomatic of trauma when divorce occurs in their families.

15. Which of the following is a correct way for classroom teachers to give understanding and support to a child whose family is in turmoil?

a. Excuse a sad child from classroom chores, knowing that the child doesn't feel like doing much.
b. Discreetly avoid any discussions with the child that might open up painful feelings.
c. Provide classroom activities and materials, such as clay and paint, that might enable the child to work through feelings.
d. Keep the child from being alone and having time to brood.

16. Which one of the following statements about objectives is *not* true?

a. An objective describes a learning outcome.
b. An objective describes where we want students to go.
c. An objective describes how to get to the outcome.
d. An objective describes the lesson focus and direction.

17. Which one of the following statements about objectives is *not* true?

a. Objectives are a communications tool aimed specifically at the students, not other audiences.
b. Objectives provide a way to evaluate student learning.
c. Objectives help focus and motivate students.
d. Objectives provide a way for teachers to measure their own effectiveness.

18. Which of the following is a good example of appropriate content for an objective?

a. Compare and contrast science fiction and fantasy.
b. Complete Unit 6 in the vocabulary book.
c. Describe the similarities and differences of setting between the stories "Wilderness Adventure" and "PS 139."
d. Solve the arithmetic problems on p. 114 in your textbook.

19. Which of the following is *not* a good example of the type of verb one should use to express the desired behavior component in an objective?

a. Calculate
b. Know
c. Define
d. Predict

20. Which of the following is *not* a good example of a learning condition given in an objective?

a. On graph paper
b. During partner practice
c. After completing the unit on World War I
d. Given a list of European countries

21. Which of the following is *not* a good example of a criterion in an objective?

   a. As assessed by the teacher
   b. With no errors
   c. For ten minutes each day
   d. To the nearest whole number

22. Which of the following would be a mistake when writing a criterion for an objective?

   a. Setting performance standards high enough to meet skills expectations.
   b. Setting realistic standards and time limits to avoid frustration.
   c. Gradually increasing expectations of accuracy as time goes by.
   d. Setting no limit to time or amount so that students are not pressured.

23. Which of the following statements is true?

   a. Write objectives that describe activities or assignments.
   b. Write objectives with creativity and complexity.
   c. Write objectives that represent important learning outcomes.
   d. Write objectives in correct form so that they will be appropriate for the students.

24. Objectives should be designed to teach something that is worth learning. Practicing skills is a good learning objective if the practice is embedded within application opportunities. Which of the following, however, may be a pointless practice?

   a. Reading to practice word attack skills.
   b. Solving problems to practice number facts and computations.
   c. Writing a composition to practice spelling and penmanship.
   d. Copying definitions of words to improve vocabulary.

25. Higher-level objectives include all of the following except:

   a. Making predictions
   b. Suggesting courses of action
   c. Memorizing important dates
   d. Providing solutions to problems

26. Which of the following is an advantage of Instructional Objectives?

   a. Since an objective must have a measurable outcome, it is easier to have low-level, and thereby easily-measured, objectives.
   b. Writing objectives forces the teacher to think about what students should be working on.
   c. Once a teacher has established a pattern for writing objectives, they all tend to be the same.
   d. Objectives tend to focus on parts of the whole picture rather than complete knowledge.

27. Strategies for establishing a verbal-linguistic learning environment include all except which one of the following?

   a. Classroom discussions
   b. Stories told by the teacher
   c. Task Cards
   d. Word walls

28. Strategies for establishing a logical-mathematical learning environment include all except which one of the following?

    a. Conducting interviews
    b. Venn diagrams
    c. Thinking of probabilities
    d. Discerning patterns

29. Strategies for establishing a tactile-kinesthetic learning environment include all except which one of the following?

    a. Large floor games
    b. Syllogisms
    c. Dance warm-ups
    d. Role playing

30. Which of the following describes a student who is a tactile-kinesthetic learner?

    a. Enjoys building models
    b. Perceives patterns and relationships
    c. Listens and responds to the spoken word
    d. Interested in writing

31. Which of the following describes a student who is a verbal-linguistic learner?

    a. Likes field trips and physical exercise
    b. Exhibits balance and dexterity
    c. Shows a knack for learning other languages.
    d. Adept at logical problem-solving

32. Which of the following describes a logical-mathematical learner?

    a. Sensitive to physical environments and systems
    b. Interested in a career as a builder
    c. Interested in a career as an engineer
    d. Reads, speaks, and writes effectively

33. All of the following describe a visual-spatial learner except:

    a. Uses clustering as a brainstorming tool
    b. Highlights with color
    c. Enjoys playing with sound
    d. Uses visual memory techniques

34. All of the following describe a musical learner except:

    a. Listens and responds with interest to a variety of sounds
    b. Wants to learn to sing or play an instrument
    c. Wants to be a sound engineer
    d. Responds well to materials of varying shapes

35. When designing a Pre-K to Grade 3 classroom, the teacher should assess the room to identify its most quiet area. This area should be reserved for:

    a. Art work
    b. Science activities
    c. A library
    d. A puppet stage

36. When arranging a classroom, which of the following are basic principles to follow?

    a. Separate noisy from quiet areas with shelves and furniture.
    b. Place materials so that they are at the children's eye level and reachable.
    c. Ensure that traffic patterns do not allow running.
    d. All of the above.

37. Having a print-rich environment includes all of the following except:

    a. Writing classroom labels in only one language to avoid confusion.
    b. Making sure print is at the children's eye level.
    c. Displaying the students' work around the classroom.
    d. Having the teacher prepare materials in front of the students to model writing.

38. If a classroom looks messy and disorganized, the effects might be all of the following except:

    a. Children displaying disruptive behavior.
    b. Children having difficulty choosing activities from amidst the chaos.
    c. Children worrying less about being neat and more about the task at hand.
    d. Children having difficulty doing clean-up chores.

39. Pervasive labeling has the effect of all of the following except:

    a. Helping children learn how to organize and store materials.
    b. Helping children to feel successful by limiting responsibility.
    c. Helping children to associate words with things.
    d. Enhancing the print-rich environment.

40. Part of the emotional environment of a classroom is the relationships between the teacher and the children. Children learn and develop well in a nurturing relationship that includes all the following except:

    a. Remains consistent in the teacher's interactions with and expectations of the children.
    b. Firmly ensures compliance with rules and routines.
    c. Empowers children with choices.
    d. Provides feedback in a positive manner.

41. The emotional balance of a classroom can be upset by conflict. Appropriate methods for a teacher to use in handling conflict do not include:

    a. Gathering information and re-capping the situation.
    b. Allowing children to come up with a solution themselves.
    c. Letting the issue drop once a solution has been agreed upon.
    d. Dealing with the conflict calmly and with a quiet voice.

42. Effective management of children with behavioral problems would include:

a. Preparing explicit instructions.
b. Following up instructions with focused, active practice.
c. Giving immediate feedback.
d. All of the above.

43. During a lesson, which of the following is the best method for classroom management?

a. Making rewards contingent on everyone doing well.
b. Promising a treat for good work to be given at the end of the week.
c. Communicating behavioral expectations clearly before the lesson starts.
d. Customizing the consequences for misbehavior to fit each student.

When answering questions 44-46, consider the follow statement:

Beyond the standard rules for classroom management, specific situations, such as lessons that call for movement or an unusual activity, necessitate further behavior management.

44. Considerations for additional behavior management include all but which one of the following:

a. Re-arranging seats to ensure compatibility and avoid conflict.
b. The teacher rather than the students selecting partners.
c. On-the-spot corrections since you can't plan ahead for what might happen.
d. Stronger reinforcements to keep students on task.

45. Additional behavioral management needs to be included in lesson planning in which of the following situations?

a. When there will be multiple transitions during the lesson.
b. When the lesson requires the use of lots of equipment.
c. When additional or unusual materials need to be distributed.
d. All of the above.

46. Behavioral management should include specific techniques for students who have difficulty staying on task. Which one of the following would *not* be appropriate?

a. Allowing such students to walk around to look at the materials that pertain to the lesson.
b. Assigning specific tasks to be completed.
c. Using response cards so that all students feel compelled to be aware and involved.
d. Not allowing peer helpers because they might harm more than help by distracting the students who have trouble staying on task.

47. Room arrangement is part of classroom management. Which one of the following is *not* true about appropriate arrangements?

a. Students don't necessarily need to see the teacher, but do need to see the blackboard, poster, or whatever demonstrates the lesson.
b. Desks should be arranged such that the teacher can get close to every student.
c. Desks or tables should be arranged to fit the activity; for example, small group discussion or independent work.
d. Teachers should select who sits where and by whom.

When answering questions 48 and 49, consider the following statement:

Good classroom management is good behavior management. If a teacher does not know how to manage time well or establish routines, there will be too many opportunities for discipline to break down.

48. In order to make the best use of time and avoid lags in time that would allow student restlessness, a teacher should do all of the following except:

    a. Check out equipment to make sure it is working before the lesson.
    b. Rely on standard clean-up rules to take care of the close of the lesson.
    c. Clearly announce rules for sharing and returning supplies before the activity starts.
    d. Have supplies or handouts ready for distribution.

49. The establishment of routines should include:

    a. How to turn in assignments
    b. What to do when finished.
    c. How to set up for partner practice.
    d. All of the above.

50. Of the following sentences, which one is a negative communication?

    a. Close the door quietly.
    b. Use your own ideas.
    c. Stop fighting over the crayons.
    d. Be ready to explain why your answer is correct.

When answering questions 51 and 52, consider the following statement:

Students want and deserve to be praised, but the way that praise is communicated can be a delicate situation.

51. Students prefer which one of the following types of praise?

    a. Public praise delivered so everyone can hear.
    b. Private, quietly delivered praise.
    c. Praise for good conduct.
    d. Praise for effort even when the work is poor.

52. Which of the following is an incorrect way to deliver praise?

    a. Make a big deal out of the praise so the student feels special.
    b. Specify the accomplishment rather than say "That's good."
    c. Back up verbal praise with a smile and warm tone.
    d. Call attention to new skills or note progress.

53. Students will be more interested in learning when they understand how the knowledge and skills learned in school can be applied in their own lives. The teacher can help students understand this connection by effectively communicating:

    a. Examples from former students of that school.
    b. Examples from personal experience.
    c. Examples from famous people.
    d. All of the above.

54. Teachers can positively communicate expectations in such a way as to make students eager to learn. Of the following statements, which one would be the least effective?

   a. "We're going to think like scientists in this class."
   b. "You might not like this practice, but it will help you to get a good grade."
   c. "I know you are all curious about how to make a puppet."
   d. "This project is one of my hobbies, so I wanted to share it with you."

55. When presenting information, effective teacher communication is best achieved when the teacher uses which of the following types of phrases?

   a. because, for example
   b. not many, not very
   c. somewhere, somehow
   d. generally, usually

56. Which of the following is an example of teachers failing to communicate effectively with their students or other teachers?

   a. The students know the lesson's objective.
   b. Assignments for 5th graders are less demanding than those for 3rd graders in the same school.
   c. All 5th grade science classes are working on photosynthesis at the same time.
   d. Students have been provided with a grading rubric for their compositions.

Questions 57 and 58 pertain to the following scenario:

> A teacher uses a mnemonic strategy of showing a series of graphics. After each graphic is described and its significance or relevance to the lesson explained, the students re-create the graphics on their own paper.

57. Which of the following is a benefit of this strategy?

   a. Assists visual and kinesthetic learners with acquisition and retention of knowledge.
   b. Assists students with linking a series of events.
   c. Assists students with grasping abstract concepts through concrete representations.
   d. All of the above.

58. Which of the following is *not* a good continuation of this lesson?

   a. Use these graphics as a review for a test.
   b. Make a game out of the graphics such as timing students to see how quickly they can put a set of jumbled graphics in order.
   c. Grade the students on how artfully they can draw the graphics.
   d. Have the students pair up to check each other's graphics for accuracy.

59. Which of the following is *not* a benefit of flexible grouping practices?

   a. Allows students to work at individual interest levels.
   b. Allows students to pick their own groups for better cooperation.
   c. Allows students to work according to readiness levels.
   d. Allows students to work on specific skills identified as deficient through assessments.

Questions 60 and 61 pertain to the following scenario:

- 138 -

Preprinted response cards or wipe-off cards are used by the students to hold up answers to questions posed by the teacher to the whole class.

60. Which of the following is *not* likely to be a result of the use of response cards?

    a. The use of response cards is a novelty that will soon grow tiresome.
    b. The use of response cards reduces daydreaming and increases on-task behavior.
    c. The use of response cards dramatically increases the number of academic responses per student.
    d. The use of response cards allows teachers to better monitor student progress.

61. Which of the following is not a component of using response cards as a strategy?

    a. Actively engages students in the lesson assessment.
    b. Can be used before, during, and after the lesson.
    c. Allows students to collaborate on answers.
    d. Enables teachers to find out what parts of the lesson need re-teaching.

62. Which of the following is a good strategy that a teacher can use with a student who has trouble maintaining attention?

    a. Provide preferential seating.
    b. Place the student in a study carrel to reduce visual distractions.
    c. Provide the student with headphones to reduce sound distractions.
    d. All of the above.

63. For students who have difficulty finishing routine assignments, the teacher should do all of the following except:

    a. Teach self-discipline about staying on task.
    b. Avoid playing games with the materials because they might add too much time to the task.
    c. Remove segments of the task; for example, don't require the student to copy word problems before calculating the answer.
    d. Divide the task into segments and allow the student to work on the parts throughout the day.

64. Some children have difficulty with a change in routine. The primary strategy for dealing with this problem is:

    a. Maintaining the same schedule as much as possible.
    b. Giving advance warning of changes such as a visitor or school assembly.
    c. Allowing students who are likely to be upset to stay next to the teacher or a friend who can comfort them.
    d. Teaching relaxation techniques.

65. The best approach to using technology in the classroom is:

    a. Expect to teach technology with your subject.
    b. Rely on the school's technology center rather than your own classroom.
    c. Use only the technology with which you are comfortable.
    d. Increasing technology will improve instruction.

66. Which of the following statements is true?

    a. Students who write compositions using the computer often take more pride in their work than those who use pen and paper.
    b. Spell check allows student to focus on content and not mechanics.
    c. Computers allow for almost effortless reorganizing and thus less time and energy.
    d. All of the above.

67. Which of the following should *not* be a consideration about using computers in the classroom?

    a. Does the state test allow for writing on computers?
    b. Is the software easy to use and fun?
    c. Will I have sufficient technical back up if anything goes wrong?
    d. Will behavior management be more difficult while students are on computers?

68. Considering that not all web sites are credible, when doing project-based learning, students doing computer research should:

    a. Find several information sources with different perspectives.
    b. Look for identifiable sponsors or authors of the site.
    c. Check for the date of the latest update.
    d. All of the above.

For questions 69-71, choose the statement that is not true.

69. The following statements deal with the availability of computers in the classroom:

    a. Numerous federal and state grants have enabled high poverty and minority schools to catch up to high socio-economic schools in number of students per computer.
    b. Only one or two computers available in your classroom may limit use to demonstrations and word processing.
    c. More than two computers in a classroom adds the possibility of doing collaboratives, independent research, portfolios, and research papers.
    d. Only about 30% or fewer students will have computers at home unless the family income is $50,000 per year or more.

70. On average, today's students who grew up with television, computers, and video games:

    a. Enjoy group activities.
    b. Participate infrequently in extracurricular activities.
    c. Love new technologies.
    d. Identify with parents.

71. When deciding how much technology to use in a lesson plan, teachers have found that:

    a. Students spend so much time alone with technology that they are sometimes better off with a plain lecture or discussion.
    b. Students enjoy electronic presentations because the information is organized for them.
    c. Students find presentations with lots of video inserts to be confusing.
    d. Students may not think critically about the content if they copy notes from a PowerPoint presentation.

72. It would be incorrect to think that because today's students are active technology users, they

    a. do not watch much television.
    b. surf the Net frequently.
    c. participate in chat rooms.
    d. play lots of video games.

73. Which of the following would be the most appropriate feedback for a teacher to give to a student if the student identifies a verb as a noun?

    a. The teacher says, "Well, that could be a noun."
    b. The teacher says, "That's a good example of a verb."
    c. The teacher says, "No, I asked for a noun."
    d. The teacher says, "Wrong again!"

74. Feedback should consist of:

    a. Specifying what was done correctly.
    b. Making suggestions for improvement.
    c. Adding a positive comment to conclude remarks.
    d. All of the above.

75. After a demonstration by the teacher, a student repeats the demonstration in front of the class. From the following list of actions, what would *not* be the best way for the teacher to give feedback?

    a. Wait to give feedback until the end if the demonstration is short.
    b. Give feedback on each step as reassurance before continuing.
    c. If a mistake is made, ask for the reason for the mistake.
    d. Re-demonstrate the correct step if the student makes a mistake, then have the student try again.

76. Besides teacher feedback, which of the following is a legitimate way for a student to get feedback on work?

    a. Using an answer key.
    b. Asking an adult volunteer.
    c. Reviewing work in student pairs.
    d. All of the above.

77. Good tests that assess student learning effectively can be difficult to construct. Of the following statements, which is *not* necessarily a bad practice in test making?

    a. The questions unevenly sample lesson content.
    b. The test is long.
    c. All questions have the same level of difficulty.
    d. The test items use examples from topics that are not familiar to all students.

78. Of the following statements, which is an advantage of multiple-choice tests?

    a. Multiple-choice tests rely on memorization rather than understanding.
    b. Multiple-choice tests cover content that is easily assessed rather than being important.
    c. Multiple-choice tests allow more assessment of content than essay tests.
    d. Multiple-choice tests often have question stems that might give away the answer to those who guess well.

79. Which of the following statements is false about short answer and completion items on a test?

    a. Short answer and completion items take more time to construct than multiple-choice items.
    b. Short answer and completion items are particularly useful in math and science courses.
    c. Short answer and completion items are particularly useful for spelling and language courses.
    d. Short answer and completion items present some of the same scoring problems as essays.

80. Which of the following statements is an advantage of essay tests?

    a. Essay tests allow students to organize their answers.
    b. Essay test grading can be highly subjective.
    c. Essay tests can cover only a small portion of the material.
    d. Essay tests favor students with good writing skills.

81. Parent involvement is a term that means:

    a. Parent education.
    b. Parent volunteers in schools.
    c. Parent service on fundraising committees.
    d. All of the above.

Questions 82 and 83 refer to the following information:

- Low-level parent involvement means that parents take part in activities that do not challenge the expertise of a teacher or decision-making powers of the school; and
- High-level parent involvement means that parents are provided opportunities to make their presence known.

82. Of the following choices, which show the *highest* level of parent involvement?

    a. Baking cookies for a class event.
    b. Going on a field trip with a child's class.
    c. Participation in a school intervention program.
    d. Attending a parent/teacher conference.

83. Of the following choices, which shows the *lowest* level of parent involvement?

    a. Parent visits to the classroom.
    b. Parent production of a school newsletter.
    c. Parent on-site observations.
    d. Parent volunteer assistance in the classroom.

84. Of the following choices, which does NOT mandate parental involvement?

    a. School-based parental education programs
    b. Head Start
    c. Title I
    d. Individuals with Disabilities Act

85. Of the following types of pre-school programs, which has mandated parental involvement?

    a. Child-care franchises
    b. Family child-care homes
    c. Head Start
    d. Non-profit child-care programs

86. Of the following choices, which has the *least* effect on student success?

    a. Good interaction skills of the parent.
    b. Socio-economic status of the parent.
    c. Self-esteem of the parent.
    d. Parent involvement in the student's academic programs.

87. For families that are low on the socio-economic scale and in need of support systems for successful child rearing, the school or pre-school should *not*:

    a. Assume the role of the parent until an intervention program can improve the parent's skills.
    b. Become one of the agencies offering services to the family.
    c. Establish an equal working relationship with the parent.
    d. Act as a form of extended family that supports the authority of the parent.

88. Teachers who have difficulty interacting with parents would benefit from:

    a. Preparing comments before meeting with parents.
    b. Sharing their fears with other teachers to elicit advice.
    c. Setting a goal to talk with a certain number of parents per week.
    d. All of the above.

89. Which is the least effective way to improve your performance as a teacher?

    a. Teach yourself with school or district audio tapes and videos on topics of best teaching practices.
    b. Subscribe to an education journal.
    c. Frequent the teacher lounge to listen to other teachers' experiences.
    d. Attend professional development conferences, seminars, and workshops.

90. The most important investment a school board, administrators, and parents can make in a school system is to provide teachers with continuous opportunities to learn because it:

    a. Deepens and broadens knowledge of content.
    b. Provides knowledge about the teaching and learning process.
    c. Is intellectually engaging and addresses the complexity of teaching.
    d. All of the above.

91. For teachers to master new content and pedagogy and be able to integrate this knowledge and skill into their practice, teachers must be given all of the following except:

    a. Time
    b. Pay incentives
    c. Support
    d. Resources

92. Of the following choices, which is true? Professional development is not

    a. site-specific since some principles of teaching are universal.
    b. about content but about strategies.
    c. necessarily job-embedded because it is an opportunity to explore other educational roles.
    d. designed by experts only but by teachers as well.

93. Of the following, which is the greatest challenge associated with professional development?

   a. Finding time to schedule professional development and do follow-up.
   b. Developing seminars on the implementation of new educational standards.
   c. Addressing the changing forms of student assessment.
   d. Providing guidelines for working with diverse populations.

94. Of the following, which is the best way to conduct professional development?

   a. Assigning the teachers to team planning while administrators have their own meetings.
   b. Doing professional development during the summer.
   c. Hiring substitutes to cover for a day of development for a group of teachers.
   d. Involving parents in planning professional development so they see its value.

95. Which of the following is the least-recommended use of technology for professional development?

   a. Watching video conferences to get seminar-style education without travel.
   b. Accessing collegial networks to exchange ideas with like teachers.
   c. Relying on distance education rather than on-campus or in-district opportunities.
   d. Using electronic bulletin boards for teaching and resource tips.

96. Which of the following is true?

   a. Pre-service training is adequate preparation for the teachers to do their work.
   b. The school district is in the business of educating students, not teachers.
   c. Teachers should spend at least 20% of their work time in professional study and collaborative work.
   d. To avoid taking time away from students, teachers should pursue professional development on their own time.

97. Laws and ethics are important areas of concern for the classroom teacher, starting with an understanding of the differences between laws and ethics. Of the following statements, which one is false?

   a. Laws are concrete, written and enacted by people.
   b. Ethics are less tangible and observable and consist of ideas.
   c. Laws are always ethical.
   d. Most laws are the codification of what society considers moral or ethical obligations.

98. Betty is a veteran teacher who has been asked by the principal to mentor a new teacher and report her observations. Betty discovers that the newcomer is a poor teacher with few disciplinary or instructional skills. Which of the following should *not* be a consideration for Betty if she is ethical?

   a. The new teacher's need for a job.
   b. Her obligation to the principal to give an accurate report.
   c. Passing off the mentoring job to another teacher.
   d. The children's need for a competent teacher.

99. Which of the following is an everyday way that teachers can ethically influence students?

   a. By setting an example in the way they do their work and care about their students.
   b. By establishing a classroom climate of respect and cooperation.
   c. By incorporating discussions of ethics into the subject matter of the lesson.
   d. All of the above.

100. Considering the due process rights of a teacher, which of the following is an incorrect statement?

    a. The principal must schedule a dismissal hearing at a reasonable time and place.

    b. A school district must justify its reasons for not rehiring a teacher, even if the teacher is on probation.

    c. The teacher must be allowed to confront and question witnesses at the dismissal hearing.

    d. The teacher must be given timely and adequate notice giving details of the reasons for the proposed suspension or dismissal.

Answers and Explanations

1. B: Lesson objectives should have an important outcome, should be useful to the students in the future, and should be at a knowledge and skill level appropriate to the students; however, activities should be planned to fit the objective, not the other way around. Every lesson plan should be concerned with an important learning outcome - trivial lessons are a waste of time and damage student interest – therefore, all lesson plans should include an important objective. The knowledge gained by a lesson should also be something students can use in the future; otherwise the lesson has no point. The lesson should also be comprehensible to the students – teaching above their skill levels leaves them unsuccessful and frustrated; teaching below their skills levels leaves them bored.

2. C: Ringing a bell is the strongest signal for getting attention from the students. Just saying something might not be heard or might be ignored because the teacher is often talking, and a hand signal might not be seen. However, a bell makes a sound different from the usual human voice and is usually louder, too, so it makes the strongest attention-getting signal. Good teachers establish certain signals with their students as a form of shortcut communication. The most common is the signal for attention. Simply saying "Good morning" or "Let's get started" are good oral signals that the teacher wants all eyes on him/her so that a change of activity can begin. Hand signals such as just holding up a hand as a signal for quiet also work well.

3. D: Answers A, B, and C, all describe appropriate and necessary elements of setting up a new lesson so that students know what the lesson is intended to do, how it can be of benefit to them, and what behavior will help them to succeed. When a teacher starts a new lesson, it is critical that the objective of the lesson is clearly communicated, that the students are helped to make a connection between the lesson and their personal experiences, and that behavioral expectations are set.

4. A: Extended practice should be part of the lesson when the teacher's evaluation shows that extended practice is needed to solidify the lesson or ensure that all students have learned the objective. The closing of the lesson is too late to try to back up and insert extended practice. When closing a lesson, it is natural to review key points, perhaps as demonstrated by work done by the students during the lesson, and giving the students a preview of the next or other related lessons builds student anticipation and desire to learn.

5. A: The teacher needs to know how well each student is doing and must teach each child. The teacher is striving for a quality learning experience for every child rather than averages or high percentages measured by a group-wide evaluation. It is true that evaluation must be part of every lesson, in some form or another, or else the teacher will not know if the objective was reached, and if some or all students need a re-teach. This evaluation can continue with retention checks in other lessons; that is, on an on-going basis, and may be repeated in overall unit tests.

6. B: The lesson plans for an experienced teacher do not have to be as detailed as they should be for a new teacher because some actions become second nature to a teacher after a while and go without saying. The steps to writing a good lesson plan do not vary with the teaching model but are the backbone of every lesson. The lesson opening, body, and closing do not need to be written in order; in fact, it is often best to write the body of the lesson first so that the teacher has had a chance to thoroughly think through the lesson before deciding on an appropriate opening. Since the lesson plan has a set pattern, all parts must be written, including pre-planning steps and editing tasks, not just the parts that will be presented to the students.

7. A: Singing a song is the answer because this is a pleasant activity that the children enjoy and that helps them to relax. Singing a song is good for a break, especially a break that transitions into a new lesson or activity. Although some songs may also enhance a lesson, the students perceive singing a fun song as just that: fun. Packing up to go home is a routine activity that is part of the classroom management structure. Playing math games is an activity that is directly related to the math curriculum and reinforces a lesson. Taking a field trip is also related to the curriculum and is supposed to be designed to illustrate or enhance a lesson.

8. C: A lesson is only one component of a unit, so the lesson plan cannot cover the whole unit. An activity plan, however, can be for an activity that incorporates several components of a unit or is a good summary activity for a unit. Whether an activity or a lesson, the opening should be something that will motivate the students to take an interest and participate in the lesson. The plans for an activity or lesson can give students an opportunity to apply previously learned skills in that subject or to integrate skills from different subjects.

9. D: All the answers are linked by the teacher's need to know more about the students' cultures. Inadequate knowledge that might lead to a misunderstanding with a student or parent needs remediation, first through recognition of any gaps of knowledge and then by various means of getting to know the cultures. Most people's knowledge about other cultures contains some stereotypes. For teachers who have a multi-cultural classroom, it would be beneficial for them to think through what they know about the cultures of the children in their classrooms to analyze whether any of that knowledge is based on stereotypes. They need to question themselves as to whether they have any first-hand knowledge about these cultures. If not, they need to devote a little time to studying about these cultures. One way to learn is to ask the children and their parents to share information about their cultures for the benefit of all.

10. B: A home that has stepparents or relatives other than the mother and father might feel ill at ease with a form that asks for only those identifications. Any teacher is likely to have a class with students who come from single-parent homes, who have divorced parents, who have stepparents and step-siblings, or who live with a grandparent or other relatives. The teacher needs to be sensitive to these various family make-ups by making forms and addressing letters in a generic manner that would fit any situation. For better communication in a multi-cultural classroom, it is a good idea to have forms and letters in whatever languages the children's parents' use. Asking early in the year about languages spoken in the home allows the teacher to customize communication to fit the response.

11. C: The offended family will be given the opportunity to educate the teacher and the class about their culture. The activity should continue so that the other students aren't denied an opportunity to share because of the teacher's mistake. Most definitely, the teacher should not compound the error by persisting in asking for something that s/he has been told is offensive. Teachers who make assumptions based on cultural stereotypes could offend students with inappropriate statements or requests. It is good practice to have the students share about their cultures in a "Show and Tell" activity, for example. However, should the teacher make a mistake about cultural practices, s/he should apologize to anyone offended and not let the matter drop but follow up with another option and continue the activity for everyone. The teacher should give careful thought to the mistake and correct any misconceptions.

12. D: Unfortunately, it is fairly common that no one tries to resolve the problem. Through fear of speaking up or ignorance of the problem, the situation continues and irritates all concerned. There are a variety of ways to solve a conflict. One is through mutual compromise; another is for one side to change. In the case of a parent/teacher cultural conflict, there could be give-and-take on both

sides, or the teacher could adjust to the cultural needs of the family, or, when the demands of the classroom cannot accommodate the cultural demands, the parents can be helped to come to an understanding of the requirements through education.

13. B: It has been shown that knowledge about the structure of one language makes it easier to pick up the structure of another. The other answer choices all play on prejudices or lack of knowledge about the best way to foster bilingualism. Schools used to discourage the use of any language but English. Some people, even teachers, still hold strong views about English-only in schools; that immigrants are an uneducated, backward group; and that assimilation into the majority culture is the best practice. This question addresses those biases while testing the knowledge of the teacher about the value of multi-language education.

14. C: Children from non-divorced families do have fewer problems than children from families of divorce. The statistic showing that the majority of children of divorce do not have serious problems may lead one to think that they do not have any more problems than children of non-divorced families. With a divorce rate of 50% in the Unites States, it is important for teachers to be cognizant of the consequences of divorce on their students. This question tests the teacher's knowledge versus assumptions about children of divorce. While it is true that children are more traumatized than the parents in a divorce, and that pre-school children are affected more than older children, nonetheless, the majority of children in a divorce situation do not have serious problems as a result. Still, they have more problems than children whose parents remain married.

15. C: Providing an outlet for the child to express feelings includes providing classroom activities and materials that would allow the child to draw or build something that is representative of that child's feelings. Sensitivity to children who are in unsettled situations at home is very important for the classroom teacher. This question addresses appropriate reactions when the teacher knows a child is in turmoil at home. In such situations, it is wise for the teacher to maintain structure for the child; excusing the child from regular classroom chores would not be a good idea. It is wise to let a child talk out feelings, so avoiding discussing feelings with the child would be to deny the child a safe outlet. Troubled children also need time to be alone, so the teacher needs to know when not to push the child into activities.

16. C: The teacher is trying to communicate to the students what the learning outcome is, not how to get there. The lesson itself provides the "how." An objective is defined as a clearly described learning outcome so that students know what they are expected to learn. It is an outline of where the teacher wants the students to go in their learning that day in class. Writing an objective on the board gives the lesson focus and direction that also helps in the selection of appropriate practice activities and evaluations.

17. A: The objective is like a public declaration for all to see – not only the students, but also other teachers, administrative staff, and parents who want to know what is going on that day and whether the objective has been clearly communicated to the students. One of the benefits of a clearly written, focused objective is that the teacher knows exactly what to evaluate – did the students learn the objective for the day? Another benefit is that the evaluation works in reverse also – providing a measure for the teacher to judge his/her own effectiveness. It is the primary purpose of an objective to focus the students on what they are to learn that day; in addition, a well-written objective might also motivate students to want to learn the day's lesson.

18. A: This objective is generic enough to emphasize knowledge and skills that would apply in a variety of situations – knowledge about science fiction and fantasy helps to evaluate a large number of reading selections. The content of an objective should be specific enough that anyone reading it

will understand the subject matter. The content should be able to stand alone and be understood without having to look up specific materials; consequently, answer B is not a good example of content because it refers to specific materials -- Unit 6 in the vocabulary book. In like manner, answer D refers to specific materials (p. 114 in the textbook). The content should also be generic enough that the emphasis is on knowledge and skills that are applicable in a number of contexts; answer C is not generic enough but could be fixed by adding the skills that would be learned from the task.

19. B: "Know" might be appropriate for a general goal or standard, but is not a measurable action. The teacher cannot know if a student truly comprehends or has learned something unless there is a demonstration of the knowledge. The behavior component of an objective states what students will do to demonstrate their learning. Thus, this component is written as an observable verb so that the outcome can be measured. Calculate, define, and predict all ask the students to do a specific, concrete task, probably written. These verbs command an action.

20. C: This response describes the learning condition rather than the evaluation condition. Objectives focus on outcomes, not on when or where the students gain the knowledge; therefore, "after completing the unit on World War I" is not a good example of an evaluation condition. Describing the evaluation condition or conditions of an objective provides additional specificity about what the student will learn. The condition can affect the difficulty level of the objective and determine the lesson and practice activities. An evaluation condition should ask students to perform a skill in isolation or in context, tell students what information or materials will be provided, or describe the setting or situation involved in the objective. Answer A is an example of materials provided – on graph paper. Answer B is an example of a setting or situation – during partner practice. Answer D is an example of information provided – given a list of European countries.

21. A: Objectives are intended to communicate clearly with students, parents, and other professionals, but "as assessed by the teacher" is not a valid criterion for acceptable performance because that leaves the objective open to interpretation. The criterion component of an objective specifies the standard of acceptable performance; that is, how well the student must do to meet the objective. Examples of criterion include demonstration of knowledge as a total number or proportion, in terms of time, as a variation, as a description or result, or a combination of these. Answer B, "with no errors," gives the total number of acceptable errors. Answer C sets the criterion in terms of time: "for ten minutes each day." Answer D describes the criterion as a variation: "to the nearest whole number" (as opposed to the nearest tenth or hundredth).

22. D: Setting an objective without a specific time or amount limit would leave students wondering if there will ever be an end to the task. A common error when writing a criterion is to set it too low, so answer A would be the correct way to write a criterion: setting performance standards high enough to meet skills expectations, especially in reading, writing, and math. Another common error is to set the criterion arbitrarily; for example, setting the accuracy rate for 80% every time, no matter the difficulty of the task, or asking that a task be performed in too short a time. Answer B is correct in directing that the teacher set realistic standards and time limits. Answer C is also a correct way to set the criterion at the right level, gradually increasing expectations for accuracy in a skill; for example, 50% by October, 65% by November, and so on.

23. C: The purpose of an objective is to represent important learning outcomes. Answer A is incorrect because objectives should be written to describe outcomes, not activities or assignments. Answer B is incorrect because objectives should be clean and simple for clarity, not creative or

complex and thus ripe for confusion. Answer D is incorrect because objectives can be well written in terms of form but still manage to be inappropriate for the students.

24. D: Although copying definitions might help to cement the meaning of a word, if the word is not one that is relevant to the lesson, it will be quickly forgotten. Answer D violates the guideline that practicing skills should be embedded within application opportunities and is busy-work practice with no point to the effort. Reading does help students to improve word attack skills, as well as many other skills, so Answer A is a worthwhile objective. If the objective is to improve number facts and computations, solving problems is a good practice, so Answer B is also a worthwhile objective. In the process of writing an essay, the student has to practice spelling and penmanship skills, so this assignment achieves a good objective, as stated in Answer C.

25. C: Memorizing dates is a low-level skill that does not require any analysis or comprehension; thus the task in Answer C is not a higher-level objective. Making predictions involves sufficient comprehension of the information given to be able to make an extension from it; this is a higher-level thinking skill and Answer A is a higher-level objective. Suggesting courses of action is also an extension of the given information and requires higher-level thinking to create a plan; thus Answer B is a higher-level objective. Similarly, providing solutions to problems involves critical thinking skills, so Answer D is a higher-level objective.

26. B: An advantage of doing objectives is that, if done properly, the exercise will cause the teacher to think about skills that the students need to learn. Answer A states an obvious problem: teachers are not supposed to be aiming for low-level skills in an objective, even if such skills are easily measurable. Answer C is a common problem: teachers in effect write the same objective day after day because they get in a rut, and it's easy to use the same pattern again and again rather than think through what objective best fits the lesson. Answer D is a problem if the teacher is so focused on the objective of the day that s/he forgets that it is supposed to fit into the big picture of the course or unit.

27. C: Task cards are a strategy best used as a manipulative for tactile-kinesthetic learners. While a task card may have writing on it, the value to tactile learners is that a card is something that the students can touch, which makes the writing more real to them. Students who are dominantly verbal-linguistic learners will learn best when listening, speaking, reading, and writing. Consequently, activities such as classroom discussions, listening to a story read by the teacher, or reading the words listed on the classroom word wall are good strategies for reaching the verbal-linguistic learners in the class.

28. A: Conducting interviews is a strategy best used for verbal-linguistic students who use speaking, such as asking questions of another person, to learn. Students who are dominantly logical-mathematical learners will learn best in the areas of mathematics, science, and logic. Strategies in these areas include using Venn diagrams to logically illustrate relationships; thinking in probabilities, which emphasizes working with numbers; and discerning patterns, which is a mathematical thinking process.

29. B: Syllogisms are a method of diagramming logical thought, a strategy that would work best with a logical-mathematical learner. Students who are dominantly tactile-kinesthetic learners will learn best when they can use their bodies or parts of their bodies, such as hands, to solve problems. Consequently, strategies such as large-floor games (those that require bodily movement over an area), dance warm-ups (also involving bodily movement), and role-playing, which allows the use of drama to illustrate a lesson, are good strategies for reaching the tactile-kinesthetic learners in the class.

30. A: A student who enjoys building models is most likely a tactile-kinesthetic learner who enjoys hands-on activities; that is, activities that allow the student to create and learn while touching related materials. Teachers discern the learning styles of students through testing or observation. A student who easily perceives patterns and relationships is likely a logical-mathematical learner. A student who listens and responds to the spoken work or who is interested in writing is likely a verbal-linguistic learner.

31. C: The ability to learn languages with relative ease is a characteristic of the verbal-linguistic learner. Teachers discern the learning styles of students through testing or observation. A student who likes field trips and physical exercise is likely a tactile-kinesthetic learner who enjoys the physical activity of a field trip or any physical exercise because such a student learns through involvement of the body. Similarly, a tactile-kinesthetic learner will exhibit greater skill with balance and dexterity. A student who is good at logical problem solving is likely a logical-mathematical learner.

32. C: A logical-mathematical learner is most likely to be interested in a career in engineering, which involves mathematics and logical problem solving. Teachers discern the learning styles of students through testing or observation. A student who is sensitive to physical environments and systems or who is interested in a career as a builder is a tactile-kinesthetic learner since these involve the use of the body in the learning/practicing process. A student who reads, speaks, and writes effectively is a verbal-linguistic learner who excels at tasks using the spoken or written word.

33. C: A student who enjoys playing with sound is most likely a musical learner who learns best when the material has rhythm and melody. Teachers discern the learning styles of students through testing or observation. A student who uses clustering as a brainstorming tool (which allows visualization of the ideas), highlights reading materials in color (which visually emphasizes important information), or uses visual memory techniques is a visual-spatial learner.

34. D: A student who responds well to materials of varying shapes is a visual-spatial learner who remembers items according to their shapes, who learns by seeing and observing, not listening to music. Teachers discern the learning styles of students through testing or observation. A student who listens and responds with interest to a variety of sounds, wants to learn to sing or play an instrument, or wants to be a sound engineer is most likely a musical learner who responds to rhythm and melody.

35. C: The library is the answer because reading requires the kind of quiet that allows the reader to become absorbed in the book. Classically, libraries are quiet places and that applies to a classroom library area as well. Children need space for art work, but not necessarily a quiet area. Science activities, since they are activities, can be noisy anyway, so a quiet area is not critical. A puppet stage is likely to produce laughter and applause, so such a noisy activity does not require a quiet area.

36. D: The answer is all of the above, because all of the choices describe practical methods of classroom design. Classrooms with a variety of activity centers need at least one place that is a quiet zone; the way to achieve quiet areas in a classroom is to eliminate distractions and muffle noise with screens, shelves, or other furniture. Children need to feel welcome and comfortable in a classroom, so it is inviting to a child to have the materials they use at eye-level where they can find what they need and reach it. Children also, however, need to understand that the classroom is a place to learn and not to roughhouse, so the classroom should be designed with traffic patterns that do not have long open stretches that would tempt children to run.

37. A: Making labels in more than one language is not confusing to the children. Rather, it is supportive of their home language (if it is not English), and bi-lingual or multi-lingual labels send the message that writing comes in a variety of shapes and languages. A print-rich environment includes labels to identify objects and work areas, print that is at a child's eye level so it can be seen easily, and print that was created by the children themselves so that they can make the connection between print and their own work. That connection between individual creation and print is reinforced when the teacher models writing by preparing posters and other written materials in front of the children.

38. C: The message will not be that the work is more important than rules and tidiness, but will be that anything goes, or that neither the teacher nor the students need care about order and cleanliness. A classroom needs to look neat and organized to show that the teacher cares and has good management. A messy or poorly organized classroom has a sense of chaos that causes disruptive behavior, especially when children are frustrated by not being able to find what they need or not having sufficient room to work. Children have difficulty choosing activities if the materials are in disarray such that they can't find all the pieces or can't clearly see what is available when the choices are piled together. If the classroom is already messy, how are children to know if they were successful at their clean-up chores or understand the need if the teacher has demonstrated a lack of concern about clean up and organization.

39. B: Labels make it easier for children to find things on their own and put them away correctly; that is, children are more independent and responsible when they can follow the labels by themselves. Labels are not a crutch that relieves children of responsibility; reading a label or icon is empowering and asks the children to follow instructions. Placing labels on as many items as possible in the classroom has the benefit of teaching the children systems of organization and storage; children learn sorting and putting things in their place so that they can be easily found when needed again. Such organization enhances the sense of structure and security for children. Labels, as print materials, naturally add to the print-rich environment of the classroom and impress the children with the value of print. Further, labels help children to associate words with actual objects, thus connecting the abstract with the concrete.

40. B: While setting rules and establishing routines is important to classroom management, the teacher should not be so firm that there is no room for flexibility and adjustments. A teacher's relationship with a child must remain consistent in terms of the teacher's interactions with the child and the expectations set for the child; a moody or fickle teacher can frustrate and anger the children. Teachers should respond to children positively and avoid negativity for the relationship to be constructive and nurturing. Although the teacher is the ultimate decision-maker in the classroom and must establish authority, sharing power with the children by guiding them into making responsible choices gives the children a sense of empowerment and a stake in the classroom situation.

41. C: There should be follow-up to the conflict resolution to make certain that the children are sticking to their agreed-upon solution and to ensure that the conflict does not re-occur. Some teachers might feel that dropping the issue will help everyone forget the conflict, but that usually is not the case. Conflicts are best handled with calmness and a quiet voice as the teacher gathers information about the conflict in order to get a complete and fair picture of the situation. Then the teacher should review the conflict with the children and ask for their ideas for ways the problem could have been prevented and ways to solve the conflict. Involving the children in the resolution of the problem teaches them self-regulation and respect for themselves and others.

42. D: All of the responses demonstrate that clear and immediate communication is the best way to deal with children with behavioral problems. Children with behavioral problems are best managed with clear, distinct communication. Therefore, potentially vague instructions must be revised prior to presentation to be as explicit as possible so the child cannot claim to have misunderstood or argue that the teacher said something else. This type of students does best when there is not a gap of time between instructions and practice, but rather by immediate involvement in the activity while the child still remembers what to do and has not yet had a chance to get distracted. The same sense of immediacy is needed for feedback or the student will not be able to connect the feedback to the activity.

43. C: Clear communication is always best for effective classroom management, especially when instructions and expectations are delineated before the lesson starts. Saying that a reward will be given "if everyone does well" is too vague and sets up conflicts. Rewards, like assessments, should be dependent on individual effort, generally. Younger children do not usually have the focus or sense of time to be able to wait for an award for a week, or to associate an award with the action that earned the reward over a week's time. Awards should be given as close to the lesson or activity for which the reward was offered as possible. "Customizing" consequences for misbehavior would be exhausting for the teacher, confusing for the children, and at risk of being interpreted as favoritism or discrimination.

44. C: The teacher should anticipate problems and be prepared with appropriate reactions rather than trying to think of what to do on the spot. Teachers need to be flexible, and unexpected things will happen, but the wise teacher will try to anticipate behavioral problems that might result from a changed situation. Stepping outside the classroom routine for special activities can result in chaos unless the teacher anticipates problems and plans for additional behavior management specific to the new situation. This planning should include how to re-arrange the seats so that the activity can proceed with sufficient space and accommodate groups or partners if needed; selecting the partners so that teams work well together; and reinforcing the rules with strong reminders of consequences.

45. D: The answer is all of the above because all of the situations described required additional pre-planning for the teacher. The types of lessons that call for additional behavior management include: 1) ones that will have multiple steps and transitions because each transition is an opportunity for students to get off task; 2) ones that will require lots of equipment because the teacher will be distracted while using the equipment or the students will be excited and lack patience when trying to use new equipment; 3) ones that require additional and unusual materials that will have to be distributed because children will again be eager to receive the materials and start trying them out.

46. D: Peer helpers are more likely to keep the restless student on task than to distract that student; therefore, peer helpers are a good idea. Allowing a student who has trouble staying on task to do a "gallery walk"; that is, to expend some energy by walking around to examine the lesson materials that are on display, is a good practice because once the student has seen the materials s/he is less likely to be distracted by wondering about them. A student who has trouble staying on task is helped by being assigned specific tasks to accomplish because breaking up the assignment into smaller jobs seems more achievable. Using response cards catches the attention of the student who has trouble staying on task and pulls that student into the lesson with the others.

47. A: The students always need to see the teacher as well as whatever is pertinent to the lesson around the room. No matter the activity or room arrangement, the teacher always needs to be able to get close to each student so that the teacher can give assistance wherever necessary. Small group

- 153 -

work, individual work, or discussions may need furniture rearrangement to best facilitate the activity, so it is standard practice to move desks and tables around to suit the lesson. When students work in pairs or teams, it is important that the teacher selects the pairs or teams to ensure compatibility and good work while avoiding problems that might result from conflicts between students or good friends sitting next to each other and being more interested in personal matters than the lesson.

48. B: The routine clean-up process may not be sufficient if extra materials or messy substances such as glue or paint have been used. Effective time management would include anticipation of the need for additional clean-up instruction and time; otherwise, students might rush or leave a mess when the routine proves insufficient for the task. Teachers shouldn't assume that the students know what to do for clean up when the situation changes. Total preparation means checking out the equipment prior to classroom use to avoid problems, having all the supplies ready so there are no delays while supplies are hunted for or pulled out of cabinets, and giving lesson-specific instructions about sharing and returning materials prior to students jumping into the lesson so that the activity does not have to be interrupted for corrective instruction or additional information.

49. D: The answer is all of the above because the A, B, and C choices are all standard to setting up routines in the classroom. A teacher who has good classroom-management skills will have certain routines in place that establish order and discipline. Among these are set routines for handing in assignments (for example, placing homework in a certain tray); for what a student should do upon completing a task (for example, take out something to read, rest head on desk, wait quietly); and for how to set up desks for partner practice (for example, turning the desks toward each other and dividing the materials). In each situation, the student knows exactly what to do and there are no questions or fussing about the steps.

50. C: While the command doesn't use "don't" or "no," it brings up a negative scenario: "fighting." It would be better to say something like "Let's share the crayons." The word "not" is a negative and some teachers find themselves saying "Don't do that"; "Don't talk"; and so forth all day long. The teacher needs to make an effort to eliminate "not," "no" and wording that indicates negatives from their commands and comments. Answer A is a good alternative to "Don't slam the door." Answer B is a positive alternative to "Don't copy." Answer D is a positive alternative to "Don't guess" and encourages critical thinking.

51. B: Students prefer private, quietly delivered praise. This way they get the praise they want, but they are not embarrassed by anything dramatic or un-cool. Answer A is incorrect because students are often embarrassed by loud praise; they don't want to stand out. Answer C is incorrect because it's not cool to be too goodie-goodie, so they don't want to be pointed out for good behavior. Answer D is incorrect because, although teachers want to give credit to students for their effort, praising work that is poor sends a confusing message to the student that poor work is acceptable; the teacher needs to communicate clearly that the effort was good, but the work still did not meet standards.

52. A: Making a big deal out of praise does not necessarily make a student feel special. Instead, it might embarrass the student with too much "gushing" that seems overdone. Answer B is a good guideline for communicating praise because being specific lets the student know exactly what s/he did correctly and will therefore be able to repeat the correct action rather than wonder what was good about the product because of vague praise. Answer C is also a good guideline for communicating praise because praise isn't convincing if the teacher does not match the words with appropriate body language and tone of voice. Answer D refers to specificity of praise again and reminds the teacher to look for opportunities for praise as in new skills or evidence of progress.

53. D: The answer is all of the above because all of the strategies are effective. It is good for the teacher to give examples of success from former students of the school because current students can best identify with those who have been where they are, so answer A is encouraging information to communicate. Although some teachers try to avoid letting students know any personal information, students find examples from the teachers' lives to be really interesting. In the case of sharing about how one can apply what was learned in school, it is a good idea for teachers to give personal examples as recommended in answer B. Just as commercials use celebrities to endorse products, so teachers can use examples from celebrities to endorse the benefits of school; answer C is a good technique for communicating the link between school and real life.

54. B: The answer uses a negative and is just like saying, "Eat your spinach because it is good for you." Kids want to do what they like, not necessarily what's good for them. Answer A is a positive communication that creates anticipation for learning because the teacher is setting expectations and giving students a goal for achieving a skill that might be interesting. Answer C sets up an expectation of curiosity that encourages students to want to find out more. Answer D is another way that a teacher can interest students who have a curiosity about the teacher's personal life, and is very inviting because it offers to share something with the students.

55. A: Words like "because" and "for example" have to be followed by a reasonably precise explanation that gives clarity to the communication. Clarity is critical to good communication. Vague or confusing language can reduce the effectiveness of presentations. Answer B gives examples of negated intensifiers; that is, the use of words such as "many" and "very" that indicate something big, but that are qualified by a "not", which communicates a nebulous state. Answer C indicates an ambiguous designation or destination – how is the student supposed to figure out needed specific information, even how to find supplies in the closet, if the directions are so vague? Answer D has words with the problem of vague probability; the student doesn't know exactly how often or what percentage.

56. B: If the 5th graders are doing less demanding work than the 3rd graders, then communication has broken down among the teachers or between the principal and teachers about the level of work that is expected of all students at that school. Students and parents alike will be wondering why the 5th graders are not being expected to do more than 3rd graders as evidence of their skills and knowledge progress. Answer A indicates effective communication if the students know the lesson's objective; such knowledge is required for good teaching. Answer C indicates that the 5th grade teachers have communicated effectively with each other and are working as a team for organized instruction. Answer D describes a situation that is good practice for communicating to students the expectations and standards of an assignment.

57. D: The answer is all of the above, because all of the options are advantages of using a series of graphics to enhance a lesson. Using a series of graphics, i.e., pictures or icons, is a good way to assist visual learners with knowledge retention. Having students make their own copies of these graphics provides kinesthetic learners with a hands-on activity to aid their learning. When the graphics are in a certain order, students are better able to understand a series of events or how the elements of the lesson are linked. Graphics also provide a concrete representation of any abstract concepts in the lesson, which clarifies the lesson for students.

58. C: The one activity that is not a good continuation of the graphics lesson would be to grade the students on the quality of their artwork in reproducing the graphics. The lesson is not about art, so the students should not be graded on their artistic skills. Doing so would only penalize those students who are not artistically inclined on a lesson where they otherwise might have success. The graphics series can be beneficial in follow-up exercises, such as using the graphics to review as

- 155 -

well as teach the lesson. If it is important for the students to learn the order in which the graphics appear, then the teacher can make sets of the graphics, divide the class into teams, then give one set to each team of students who will then compete to see which team can put the graphics in order in the fastest time.

59. B: Allowing students to pick their own groups defeats the purposes outlined above and will most likely result in groups that were chosen by the students so that they could be with friends rather than good working partners. Flexible grouping is designed to put students together in groups that work well for various purposes. One type of group would be one in which the students can work according to similar interests. Others would group students according to readiness levels or specific skill levels. In other words, the grouping would be teacher-selected according to assessments that indicate the needed diversity or similarities to make the group efficient.

60. A: Experience shows that the practice does not grow old but remains an effective tool that the students enjoy using because it is quick, active, and does not involve individual pressures. Using response cards involves all of the students at the same time, so students who might otherwise daydream or be reluctant to give an answer are swept up into the activity; they have less fear of answering when part of a group and can't easily go off task when everyone around is engaged. Using response cards for just 30 minutes per day instead of hand raising elicits more than 3,700 additional academic responses during the school year (Harvard et al., 1996), so it is a highly effective method for engaging students in lessons. Using response cards also allows teachers to assess student understanding of the lesson in a glance.

61. C: As an assessment tool that checks individual responses, using response cards is not designed for group or pair work where a stronger student might be able to pick the answers for a weaker student who would then not be identified for remediation. Using response cards actively engages students in an assessment since they must make a choice and physically raise a card. The strategy is one that can be used as a pre-assessment before a lesson that might also attract student interest in the upcoming lesson. The strategy can also be used during the lesson to check understanding and progress, and of course, after the lesson as a quick assessment of mastery. As an assessment tool, using response cards, perhaps in shorter question sets, enables teachers to find the areas that need re-teaching.

62. D: The answer is all of the above because all of the first three strategies are legitimate. A student who can disappear in the crowd of a classroom is more likely to wander off task; however, a student who is given preferential seating at a desk near the teacher or other adult, or with a group of quiet students, or away from high traffic areas, or at a desk alone rather than at a table with other students will be more likely to keep his/her attention on the subject. Sometimes, a student who is easily distracted needs to be placed in a study carrel where visual distractions can be minimized. Another strategy for reducing distractions is to eliminate sounds through the use of headphones – the student hears only the lesson, not all the other noises in the classroom.

63. B: It helps students to stick to a task if the task is made more fun by adding novelty to it through games or personal interest materials. For students who have difficulty staying with and completing routine tasks, the teacher can employ certain strategies that will encourage the child to stick with the work. One way is to explain to the students about the importance of remaining on-task and monitoring oneself. Another way is to eliminate any part of the routine that really isn't necessary, such as copying sentences. Still another way is to break up the task into smaller time commitments. In this way, the student doesn't get too bored before being allowed to go to something else, but is nonetheless required to come back in a timely manner to finish.

64. A: One has to have the regular routine first, and then one can have remedial strategies for breaks in the routine. Some students, especially the youngest students, have difficulty coping with change; they need the stability of routine and find deviations from the norm to be threatening or frightening. The primary strategy for dealing with this situation is to maintain the posted schedule as much as possible. When visitors or special events do occur, it helps, of course, to prepare the students by telling them in advance of the change in schedule. Those children who are still disturbed by the change can be helped by being near someone they trust during the visit or activity. The teacher can even teach relaxation techniques to the students and suggest these techniques when a student appears to be having anxiety over a change in routine.

65. C: The best approach for a teacher in regards to using technology in the classroom is to use only the technology with which s/he is comfortable so that the technology does not complicate or distract from the lesson. Answer A is not the best approach because while the teacher should know enough to demonstrate the technology used in the classroom, it is not the teacher's job to teach technology; therefore, the teacher should not be hesitant to use technology out of fear of having to become a technical expert. Answer B is not the best approach because the teacher needs to find a balance between using the technology center and working with computers in the classroom. It is more convenient to stay in the classroom, but the technology center exists to expand capabilities. Answer D is not the best approach because while increasing technology might improve instruction, there is no guarantee; only better teaching can improve instruction.

66. D: The answer is all of the above because all of the statements about the benefits of student computer use for compositions are true. Answer A is true because students do not have to worry about penmanship and neatness when writing on a computer, so they find the product more attractive and likely to get a better grade. Answer B is true because the students don't have to worry about their spelling, or grammar for that matter, if they use the spelling and grammar checks. This means that they can relax and concentrate on the content itself. Answer C is true because the cut-and-paste feature of the word processor allows for easy reorganizing and rewriting, which saves time and energy.

67. A: The research shows that instruction and student progress are greatly aided by the use of computers. Some states actually forbid the use of computers in certain areas because computers can't be used on the state test, but this prohibition ignores the benefits of computer instruction and the ability of students to transition to testing without computers. Many teachers have serious trepidations about using computers in the classroom. When trying to figure out whether they can handle the technology or whether there will be sufficient benefit from using computers, teachers should ask if the software is complicated and boring or easy to use and fun for the students. Teachers should also ask whether there will be sufficient technological support if anything should go wrong. If the teacher is software and hardware with insufficient technical support, h/she runs the risk of having the software running on only a few computers, or multiple computers not working properly. Teachers should be concerned about the effect of computers on student behavior; on this issue they should be reassured that student behavior is generally better when students, who love technology, can be engaged by a computer.

68. D: The answer is all of the above, because all of the statements in A, B, and C are issues that should be considered when doing research, and all students should be taught these precautions about reliable sources. Considering the unreliability of some web sites, students should be cautioned, as mentioned in answer A, to find several information sources with different perspectives as a way to get a balanced view of the issue being researched; phony web sites should become obvious by comparison. Answer B gives advice about another way to check the credibility of a web site by making sure the web site has an identified author or institutional sponsor; if

- 157 -

whoever is behind the web site is unidentified, the web site is suspicious. Answer C advises students to check for the latest date of update; if the last time the site was updated is years ago, then the information could be out-of-date.

69. A: Despite the large number of federal and state grants to help schools with high poverty and minority populations to catch up with schools in higher socio-economic areas, the poorer schools still lag behind in technology. Answer B is a true statement about the limitations placed on the teacher and students if there are not enough computers available for use in the classroom; not much more can be done than demonstrations and the occasional individual work. Answer C is true in that having more than two computers in the classroom allows more student access for collaboratives; allows more time on computers for students since they don't have to share as much; and enables students to work on more complex projects, such as research and portfolios. Answer D is true and very important to know; while we assume that all kids are fans of technology, that does not mean that they have access to technology at home, and the income level for having a home computer is perhaps surprisingly high.

70. B: Just as students use group activities as perhaps an antidote to all the time spent alone with technology, students are signing up for extracurricular activities just as much and more than was the norm in pre-computer days. The answers to this question may be surprising. Although students who have grown up with television, computers, and video games are thereby isolating themselves to activities done alone, answer A is true because, in contrast, they enjoy group activities. Answer C is perhaps obvious because students who dwell on technology love even more new technology. Answer D, that students identify with parents, is true because their toys are not for childhood only but are much the same that the parents use for work and play; technology has brought the worlds of parents and children closer together in daily activities.

71. C: Technology-loving students find lots of video insets in a presentation engaging and are not confused by them. Answer A is true because, just as students turn from their technology used alone to do group work or participate in extracurricular activities, students want a break from all that technology on occasion and like to have a plain lecture or discussion. When a written presentation is given by the teacher, such as a PowerPoint, obviously it will be organized more than a verbal presentation, and students like the clarity as stated in answer B. Answer D is true in that the negative side to a computerized presentation is that the students will just copy the nice, organized notes and not think critically about the content.

72. A: Somehow students still find time for lots of television while still surfing the Net, participating in chat rooms, and playing video games. The connection is that television is another medium that provides images and entertainment and is, therefore, part of the technology package for students. It might be easy to assume that technology enthusiasts among students do not watch much television because they are indeed busy surfing the Net (answer B), participating in chat rooms (answer C), and playing lots of video games (answer D).

73. B: The teacher corrects the student in a nice way by saying "good example," but identifies the form of speech in the mistaken answer and can then go back to the search for an example of a noun. Answer A would not be appropriate; while the teacher is trying to be nice, to say that a verb could be a noun is misinformation that could confuse students. Answer C is insufficient; the teacher should say nicely, "No, that's a verb. I need a noun." Just saying, "No, I asked for a noun." doesn't let the student know the form of speech for the answer that was given. Answer D is rude and might hurt the student's feelings even if delivered in a teasing manner.

74. D: Answers A, B, and C are all hallmark ingredients of good feedback. Answer A is correct in that feedback should contain what the student did right and what the student did wrong. Being clear and specific about what is correct and incorrect helps the student to see the difference. Answer B is correct in that feedback should also contain suggestions for improvement. Examples of situations where there is room for improvement include those in which an answer is correct but does not have an explanation or one that could be extended for more critical thinking. Answer C is correct in that feedback should always end on a positive note; even when the feedback involves correcting a mistake, there are ways to encourage the student to try again or to tell the student that there are signs of improvement.

75. C: The point is to learn the correct method for the demonstration, not to probe the reasons for the mistake. Questioning the student about the mistake will probably get an "I don't know" response and make the student more nervous from being challenged to explain him or herself. Answer A is a good suggestion because in the case of a short presentation, it is best to give feedback at the end rather than interrupt the student, which might be upsetting. This is especially true if the feedback involves correcting a mistake. Answer B is a good way to give feedback in a longer presentation that has steps to it because the feedback will then be fresh and pertinent to each step. This is preferable to the student or audience trying to think back in order to connect a step to the feedback. Answer D is a good method for feedback when a step-by-step presentation is given and it is important that the step be done correctly for the rest of the demonstration to work. The teacher should re-demonstrate the step, and then allow the student to try again. It is important to let the student try again; otherwise, the correction will look like teacher interference and the student will not learn how to do the step.

76. D: Answers A, B, and C are all variations on feedback that give students some independence while allowing the teacher more personal time with those who need intensive assistance. If the teacher is not available to give feedback, it is acceptable to allow the student to refer to an answer key, as in Answer A. The key provides enough information for the student to know what was correct and what was incorrect and be able to go on from that point; usually in this situation the teacher has established a routine for continuing, depending on the student's score. By allowing students to ask another adult for help, Answer B provides another alternative when the teacher is unavailable to give feedback. Of course, this works only if there is another adult present, but on many activities and exercises, any adult should be able to explain the lesson and interpret the student's results. Answer C, allowing students to work in pairs and critique each other, is a good method of feedback that frees up the teacher's time and often is less stressful for students. Assuming the students are well disciplined, they will enjoy working with each other and often will find it less stressful to make a mistake in front of a classmate than the teacher. This method is best for low-level skills and drills.

77. B: Although some educators think a long test is too taxing for students and graders, a long test actually gives the students more opportunities to show what they know and gives the teacher more opportunities to cover the entire lesson. Answer A describes a problem with test making in that uneven sampling of the lesson content can mean that students could study hard in an area where the teacher hardly asks a question. Students feel deceived in such circumstances and it is unfair if students studied, but did not concentrate where the teacher did. Answer C describes a problem with test where all the questions have the same level of difficulty and thus do not challenge the students or provide a way to separate lower and higher achievers. Answer D presents another problem in test making when references or allusions are made to topics unfamiliar to some students; in these cases, the students cannot answer questions because they have not been presented with the information about those topics.

78. C: While multiple-choice assessment might be intellectually shallower, it can cover more territory than essay questions, which are more focused. Answer A is not an advantage of multiple-choice tests because, while some information needs to be memorized, critical thinking is even more important and multiple-choice tests do not allow for critical thinking as much as mere memorization. Answer B is not an advantage because, although teachers are always looking for an easy way to do assessment and save time, multiple-choice tests do not necessarily cover the important material as completely as essay tests. Answer D is not an advantage because the nature of a multiple-choice question stem is such that it often can't help but give away the answer to students who are able to deduce or guess well.

79. A: It is not true that it takes more time to construct short-answer and completion questions than multiple-choice questions; on the contrary, it takes less time to construct the short-answer and completion questions, but probably more time to grade them. Answer B is true in that short-answer and completion test items are especially useful in math and science because it is necessary to test whether students are able to recall formulas or equations. Answer C is true in that short-answer and completion test items are especially useful for spelling and language courses where specific bits of information often are required in order to do more complex problem-solving tasks. Answer D is true about short-answer and completion test items in that they are like mini-essays and therefore present some of the same scoring problems related to time and subjectivity as essays.

80. A: One advantage of an essay test or question is that the nature of the answer allows the student to think things through and organize the answer rather than trying to fit into the test form. Answer B is a disadvantage of essay tests in that grading can be highly subjective and therefore not necessarily consistent or fair. Answer C is a disadvantage of essay tests in that essay questions are focused on a specific area and do not give broad coverage to the material. This specificity reduces the opportunities for a student to do well. Answer D is a disadvantage of essay tests in that good written answers must be organized, legible, and must employ correct spelling and grammar. The advantage in answering essay questions goes to students who are talented in writing and not necessarily to those who have the best answers.

81. D: This answer reflects the variety of choices. According to *Home, School, and Community Relations* by Carol Gestwicki, the understanding of the term "parent involvement" is often much narrower than all of the opportunities for involvement that exist. Teachers might think that parent involvement is just keeping parents informed about their student's progress, but it also involves a variety of activities in which parents might engage to assist or improve the school. Therefore, it is important for educators to know a wide variety of ways that parents can be encouraged to undertake involvement. This question addresses the breadth of teachers' knowledge in this area.

82. C: Participating in an intervention program requires more intense involvement than just a one-time activity such as baking cookies, going on a field trip, or even visiting with the teacher. Once the educator is aware of the choices for parent involvement, it is also important to understand the difference between high and low levels of involvement. In this manner, parents who are involved only at a low level can be invited to higher levels that will result in a better understanding of the school and classroom situation and thus improve relations between parents and the school. This question tests the educator's understanding of low and high levels of parental involvement.

83. B: Although a newsletter requires quite a bit of time, it does not involve the parent with the students. Parents sitting in on classes, observing the functions of the school, or actually assisting in the classroom are examples of higher involvement. Once the educator is aware of the choices for parent involvement, it is also important to understand the difference between high and low levels of involvement. In this manner, parents who are involved only at a low level can be invited to higher

- 160 -

levels that will result in a better understanding of the school and classroom situation and thus improve relations between parents and the school. This question tests the educator's understanding of low and high levels of parental involvement.

84. A: School-based parental education programs are available to parents, but attendance is voluntary, not mandatory. The other choices are all federal programs with mandated parental involvement. Of the various types of motivation designed to bring about parent involvement in schools, one is legal mandate. It is important for parents and teachers to know that enrollment of a child in certain types of schools requires a commitment from the parents to participate in school matters. This question tests the knowledge of the educator concerning programs that mandate or do not mandate parent involvement. Such knowledge involves an awareness of which programs are government-sponsored and which are not.

85. C: This choice is a federal program with mandated parental involvement while the other three are non-federal programs that set their own levels of parental involvement. Of the various types of motivation designed to bring about parent involvement in schools, one is legal mandate. It is important for parents and teachers to know that enrollment of a child in certain types of schools requires a commitment from the parents to participate in school matters. This question tests the knowledge of the educator concerning programs that mandate or do not mandate parent involvement. Such knowledge involves an awareness of which programs are government sponsored and which are not.

86. B: Socio-economic factors, while important, are still not as important to a child's academic success as quality parental involvement. Good parenting is so important that all factors directly related to the parent are more important than the effects of the social or economic situation of the family. Even in the midst of poverty and lower-class status, the parent can effectively prepare the child for school and support the child's progress. However, parents need sufficient self-esteem to believe that their contribution is valuable enough to make the effort. With so much emphasis on special strategies for children of poverty, coupled with the emphasis on the effects of poverty, the overriding influence of a parent may be forgotten by educators. Therefore, this question tests the awareness of the educator concerning the critical nature of good parenting.

87. A: Schools can provide intervention programs to improve parenting skills, but they cannot assume the parenting role in the interim even if it seems that the school is being placed into a position to take that role. Educators are well aware that schools need to take an active role in community education, as well as that of the children, in order to improve the abilities of the parents to successfully promote the academic progress of their children. Schools partner with other agencies to assist in the delivery of needed services, attempt to involve the parent in the child's education, and offer to be an extension of the family in the academic setting. However, the interaction does not extend to actually usurping the authority of the parents, even when the parents have poor parenting skills.

88. D: A, B, and C are all effective methods for overcoming difficulties with interacting with parents. Teachers get into the business of teaching to work with children, not parents. Consequently, some may feel very ill at ease with parents or see parents as interfering with their classrooms. Some teachers may be fine with children, but timid around adults. To remedy this problem, it is helpful for these teachers to prepare their comments and set an agenda in advance of a parent meeting, so that the teacher has more confidence and is less likely to say something unintended. It is also helpful for teachers to share their concerns, learn from the experience of others, and find out that other teachers share the same fears. It is also good personal discipline and helpful to classroom

management if teachers set goals on reaching a certain number of parents each week. This goal setting pressures the teacher into completing calls when they are reluctant to make contact.

89. C: Although teachers can pick up good tips from each other, too often the lounge is the place where teachers go to gripe and hide instead of sharing and collaborating. Answer A is an acceptable way to pursue professional development. The tapes and videos are there for the teachers' benefit and can be an effective means of learning. Answer B is an excellent method of maintaining knowledge in the field; subscribing to an education journal should be a given for any teacher. Answer D is obviously a good way to improve teacher performance since conferences, seminars, and workshops are designed for that purpose.

90. D: The answer is all of the above, because those who provide professional development need to make sure that it covers not only content, but also overall teaching skills in a way that is stimulating and helpful to the teachers. Answer A refers to the type of professional development that is specific to content knowledge. Deepening and broadening content knowledge enables teachers to better transmit the content to the students. Answer B refers to the type of professional development that focuses on the teaching and learning process in general and refreshes the skills of the teachers. Answer C refers to the way professional development should be delivered so that the teachers are intellectually engaged and aided in their quest for solutions to the complexities of teaching.

91. B: Although pay incentives certainly encourage teachers to pursue professional development, teachers do not have to be given extra pay to attend, and should not need pay incentives to want to further their teacher education. Answer A lists a critical need of teachers when it comes to professional development: time. With all their duties and the requirements of the teaching calendar, it is very difficult to find time for professional development. Answer C, support, is necessary for teachers to be able to participate in professional development – support from administrators, fellow teachers, and parents. Answer D is an important aspect of professional development because, even when teachers can find the time, they need the monetary resources to attend and then the resources of supplies and materials to follow up on their training.

92. D: Professional development is not a trickle-down process but rather a collaboration of experts and teachers sharing research and experience. Answer A is not true because, although some principles of teaching are universal, a priority of professional development is to help the teachers where they are in order to help with site-specific needs. Answer B is not true because, although some professional development might be about classroom strategies, other types of professional development are definitely aimed at improving content knowledge. Answer C is not true because, like Answer A, although teachers should be aware of other opportunities in the field of education, a priority of professional development is to help the teacher with the job at hand.

93. A: Although answers B, C, and D are all challenging tasks of professional development, studies show that the biggest challenge is finding the time in the crowded school calendar to present the information and do follow-up. Answer B is certainly a challenge in that the development of seminars to teach how to implement new educational standards is often complex and limited by time restraints, but this challenge is just part of the business of professional development. Answer C is a challenge because addressing any form of change requires developing adequate explanations and demonstrating how to implement the changes, often while meeting resistance from the constituent audience. Answer D is a challenge because it involves intensive research into the diverse populations and figuring out best practices.

94. D: Involving parents in planning professional development is a good way to make them a part of the school community and strengthen understanding of the goals of the school. It is the best of the

choices for this question. Answer A is not a good way to conduct professional development because administrators should be involved in and supportive of team planning and all other aspects of teacher collaboration, not off to the side acting like a separate unit. Answer B is an acceptable way of doing professional development because it takes advantage of the teacher's free time and allows for more extended courses; however, summer professional development means that the teachers have to give up their vacation time and will not be able to immediately apply what they have learned in the classroom, which might mean a loss of momentum. Answer C is done occasionally, but removing a whole group of teachers from the school is disruptive and the quality of instruction might suffer with substitutes.

95. C: Although distance education may be more convenient, it is very important for teachers to collaborate with other teachers, to be involved in their school community, and to enjoy the social aspect of meeting with other teachers and educational professionals. Hiding out at home with the computer is not the best way to pursue professional development. Answer A is a good way to get professional development through technology because video conferences online are just as professionally prepared and have just as important topics as live seminars. Answer B is a good way to get professional development because exchanging information with other teachers is a valid method for educating oneself about content or best practices. Answer D is a good way to get professional development because, like Answer B, networking with other teachers is an excellent source of information.

96. C: What is true is not that teachers should spend less time or only their own time for professional development, but that teachers should actually spend more time--at least 20% of their work time--in professional study and collaborative work. Professional development is an essential part of teaching and it is, therefore, legitimate to provide professional development opportunities during work time. Furthermore, it is also reasonable to expect teachers to incorporate continuous learning for themselves during the school day. Answer A is what some critics of time spent on professional development say, but it shows a lack of understanding of the complexity and needs of the classroom teacher. Answer B is also a common comment of critics of the educational system, but this criticism does not exhibit an understanding of the changes in education that require teachers to need education themselves in order to keep up. Answer D is another common complaint from people who resent teachers being out of the classroom for professional development. Such complaints show a lack of understanding about the need for extensive, continuous professional development and a failure to recognize that time restraints might require taking teachers out of the classroom to accommodate the requirement.

97. C: While many laws are based on ethics, not all laws are ethical. Examples of unethical laws include the Jim Crow laws in the United States that restricted the civil rights of black people, or laws such as those imposed in Nazi Germany that permitted taking the lives and property of Jews. Answer A is correct in that laws are written and therefore are not just ideas but are concrete and enacted by people of authority. Answer B is correct in that ethics are a personal code enforced by a person's own conscience; they are not written down but are ideas. Answer D is correct in that society transfers many of its ethics into laws to codify them.

98. C: If Betty is an ethical person, she will not consider trying to avoid her responsibilities in the situation. Ignoring a problem and hoping it will go away or passing off a problem to someone else is not ethical behavior. Answer A is a consideration in that Betty's ethics include sympathy for someone needing a job; Betty does not want to cause hardship to another person. Answer B is a consideration in that Betty has an ethical responsibility to comply with the principal's request. Answer D is a consideration in that Betty's ethics dictate that the students should come first; therefore, she needs to make sure they have a competent teacher.

99. D: The answer is all of the above because Answers A, B, and C are all everyday ways that teachers can ethically influence students. Answer A is an everyday way that teachers can ethically influence students. Teachers are tightly restricted on what they can convey to students and are thus warned to stay away from anything potentially controversial, but setting a good example in terms of a work ethic and a caring personality are certainly acceptable as ethics to be passed on to students. Answer B, establishing a classroom climate of respect and cooperation, is not only an acceptable means of transmitting ethics; such an environment is essential for good teaching. Answer C is an everyday way that teachers can share ethical values with their students, and have students share those values among themselves. To accomplish this sharing, however, the teacher must ensure that the classroom discussion of ethics stays on the subject matter of the lesson and does not result in anyone trying to force any particular viewpoint on others.

100. B: A school district does not have to justify its reasons for not rehiring a teacher who is on probation, as unfair as that might seem, and it is clearly specified in a probationary contract that the teacher can be dismissed without reason. Answer A is a correct statement because it is a requirement that dismissal hearings be scheduled at a reasonable time and place to avoid unfair treatment. Answer C is a correct statement because, at a dismissal hearing, due process requires that the defendant be able to confront and question witnesses so that both sides are heard. Answer D is a correct statement in that the teacher must be given sufficient time to prepare a proper defense and possibly hire an attorney. Additionally, the teacher must be provided with details about the reasons for dismissal in order to know what to address at the hearing. Denying sufficient time and information to prepare a defense would be unfair.

How to Overcome Test Anxiety

Just the thought of taking a test is enough to make most people a little nervous. A test is an important event that can have a long-term impact on your future, so it's important to take it seriously and it's natural to feel anxious about performing well. But just because anxiety is normal, that doesn't mean that it's helpful in test taking, or that you should simply accept it as part of your life. Anxiety can have a variety of effects. These effects can be mild, like making you feel slightly nervous, or severe, like blocking your ability to focus or remember even a simple detail.

If you experience test anxiety—whether severe or mild—it's important to know how to beat it. To discover this, first you need to understand what causes test anxiety.

Causes of Test Anxiety

While we often think of anxiety as an uncontrollable emotional state, it can actually be caused by simple, practical things. One of the most common causes of test anxiety is that a person does not feel adequately prepared for their test. This feeling can be the result of many different issues such as poor study habits or lack of organization, but the most common culprit is time management. Starting to study too late, failing to organize your study time to cover all of the material, or being distracted while you study will mean that you're not well prepared for the test. This may lead to cramming the night before, which will cause you to be physically and mentally exhausted for the test. Poor time management also contributes to feelings of stress, fear, and hopelessness as you realize you are not well prepared but don't know what to do about it.

Other times, test anxiety is not related to your preparation for the test but comes from unresolved fear. This may be a past failure on a test, or poor performance on tests in general. It may come from comparing yourself to others who seem to be performing better or from the stress of living up to expectations. Anxiety may be driven by fears of the future—how failure on this test would affect your educational and career goals. These fears are often completely irrational, but they can still negatively impact your test performance.

> **Review Video: 3 Reasons You Have Test Anxiety**
> Visit mometrix.com/academy and enter code: 428468

Elements of Test Anxiety

As mentioned earlier, test anxiety is considered to be an emotional state, but it has physical and mental components as well. Sometimes you may not even realize that you are suffering from test anxiety until you notice the physical symptoms. These can include trembling hands, rapid heartbeat, sweating, nausea, and tense muscles. Extreme anxiety may lead to fainting or vomiting. Obviously, any of these symptoms can have a negative impact on testing. It is important to recognize them as soon as they begin to occur so that you can address the problem before it damages your performance.

> **Review Video: 3 Ways to Tell You Have Test Anxiety**
> Visit mometrix.com/academy and enter code: 927847

The mental components of test anxiety include trouble focusing and inability to remember learned information. During a test, your mind is on high alert, which can help you recall information and stay focused for an extended period of time. However, anxiety interferes with your mind's natural processes, causing you to blank out, even on the questions you know well. The strain of testing during anxiety makes it difficult to stay focused, especially on a test that may take several hours. Extreme anxiety can take a huge mental toll, making it difficult not only to recall test information but even to understand the test questions or pull your thoughts together.

> **Review Video: How Test Anxiety Affects Memory**
> Visit mometrix.com/academy and enter code: 609003

Effects of Test Anxiety

Test anxiety is like a disease—if left untreated, it will get progressively worse. Anxiety leads to poor performance, and this reinforces the feelings of fear and failure, which in turn lead to poor performances on subsequent tests. It can grow from a mild nervousness to a crippling condition. If allowed to progress, test anxiety can have a big impact on your schooling, and consequently on your future.

Test anxiety can spread to other parts of your life. Anxiety on tests can become anxiety in any stressful situation, and blanking on a test can turn into panicking in a job situation. But fortunately, you don't have to let anxiety rule your testing and determine your grades. There are a number of relatively simple steps you can take to move past anxiety and function normally on a test and in the rest of life.

> **Review Video: How Test Anxiety Impacts Your Grades**
> Visit mometrix.com/academy and enter code: 939819

Physical Steps for Beating Test Anxiety

While test anxiety is a serious problem, the good news is that it can be overcome. It doesn't have to control your ability to think and remember information. While it may take time, you can begin taking steps today to beat anxiety.

Just as your first hint that you may be struggling with anxiety comes from the physical symptoms, the first step to treating it is also physical. Rest is crucial for having a clear, strong mind. If you are tired, it is much easier to give in to anxiety. But if you establish good sleep habits, your body and mind will be ready to perform optimally, without the strain of exhaustion. Additionally, sleeping well helps you to retain information better, so you're more likely to recall the answers when you see the test questions.

Getting good sleep means more than going to bed on time. It's important to allow your brain time to relax. Take study breaks from time to time so it doesn't get overworked, and don't study right before bed. Take time to rest your mind before trying to rest your body, or you may find it difficult to fall asleep.

> **Review Video: The Importance of Sleep for Your Brain**
> Visit mometrix.com/academy and enter code: 319338

Along with sleep, other aspects of physical health are important in preparing for a test. Good nutrition is vital for good brain function. Sugary foods and drinks may give a burst of energy but this burst is followed by a crash, both physically and emotionally. Instead, fuel your body with protein and vitamin-rich foods.

Also, drink plenty of water. Dehydration can lead to headaches and exhaustion, especially if your brain is already under stress from the rigors of the test. Particularly if your test is a long one, drink water during the breaks. And if possible, take an energy-boosting snack to eat between sections.

> **Review Video: How Diet Can Affect your Mood**
> Visit mometrix.com/academy and enter code: 624317

Along with sleep and diet, a third important part of physical health is exercise. Maintaining a steady workout schedule is helpful, but even taking 5-minute study breaks to walk can help get your blood pumping faster and clear your head. Exercise also releases endorphins, which contribute to a positive feeling and can help combat test anxiety.

When you nurture your physical health, you are also contributing to your mental health. If your body is healthy, your mind is much more likely to be healthy as well. So take time to rest, nourish your body with healthy food and water, and get moving as much as possible. Taking these physical steps will make you stronger and more able to take the mental steps necessary to overcome test anxiety.

> **Review Video: How to Stay Healthy and Prevent Test Anxiety**
> Visit mometrix.com/academy and enter code: 877894

Mental Steps for Beating Test Anxiety

Working on the mental side of test anxiety can be more challenging, but as with the physical side, there are clear steps you can take to overcome it. As mentioned earlier, test anxiety often stems from lack of preparation, so the obvious solution is to prepare for the test. Effective studying may be the most important weapon you have for beating test anxiety, but you can and should employ several other mental tools to combat fear.

First, boost your confidence by reminding yourself of past success—tests or projects that you aced. If you're putting as much effort into preparing for this test as you did for those, there's no reason you should expect to fail here. Work hard to prepare; then trust your preparation.

Second, surround yourself with encouraging people. It can be helpful to find a study group, but be sure that the people you're around will encourage a positive attitude. If you spend time with others who are anxious or cynical, this will only contribute to your own anxiety. Look for others who are motivated to study hard from a desire to succeed, not from a fear of failure.

Third, reward yourself. A test is physically and mentally tiring, even without anxiety, and it can be helpful to have something to look forward to. Plan an activity following the test, regardless of the outcome, such as going to a movie or getting ice cream.

When you are taking the test, if you find yourself beginning to feel anxious, remind yourself that you know the material. Visualize successfully completing the test. Then take a few deep, relaxing breaths and return to it. Work through the questions carefully but with confidence, knowing that you are capable of succeeding.

Developing a healthy mental approach to test taking will also aid in other areas of life. Test anxiety affects more than just the actual test—it can be damaging to your mental health and even contribute to depression. It's important to beat test anxiety before it becomes a problem for more than testing.

> **Review Video: Test Anxiety and Depression**
> Visit mometrix.com/academy and enter code: 904704

Study Strategy

Being prepared for the test is necessary to combat anxiety, but what does being prepared look like? You may study for hours on end and still not feel prepared. What you need is a strategy for test prep. The next few pages outline our recommended steps to help you plan out and conquer the challenge of preparation.

Step 1: Scope Out the Test

Learn everything you can about the format (multiple choice, essay, etc.) and what will be on the test. Gather any study materials, course outlines, or sample exams that may be available. Not only will this help you to prepare, but knowing what to expect can help to alleviate test anxiety.

Step 2: Map Out the Material

Look through the textbook or study guide and make note of how many chapters or sections it has. Then divide these over the time you have. For example, if a book has 15 chapters and you have five days to study, you need to cover three chapters each day. Even better, if you have the time, leave an extra day at the end for overall review after you have gone through the material in depth.

If time is limited, you may need to prioritize the material. Look through it and make note of which sections you think you already have a good grasp on, and which need review. While you are studying, skim quickly through the familiar sections and take more time on the challenging parts. Write out your plan so you don't get lost as you go. Having a written plan also helps you feel more in control of the study, so anxiety is less likely to arise from feeling overwhelmed at the amount to cover.

Step 3: Gather Your Tools

Decide what study method works best for you. Do you prefer to highlight in the book as you study and then go back over the highlighted portions? Or do you type out notes of the important information? Or is it helpful to make flashcards that you can carry with you? Assemble the pens, index cards, highlighters, post-it notes, and any other materials you may need so you won't be distracted by getting up to find things while you study.

If you're having a hard time retaining the information or organizing your notes, experiment with different methods. For example, try color-coding by subject with colored pens, highlighters, or post-it notes. If you learn better by hearing, try recording yourself reading your notes so you can listen while in the car, working out, or simply sitting at your desk. Ask a friend to quiz you from your flashcards, or try teaching someone the material to solidify it in your mind.

Step 4: Create Your Environment

It's important to avoid distractions while you study. This includes both the obvious distractions like visitors and the subtle distractions like an uncomfortable chair (or a too-comfortable couch that makes you want to fall asleep). Set up the best study environment possible: good lighting and a comfortable work area. If background music helps you focus, you may want to turn it on, but otherwise keep the room quiet. If you are using a computer to take notes, be sure you don't have any other windows open, especially applications like social media, games, or anything else that could distract you. Silence your phone and turn off notifications. Be sure to keep water close by so you stay hydrated while you study (but avoid unhealthy drinks and snacks).

Also, take into account the best time of day to study. Are you freshest first thing in the morning? Try to set aside some time then to work through the material. Is your mind clearer in the afternoon or evening? Schedule your study session then. Another method is to study at the same time of day that you will take the test, so that your brain gets used to working on the material at that time and will be ready to focus at test time.

Step 5: Study!

Once you have done all the study preparation, it's time to settle into the actual studying. Sit down, take a few moments to settle your mind so you can focus, and begin to follow your study plan. Don't give in to distractions or let yourself procrastinate. This is your time to prepare so you'll be ready to fearlessly approach the test. Make the most of the time and stay focused.

Of course, you don't want to burn out. If you study too long you may find that you're not retaining the information very well. Take regular study breaks. For example, taking five minutes out of every hour to walk briskly, breathing deeply and swinging your arms, can help your mind stay fresh.

As you get to the end of each chapter or section, it's a good idea to do a quick review. Remind yourself of what you learned and work on any difficult parts. When you feel that you've mastered the material, move on to the next part. At the end of your study session, briefly skim through your notes again.

But while review is helpful, cramming last minute is NOT. If at all possible, work ahead so that you won't need to fit all your study into the last day. Cramming overloads your brain with more information than it can process and retain, and your tired mind may struggle to recall even previously learned information when it is overwhelmed with last-minute study. Also, the urgent nature of cramming and the stress placed on your brain contribute to anxiety. You'll be more likely to go to the test feeling unprepared and having trouble thinking clearly.

So don't cram, and don't stay up late before the test, even just to review your notes at a leisurely pace. Your brain needs rest more than it needs to go over the information again. In fact, plan to finish your studies by noon or early afternoon the day before the test. Give your brain the rest of the day to relax or focus on other things, and get a good night's sleep. Then you will be fresh for the test and better able to recall what you've studied.

Step 6: Take a practice test

Many courses offer sample tests, either online or in the study materials. This is an excellent resource to check whether you have mastered the material, as well as to prepare for the test format and environment.

Check the test format ahead of time: the number of questions, the type (multiple choice, free response, etc.), and the time limit. Then create a plan for working through them. For example, if you have 30 minutes to take a 60-question test, your limit is 30 seconds per question. Spend less time on the questions you know well so that you can take more time on the difficult ones.

If you have time to take several practice tests, take the first one open book, with no time limit. Work through the questions at your own pace and make sure you fully understand them. Gradually work up to taking a test under test conditions: sit at a desk with all study materials put away and set a timer. Pace yourself to make sure you finish the test with time to spare and go back to check your answers if you have time.

After each test, check your answers. On the questions you missed, be sure you understand why you missed them. Did you misread the question (tests can use tricky wording)? Did you forget the information? Or was it something you hadn't learned? Go back and study any shaky areas that the practice tests reveal.

Taking these tests not only helps with your grade, but also aids in combating test anxiety. If you're already used to the test conditions, you're less likely to worry about it, and working through tests until you're scoring well gives you a confidence boost. Go through the practice tests until you feel comfortable, and then you can go into the test knowing that you're ready for it.

Test Tips

On test day, you should be confident, knowing that you've prepared well and are ready to answer the questions. But aside from preparation, there are several test day strategies you can employ to maximize your performance.

First, as stated before, get a good night's sleep the night before the test (and for several nights before that, if possible). Go into the test with a fresh, alert mind rather than staying up late to study.

Try not to change too much about your normal routine on the day of the test. It's important to eat a nutritious breakfast, but if you normally don't eat breakfast at all, consider eating just a protein bar. If you're a coffee drinker, go ahead and have your normal coffee. Just make sure you time it so that the caffeine doesn't wear off right in the middle of your test. Avoid sugary beverages, and drink enough water to stay hydrated but not so much that you need a restroom break 10 minutes into the test. If your test isn't first thing in the morning, consider going for a walk or doing a light workout before the test to get your blood flowing.

Allow yourself enough time to get ready, and leave for the test with plenty of time to spare so you won't have the anxiety of scrambling to arrive in time. Another reason to be early is to select a good seat. It's helpful to sit away from doors and windows, which can be distracting. Find a good seat, get out your supplies, and settle your mind before the test begins.

When the test begins, start by going over the instructions carefully, even if you already know what to expect. Make sure you avoid any careless mistakes by following the directions.

Then begin working through the questions, pacing yourself as you've practiced. If you're not sure on an answer, don't spend too much time on it, and don't let it shake your confidence. Either skip it and come back later, or eliminate as many wrong answers as possible and guess among the remaining ones. Don't dwell on these questions as you continue—put them out of your mind and focus on what lies ahead.

Be sure to read all of the answer choices, even if you're sure the first one is the right answer. Sometimes you'll find a better one if you keep reading. But don't second-guess yourself if you do immediately know the answer. Your gut instinct is usually right. Don't let test anxiety rob you of the information you know.

If you have time at the end of the test (and if the test format allows), go back and review your answers. Be cautious about changing any, since your first instinct tends to be correct, but make sure you didn't misread any of the questions or accidentally mark the wrong answer choice. Look over any you skipped and make an educated guess.

At the end, leave the test feeling confident. You've done your best, so don't waste time worrying about your performance or wishing you could change anything. Instead, celebrate the successful completion of this test. And finally, use this test to learn how to deal with anxiety even better next time.

Important Qualification

Not all anxiety is created equal. If your test anxiety is causing major issues in your life beyond the classroom or testing center, or if you are experiencing troubling physical symptoms related to your anxiety, it may be a sign of a serious physiological or psychological condition. If this sounds like your situation, we strongly encourage you to seek professional help.

Thank You

We at Mometrix would like to extend our heartfelt thanks to you, our friend and patron, for allowing us to play a part in your journey. It is a privilege to serve people from all walks of life who are unified in their commitment to building the best future they can for themselves.

The preparation you devote to these important testing milestones may be the most valuable educational opportunity you have for making a real difference in your life. We encourage you to put your heart into it—that feeling of succeeding, overcoming, and yes, conquering will be well worth the hours you've invested.

We want to hear your story, your struggles and your successes, and if you see any opportunities for us to improve our materials so we can help others even more effectively in the future, please share that with us as well. **The team at Mometrix would be absolutely thrilled to hear from you!** So please, send us an email (support@mometrix.com) and let's stay in touch.

If you'd like some additional help, check out these other resources we offer for your exam:

http://MometrixFlashcards.com/IndianaCORE

Additional Bonus Material

Due to our efforts to try to keep this book to a manageable length, we've created a link that will give you access to all of your additional bonus material.

Please visit http://www.mometrix.com/bonus948/incoreelemed to access the information.